Veering

The Frontiers of Theory

Series Editor: Martin McQuillan

Visit the Frontiers of Theory website at www.euppublishing.com/series/tfot

Veering

A Theory of Literature

Nicholas Royle

Edinburgh University Press

To Jinan

© Nicholas Royle (b. 1957), 2011, 2012

First published in hardback by Edinburgh University Press 2011

Edinburgh University Press Ltd
22 George Square, Edinburgh EH8 9LF

www.euppublishing.com

Typeset in 10.5/13 pt Sabon
by Servis Filmsetting Ltd, Stockport, Cheshire, and
printed and bound in Great Britain by
CPI Group (UK) Ltd, Croydon, CR0 4YY

A CIP record for this book is available from the British Library

ISBN 978 0 7486 3654 9 (hardback)
ISBN 978 0 7486 5508 3 (paperback)

Contents

Series Editor's Preface

Since its inception, Theory has been concerned with its own limits, ends and afterlife. It would be an illusion to imagine that the academy is no longer resistant to Theory but a significant consensus has been established and it can be said that Theory has now entered the mainstream of the humanities. Reaction against Theory is now a minority view and new generations of scholars have grown up with Theory. This leaves so-called Theory in an interesting position which its own procedures of auto-critique need to consider: what is the nature of this mainstream Theory and what is the relation of Theory to philosophy and the other disciplines which inform it? What is the history of its construction and what processes of amnesia and the repression of difference have taken place to establish this thing called Theory? Is Theory still the site of a more-than-critical affirmation of a negotiation with thought, which thinks thought's own limits?

'Theory' is a name that traps by an aberrant nominal effect the transformative critique which seeks to reinscribe the conditions of thought in an inaugural founding gesture that is without ground or precedent: as a 'name', a word and a concept, Theory arrests or misprisions such thinking. To imagine the frontiers of Theory is not to dismiss or to abandon Theory (on the contrary, one must always insist on the it-is-necessary of Theory even if one has given up belief in theories of all kinds). Rather, this series is concerned with the presentation of work which challenges complacency and continues the transformative work of critical thinking. It seeks to offer the very best of contemporary theoretical practice in the humanities, work which continues to push ever further the frontiers of what is accepted, including the name of Theory. In particular, it is interested in that work which involves the necessary endeavour of crossing disciplinary frontiers without dissolving the specificity of disciplines. Published by Edinburgh University Press, in the city of Enlightenment, this series promotes a certain closeness to that spirit: the continued exercise of critical thought as an attitude of inquiry which counters modes of closed or conservative opinion. In this respect the series aims to make thinking think at the frontiers of theory.

Martin McQuillan

Advertisement

1. Veering is kinetic and dynamic. At once literal and figurative, it offers a mobile arsenal of images and ideas for thinking differently about literature – about genre, plot and narration, character and point of view, voice, tone and music, authorial intention and desire. It opens up new possibilities for responding to what is on the move and uncertain in the very moment of reading, to what is slippery, unpredictable and chancy in the experience of literature.

2. Veering impels us towards new questions about aesthetics. A literary text is composed of forces. It is a work of veering. The literary work may veer well or beautifully, in a shift or turn that pleases, surprises, thrills, fascinates. Or it can veer poorly, ineffectually, clumsily. The 'twist in the tale', for example, is hardly ever a veering worthy of the name. The manner in which a literary work veers is closely related to what might be called the signature or signature-effect of the writer. Analysis here promises something like a perverse science of literature: the art of veering.

3. Veering involves an economy of desire. Everybody veers in his or her own fashion. But this is never simply a matter of choice, volition or 'personal preferences'. There is always something *other* about veering. Veering offers fresh slants on the classical notion of clinamen ('leaning', 'inclination') as a basis for thinking about the strangeness of life, the singularity of being in the world, as well as about that peculiar thing we call literature.

4. Veering is not human, or not only human. Other animals veer. So do objects, such as stars. The theory of veering is non-anthropocentric. It gets away from the supposition that we human animals are at the centre of 'our' environment. As we will see, the word 'environment' has veering – the French verb, *virer*, 'to turn' – inscribed

within it. Veering orients us towards a new understanding of 'the environment'.

5. This study is deeply interested in words, in where they come from, how they work, and what they can do. It is about the love of language (*philology*). But it is also about what is non-verbal, beyond words, other than language. There is something irreducibly, stubbornly physical and phenomenal about veering. Mostly it seems – like reading itself – to be something that happens in silence.

Chapter 1

Casting Off

Like glass, the illusion shattered: a car hummed like a hornet towards them, veered, showed its scarlet tail-light, streaked away up the road. (Elizabeth Bowen)[1]

Strange, the sort of loyalty that reading gives birth to in us. (Maurice Blanchot)[2]

This book is a twisted love story. It is also a theory of literature. Mostly it is about the love of one word: 'veering'. This word does not occur with enormous frequency, either in literature or in everyday language, but that is perhaps part of its charm. In the pages that follow I explore 'veering' as a sort of pivot for thinking about literature and its relation to the world.

It may seem an odd or unpropitious time to be offering a theory of literature. It is the sort of thing one associates with fifty years ago, with the writings of Roland Barthes (*Theory of the Text*) or Harold Bloom (*The Anxiety of Influence: A Theory of Poetry*). Theory has, as they say, had its day. Books with titles such as *After Theory* and *Post Theory* have been around for some time. Indeed there are not a few people who suppose that literature, also, has had its day. The love of literature is thus perceived to be in decline, if not actually doomed. More passion is aroused by film, television, the internet, gaming and so on. As a subject of study, literature seems to have become largely absorbed into a broader, more diffuse area, sometimes given the name 'cultural studies' or 'cultural history'. Technologically and otherwise, the world itself seems to be shrinking and speeding up in ways that make a love of literature increasingly peripheral, a diminished thing.

But who is to say what is an odd or unpropitious time when it comes to literature? Especially if, as I want to suggest, we come to think of veering as an experience of time as much as space.

*

'Veering' is a verb, an adjective and also a noun. As an adjective it means 'Changing course or direction; turning round, revolving', or (in a figurative sense) 'Vacillating, variable, changeful'; as a noun 'veering' refers to 'The action or fact of changing course or direction' (as in the case of the wind, or a ship, or again, figuratively, anything at all). Veering is an old word 'of obscure origin' (see *Oxford English Dictionary*, 'veer', v.2), but is connected to the French verb *virer*, to turn or turn around. In the essays and other pieces assembled in this book, we will be exploring 'veering' as it shows up in literary works – from Ben Jonson to J. H. Prynne, from George Eliot to Stephen King. More generally, veering will come to provide new ways of thinking about a wide range of literary topics and critical concepts, including narrative structure, voice and point of view, character and desire, digression, authorial intention, wordplay, intertextuality and genre itself. In the process, the figure and concept of veering are linked to the emergence of what I call the literary turn.

Veering is intimately bound up with 'environment', a word with the French verb *virer* at its heart. This book, in turn, has the question of the environment and environmentalism at its heart. Indeed it would seem impossible today to imagine proposing a 'theory of literature' that does not engage with this question. Everything that might once have comfortably associated literature with 'nature' is over. The concept of environment ('the environment' and multiple 'environments') – above all in relation to environmental degradation and climate change – has become a focus for some of the most challenging and urgent issues of our time. As Timothy Clark remarks:

> *the environment* functions as a term to name what there is once the older term *nature* seems inadequate, sentimental or anachronistic. In the limited sense of places unaffected by human activity there is no 'nature' as such left on the planet, but there are various 'environments', some more pristine than others.[3]

'Environment' is a complex and far-reaching word – a word, in effect, of unbounded significance. As Clark goes on to note, 'the "environment" ... is, ultimately, everything'.[4] The pages that follow do not seek directly to analyse – let alone propose any solution to – the 'question of the environment'. Rather they are concerned with a sort of *détournement* (as Guy Debord termed it) – with a twisting or turnabout that pivots on the *veering* in 'environment'.[5] They are concerned with the idea that, in order to apprehend the meaning of 'environment', it is first of all necessary to reckon with *veering*. Analysis of the latter discloses new perspectives on the former. Above all, the theory of veering is concerned to interrogate and displace all thinking of an environment in straightforwardly anthropocentric terms: if an environment *environs*, it does not merely environ the human. The human animal is not at the centre of the world.

'Veering' involves contemplating all sorts of turns, funny and otherwise. We speak of the wind veering, of a boat or other vessel veering, and of a person veering. But it is not confined to the human. Under the meaning of 'to veer' as 'To turn round or about; to change from one direction or course to another' ('veer', v. 2, sense 3), the *OED* first offers cases in terms 'Of things' (sense 3a) and then 'Of persons or animals' (sense 3b). Under this latter heading it gives, in particular, instances of horses veering. So, for example: 'The amazed horse veered quickly to one side, and stopped as if stricken to stone' (1879). A considerable and perhaps surprising weight falls here on the great dictionary's classificatory phrase, 'of persons *or* animals'. How are we to construe that 'or'? What is at stake in this seemingly straightforward, commonsensical distinction between 'persons' on the one hand, and 'animals' on the other? The 'or' here might be described as a sort of category mistake, a deluded effect of anthropocentrism. Persons *are* animals, and, at least in the context of the English language, 'veering' is one of the richest and most intriguing words testifying to this. *Veering is what living creatures do*, human or otherwise.

In this book, we will encounter all kinds of creatures veering: birds, reptiles, insects, mammals, fish and so on. 'Veering' offers, among other things, a way of trying to think the human and non-human animal together, even while it remains necessary to reckon with what is singular about veering in each and any instance. Veering in other animals can offer a way of describing what is attractive, even erotic in human movement. Thus in John Berger's novel *To the Wedding*, we read: 'Now she touches Gino's cheek and turns to dance alone for him. Poised like a bird facing the wind, she lets herself veer and be swept back over the same spot again and again and again whilst her hands pluck the rhythms from the air.'[6] 'Like a bird' is a comparative metaphor, it is not '*the same as* a bird'. Yet Berger, along with many other writers we will be considering in the following pages, seems alert to a complexity and ambiguity in the word 'veer' that prompts us to sense an effacement between the human and non-human animal. Perhaps more provokingly than any other kinds of writing, literary works draw us into an engagement with the uncanny, non-anthropocentric character of veering.

At the same time, the uncanniness of veering doubtless emerges from a sense of the human – the familiar, all too familiar, familiar yet strange, strangely familiar, and so on. There is, in Don DeLillo's striking phrase, a 'human veer'. This term appears in his novel *Underworld* (1997), in a

passage describing New York from what is perhaps too easily called a
bird's-eye view:

> This was Klara Sax's summer at the roofline. She found a hidden city above
> the grid of fever streets. Walk and Dont Walk. Ten million bobbing heads
> that ride above the tideline of taxi stripes, all brain-waved differently, and
> yes the street abounds in idiosyncrasy, in the human veer, but you have to
> go to roof level to see the thing distinct, preserved in masonry and brass.
> She looked across the crowded sky of ventilators and antennas and suddenly
> there's a quirk, some unaccountable gesture that isolates itself.[7]

It might be said that all of DeLillo's novels are concerned with this
'human veer', both in macroscopic terms and at the level of tiny details
that call for but defy language ('all brain-waved differently', 'a quirk',
'some unaccountable gesture'). DeLillo is one of the most perceptive and
poetic contemporary thinkers of what *Underworld* elsewhere evokes
as 'the little delves and swerves that make a state of being' (338). And
like John Berger, he is sharply attuned to the ways in which veering is
not necessarily – and on many occasions not at all – human. Thus at
another moment in *Underworld*, we read about how a man called Brian
'watched several gulls veering near and saw a hundred other gulls positioned on a slope, all facing the same way, motionless, regardful, joined
in consciousness, in beautiful empty birdness, waiting for the signal to
fly' (186). There is something Hitchcockian and eerie, perhaps, about
this scene of present and prospective veering, these gulls 'joined in consciousness'. Birds veer, people veer. Horses veer, wolves veer, deer veer.[8]
Every veering is singular, even cryptic.

Veering is physical, it involves a moving body or force. But we also
speak of veering in a psychological context, of someone veering away
from some goal or aspiration, for example, or veering between one thing
and another. Veering can be deliberate or unintentional. Either way,
there is a suggestion of something sudden, unexpected or unpredictable.
Moreover veering as a movement does not necessarily depend on any
logic of origin or destination: it is an uncertainly perverse, unfinished
movement *in the present*. Veering, then, entails an experience or event of
difference, of untapped and unpredictable energy. Veering back, round,
down, up, towards, about, over, away, off: it might go anywhere.[9] At
the same time, as I hope to show, there is an aesthetics at issue (and here,
again, the question of distinctions and crossings between the human and
non-human is crucial): veering can be awkward, inadvertent, clumsy;
but it can also be beautiful, graceful, canny.

Just in case the reader may be supposing that I am interested only
in tracking down this one word, *veering*, in seeking it out and netting

it, as if I were some kind of demented lepidopterist of language, let me clarify. While 'veering' is indeed, I believe, a rich and strange word that merits the most detailed and careful analysis, perhaps its greatest fascination has to do with what is non-linguistic, beyond or other than language. Veering is physical and phenomenal: it is a *force* or *play of forces*. Given that our primary focus is literature, there will inevitably be close attentiveness to the 'words on the page', to the specific vocabulary as well as the syntax and rhetorical structure of the specific work under consideration, as well as to its historical context. But, at the same time, my concern is to elaborate an understanding of veering that goes beyond any traditional enclosure of 'literature' and that cannot be confined or reduced to any kind of 'mere theory', 'linguisticism' or 'wordplay'. Veering is not only human, as we have noted: it goes, as it were, all the way down and all the way out. It is about literature, but it is also about anthropocentrism, the environment, space and time.

To investigate the figure and concept of veering, then, we must be prepared to shift between the micrological and the macrological, the 'example' and its beyond, the singular and the general. This book is largely focused on the English language and literature in English. From the start, however, we must contend with the fact that there is no single, self-contained language. To engage with the verb 'to veer' is to find ourselves in Latin, French and other so-called foreign waters. We are already adrift. We must turn and turn about. Besides 'veer' itself and other words linked to the French *virer*, for example, there are all the words related to the Latin verb *vertere* ('to turn'), such as 'verse', 'version', 'versification', 'subvert', 'pervert', 'advert', 'avert', 'vertigo', *'vice versa'* and so on. Then there are the inexhaustible riches of the word 'turn' (from the Latin *tornāre*, 'to turn in a lathe', from *tornus*, 'turner's wheel', from Greek *tornos*, 'lathe') – from the good turn to speaking out of turn to the turn of the screw to the linguistic turn, etc. There are also those perhaps more classical-looking terms, such as 'trope' and 'tropology' (that is, the study of rhetorical figures as, literally in ancient Greek, 'turns') and 'clinamen' (literally 'inclination', 'leaning' or 'swerve'), which in their distinctive ways help provide a vocabulary for our topic. And finally there are the innumerable related or analogous words for 'veering', such as 'whirling', 'swerving', 'swirling', 'whiffling', 'tilting', 'twisting', 'diverging' and 'deviating', as well as a host of related others whose force and significance is in play in the pages ahead: 'detour', 'digression', 'seduction', 'zigzag' and so on. My concern is with how veering gives a new turn to thinking about all these various terms and figures.

*

This study has a particular historical inflection. 'Veering' is originally associated with the nautical and elemental (a ship or the wind). In the course of the seventeenth century it comes to be used also, however, as a word to describe alterations or changeableness in people (*OED*, 'veer', v. 2, sense 4a), or in thoughts and feelings (sense 4b). Thus in John Dryden's *Amphitryon* (1690), for example, a character is compared to the 'Weather-cock of Government' that 'veers'.[10] Correspondingly, the speaker in 'The Jacks Put to their Trumps', a poem first published in 1714, describes how others 'at last veer'd quite about, / And joyn'd in my disgrace'.[11] The character and potential of 'veering' alters further, in a subtle but significant way, around the end of the eighteenth century. I take Wordsworth as a key figure here. There is a shift away from the more immediately nautical or elemental, and from a figurative sense of veering, based on such usages, attributed to something or to someone else. In a supplementary but new and distinctive turn, we see the emergence of veering as a form of self-description, that is to say, as a differently freighted word applicable to one's own body, feelings, thoughts and memories. At an otherwise seemingly unremarkable moment in *The Prelude* (1805), Wordsworth describes *himself* as 'veering'.[12]

Through the nineteenth century and beyond, the sense and connotations of the word 'veer' (and its cognates) are supplemented and modulated, acquiring a new dimension of interiority. An early and indicative example here is Tennyson's 'Madeline' (1830), in which the eponymous young woman is repeatedly portrayed as '[e]ver varying':

> A subtle, sudden flame,
>   By veering passion fanned,
>   About thee breaks and dances:
>   When I would kiss thy hand,
> The flush of angered shame
>   O'erflows thy calmer glances,
> And o'er black brows drops down
> A sudden-curvèd frown.[13]

'Ever-varying Madeline' is evidently ever-veering, though the ambiguity of the flame that 'breaks and dances' adds a further twist: the 'veering passion' seems to be at once external (capable of fanning a flame around or 'about' her) and internal (as in a conventional image of 'passion' within), to be something shifting *within* her *and* something *between* her and the speaker.

Perhaps inevitably, however, it is in the expansiveness of narrative fiction, and above all in the novel, that this new stress on the vagaries of interiority or interiorizing movement is most marked. Thus, for example, in Wilkie Collins's *The Moonstone* (1868), Mr Franklin is going up to bed, having just declined a brandy-and-soda: 'On the landing, however, either his cousin persuaded him, or he veered about and changed his mind as usual.'[14] And in Collins's slightly later novel, *The Law and the Lady* (1875), we encounter a bizarre character called Miserrimus Dexter, shouting megalomaniacal fantasies about being the author of *King Lear* or being Napoleon and wildly propelling himself about on 'a high chair on wheels', a strange embodiment of 'man and machinery blended in one'. Momentarily stopping, and focusing his eyes on the narrator, we are told: 'His mind instantly veered back again to Shakespere and King Lear.'[15] Correspondingly, in Thomas Hardy's *Jude the Obscure* (1896), Jude reminisces about Sue as a woman whose 'intellect broke, and she veered round to darkness', while in Henry James's *The Awkward Age* (1899), the narrator describes how, as she was speaking, 'the Duchess had veered a little to indulgence'.[16] From Tennyson to George Eliot to Herman Melville to D. H. Lawrence and on into more contemporary literature, veering is picked up as a figure either to describe inner states per se, or to describe the external world in a way that seems to mirror, indicate or enact interior states. 'States', however, transpires to be a misnomer: as we shall discover, the work that 'veering' does, in a range of literary texts, is to call into question the very notion and possibility of a state, of stability or stabilization.

'Veering', in fact, impels us to think afresh and otherwise about the borders or opposition between interior/exterior or inner/outer. Its appearance in literature and other kinds of discourse, from Wordsworth to the present, consistently seems to prompt larger questions of interior and exterior worlds, meaning and intention, rhythm and movement, chance and desire, purpose and end. We might illustrate this with a couple of contemporary examples, one (at least ostensibly) literary, the other (at least ostensibly) not. First of all, then, a further brief extract from DeLillo's novel *Underworld*:

> A car comes veering off the avenue and Cotter stops to let it go by. Then he feels something shift around him. There's a ripple in the pavement or the air and a scant second in a woman's face nearby – her eyes shift to catch what's happening behind him. He turns to see Bill coming wide and fast and arm-pumping.[17]

The 'veering' of the car seems at once prelude to *and part of* a more general and unsettling 'shift[ing]' and 'rippl[ing]'. As elsewhere in DeLillo's work, veering combines a sense of beauty and surprise with scientific detachment and objectivity: it presages the trembling and unstable mixture of what is hallucinatory ('a ripple in the pavement or the air') and actual ('what's happening').

The second example comes from the so-called mainstream media, *The Guardian* newspaper, and has to do with the real world, not (ostensibly) with literature. But let us also note by way of anticipation: what makes 'veering' so complex, intriguing and potentially productive as a critical concept is that it disturbs presuppositions about the literal and figurative, the physical and psychological, the external and internal, the literary and the real. Thus we will find ourselves trying to reckon, in the pages ahead, with a veering that goes beyond, traversing or zigzagging through all such distinctions. Here is Martin Woollacott, writing about Israel, Palestine and US policy since 1945: 'Reagan backed Iraq against Iran to the point of providing target data for Saddam's chemical strikes on Iranian troops and, veering between extreme bellicosity and extreme timidity, meddled disastrously in Lebanon.'[18] The US (under President Reagan) behaved catastrophically in Lebanon by veering in its policy between one thing and another. Woollacott's use of 'veering' here is illustrative of a certain pejorative connotation: veering is bad; you should not veer, especially if you are the US president, dealing with issues of grave international concern, indeed with terrible suffering and injustice. Another book might be written about the enormities of veering in foreign policy, concerning the US, Britain and Israel, in particular, as a calculated strategy for doing nothing at all or at any rate for inhibiting, deferring or stalling any lasting or effective 'peace agreement' in the Middle East. Suffice here merely to point up the oddities of the word as a kind of verbal nomad. Reagan (or the US government under Reagan) is described as veering between one thing and another. Veering entails a movement between: it entails 'extreme bellicosity' and 'extreme timidity' while also, in effect, being neither one nor the other. This peculiar neither-nor but also both-at-the-same-time corresponds to the question of location. *Where* is this veering to which Woollacott refers? Is it in Ronald Reagan's head? Is it a description of a psychological state or of the actual economic, military, social, ethical and political consequences of that state?

As I hope to make clear, analysis of the concept and figure of veering opens up new ways of thinking about literature and literary genres (the novel, poetry, drama, creative writing), as well as about critical and autobiographical discourse. But it is scarcely to be confined to these. The question of veering is not separable, ultimately, from much grander and more classical kinds of problem: the question of the nature of the self, desire and beauty, responsibility and justice. The historical trajectory of 'veering' is inextricably related to developments in science and psychology, secularization, the history of sexuality and, especially from the early twentieth century, to the impact of new conceptions of time and space (Einstein and others) as well as the human mind (Freud and others).

In one direction, then, veering leads into the farthest reaches of time and space – into what Richard Panek describes as the 'swirl of billions of stars', a 'universe in motion in more ways than anyone had ever imagined'.[19] Such are the veerings of the universe – and of the 'giddy language' of cosmology and astronomy: seeing beyond seeing, moving back billions of years towards when or how the universe began, the elusive character of dark matter and dark energy, redshifts and blueshifts, elliptical and spiral galaxies, galactic rotation curves and deviations, the abruptly rising light curves of supernovae, neutron stars spinning round hundreds of times per second . . .[20] And in another direction, veering leads into the human body and the nature of desire, thinking and feeling. Tennyson's Madeline provides a sort of prototype here: his/her 'veering passion' could be said to prefigure the emergence of a new interest (both scientific and literary) in desire as veering, as well as of a psychological language concerned with ambivalence and (more problematically) deviance and the perverse. Love veers, as Dryden was perhaps the first explicitly to make clear.[21] Desire is a veering thing and, as will become evident in the pages ahead, veering is intricately entwined with the emergence and history of what we called 'queer'. However you may want to think about it, veering is not straight. To focus on veering in literature (and beyond) is to engage with new and perhaps unexpected, even unheard-of orientations.[22]

There is a shift, then, in little more than a century, from a 'veering round' of the human subject in Wordsworth to the 'veering round' of the universe itself in Lawrence.[23] That is just one of the trajectories traced in this book. Our peregrinations take us by way of, among others, Milton, Coleridge, Lewis Carroll, George Meredith, Proust, Joyce, Sylvia Townsend Warner, Nabokov, Elizabeth Bowen, Alan Bennett, Amitav Ghosh and Keston Sutherland. There are excursions, of varying intensity and length, into the critical and philosophical writings of Montaigne, Freud, Adorno, Raymond Williams, Blanchot, Derrida, Cixous and Deleuze. We are interested in how 'veering' might cast new light on three interrelated questions: What is literature? What is its value or force? Why might the question of literature today be important, perhaps more important than ever? We drift, however, into unanticipated times and spaces. At once applicable to the small (atoms, non-human animals, the human body, human thoughts and feelings) and to the inconceivably vast (the environment, the stars, the universe and plural universes), veering becomes a new figure through which to reflect not only on literature, but on everything else besides.

Notes

Unless otherwise indicated, all dictionary definitions are from the *Oxford English Dictionary* (hereafter *OED*), 2nd edition (Oxford: Oxford University Press, 1989), in its latest online version (at http://www.oed.com).

All quotations from Freud are from *The Standard Edition of the Complete Psychological Works of Sigmund Freud* (hereafter *SE*), 24 vols, trans. and ed. James Strachey, in collaboration with Anna Freud, assisted by Alix Strachey and Alan Tyson, and editorial assistant Angela Richards (London: Vintage, 2001).

1. Elizabeth Bowen, 'Mysterious Kôr', in *The Collected Stories of Elizabeth Bowen* (Harmondsworth: Penguin, 1983), p. 731.
2. Maurice Blanchot, *The Book to Come*, trans. Charlotte Mandell (1959; Stanford: Stanford University Press, 2003), p. 150.
3. Timothy Clark, *The Cambridge Introduction to Literature and the Environment* (Cambridge: Cambridge University Press, 2011), p. 6.
4. Clark, *Literature and the Environment*, p. 203.
5. See Guy Debord and Gil J. Wolman, 'A User's Guide to Détournement', and Guy Debord, 'Détournement as Negation and Prelude', in *Situationist International Anthology*, rev. and expanded edn, ed. and trans. Ken Knabb (Berkeley: Bureau of Public Secrets, 2006), pp. 14–21, 67–8 and *passim*. Veering, as I attempt to elaborate it in this book, thus corresponds in numerous ways with the work of Timothy Morton, not least as regards a linking of 'the environment' and environmentalism with the uncanny. 'Ecological experience', Morton argues, is strangely 'curved'. He writes: 'The more ecological awareness we have, the more we experience the uncanny. Any environmentalism that edits this out is incomplete. If there is an inevitable experiential dimension of ecology, there is an inevitable psychological dimension. This psychological dimension includes weird phenomena that warp our psychic space. There is no smooth, flat, immediate ecological experience. It's all curved.' See Timothy Morton, *The Ecological Thought* (Cambridge, MA: Harvard University Press, 2010), p. 54.
6. See John Berger, *To the Wedding* (London: Bloomsbury, 2009), pp. 197–8.
7. Don DeLillo, *Underworld* (London: Picador, 1999), p. 371. Further page references are to this edition and are given parenthetically in the main body of the text.
8. Thus, for example, in George Eliot's *Daniel Deronda*, ed. Barbara Hardy (Harmondsworth: Penguin, 1967), 'lively horses . . . veered about' (p. 102); in Jack London's *White Fang* (London: Thomas Nelson, n.d.), 'a gaunt old wolf . . . was addicted to crowding [the she-wolf], to veering towards her till his scarred muzzle touched her body, or shoulder, or neck' (p. 46); and in J. Walker McSpadden and Charles Wilson's *Robin Hood and His Merry Outlaws* (London: Associated Newspapers, 1920), 'the stag veer[ed] about and fix[ed] its glances rigidly on the bushes to the left side of the glade' (p. 217).

9. Of the numerous possibilities of prepositions that turn up with the verb 'to veer', perhaps the least common is 'up' (or 'upward'). But see, for example, David Bromwich's 'The Confessions of Bill', a review of Taylor Branch's *The Clinton Tapes: Wrestling History with the President* (New York: Simon and Schuster, 2009), in *The New York Review of Books*, 24 October 2009: 'How was Clinton able at once to govern and to observe, with a semblance of detachment, the trial that almost drove him out of the presidency? A mood of oppression may sometimes be detected in the tapes made during the impeachment; but even then his spirits veer upward to gallows humor and a strange sort of exhilaration.' We encounter another instance of 'veering up' in the work of Philip Roth, in Chapter 10 'Veering with Lawrence', below.

10. Thus Phædra accuses Gripus: 'thou Weather-cock of Government; that when the Wind blows for the Subject, point'st to Priviledge; and when it changes for the Soveraign, veers to Prerogative'. See *Amphitryon*, V, i, 13–16, in *The Works of John Dryden*, vol. 15, ed. Earl Miner (Berkeley: University of California Press, 1976).

11. See *Early English Poetry, Ballads, and Popular Literature of the Middle Ages*, vol. 1 (London: The Percy Society, 1840), p. 137. The poem was formerly attributed to Jonathan Swift.

12. William Wordsworth, *The Prelude 1799, 1805, 1850*, ed. Jonathan Wordsworth, M. H. Abrams, and Stephen Gill (New York: Norton, 1979), Book 4 (1805 text), l. 14. I discuss this in more detail in Chapter 6 'On Critical and Creative Writing', below.

13. See Alfred Tennyson, 'Madeline', ll. 27–35, in *The Poems of Tennyson*, ed. Christopher Ricks (London: Longmans, 1969), pp. 192–3. In rhyming it with 'thine' (ll. 2, 10 and 17) and 'divine' (l. 16), Tennyson inscribes the very name of Madeline with the force of making a line, though palpably not a straight one. 'Ever-varying Madeline' occurs at ll. 3, 18 and 27.

14. Wilkie Collins, *The Moonstone*, ed. J. I. M. Stewart (Harmondsworth: Penguin, 1986), p. 114.

15. See Wilkie Collins, *The Law and the Lady*, ed. Jenny Bourne Taylor (Oxford: Oxford World's Classics, 1999), pp. 206–7. I came across a reference to this later Collins novel thanks to a quite bizarre little publication called *Veering: Webster's Quotations, Facts and Phrases* (San Diego: Icon, 2008). I acquired this item (at extraordinary expense – it cost almost £30, though it is a flimsy pamphlet of just thirty-two pages) only after the bulk of the present study was completed. It consists of lists of 'Familiar Quotations' (many of which have nothing to do with the word 'veering' as such: for example, 'A good way to change somebody's attitude is to change your own' (Anonymous) or 'Change in all things is sweet' (Aristotle)), 'Use in Literature', 'Nonfiction Usage', 'Encyclopedic Usage' (including seemingly random instances of 'veer' as a proper name, such as 'Lieutenant Commander N. R. Van der Veer' ['N. R.'? What do those initials stand for?] and 'Vander Veer Botanical Park') and, finally, 'Lexicographic Usage'. It is – a shade suspiciously? – printed by 'Amazon.co.uk, Ltd., Marston Gate'. I had found it on the Amazon website, while (as a character in a novel might say) veering about on the net. I confess it was difficult not to feel a quiver of strange paranoia: was this peculiar and absurdly expensive

publication not only printed, but actually generated, specifically for me? Should I feel pleased or threatened? Was it an aid or hindrance? And what sort of weird shadow or double of my book, cast in advance?

16. See Thomas Hardy, *Jude the Obscure* (London: Macmillan, 1974), p. 419, and Henry James, *The Awkward Age* (New York: Norton, 1969), p. 69.

17. DeLillo, *Underworld*, p. 56.

18. Martin Woollacott, reviewing Patrick Tyler's book about Israel and Palestine and US policy since 1945, *A World of Trouble: America in the Middle East* (London: Portobello Books, 2009), in *The Guardian*, Review section (7 February 2009), p. 6. For Tyler's discussion of Reagan's veering, see, for example, pp. 268 and 281.

19. Richard Panek, *The 4% Universe: Dark Matter, Dark Energy, and the Race to Discover the Rest of Reality* (Oxford: Oneworld, 2011), p. 39.

20. Panek offers a compelling account not only of these topics but also of the desires and compulsions, rivalries and friendships driving the major figures responsible for discoveries and advances in the field. For the phrase 'giddy language' in particular, see p. 57.

21. I discuss Dryden's work more fully below, especially in Chapter 2 'Reading a Novel'.

22. For a thought-provoking exploration of this topic from a specifically phenomenological angle, see Sara Ahmed, *Queer Phenomenology: Orientations, Objects, Others* (Durham, NC: Duke University Press, 2006). As Ahmed notes in her Introduction: 'To queer phenomenology is to offer a different "slant" to the concept of orientation itself' (4).

23. For a detailed reading of Lawrence in this respect, see Chapter 10 'Veering with Lawrence', below.

Chapter 2

Reading a Novel

On with your Story in a direct Line, and fall not into your
Crooks and your Transversals. (Cervantes)[1]

She came around a curve . . . and then saw – too late – several
large, splintered pieces of wood scattered across the road.
There were rusty nails jutting from many of them. She jounced
across the pothole that had probably dislodged them from
some country bumpkin's carelessly placed load, then veered for
the soft shoulder in an effort to get around the litter, knowing
she probably wasn't going to make it; why else would she hear
herself saying *Oh-oh*? (Stephen King)[2]

When you read a novel, as you become involved, you veer. You come to
realize that you have veered into it and you go on veering. It is not like a
movie or computer game or conversation or session with a psychothera-
pist, it is another world. It is not simply a separate world, a utopic place.
Falling in love with a novel, letting yourself be seduced, drifting into its
strange expanse that is really neither surface nor depth, you are certainly
a pervert of sorts, a reader pleasurably submitting to that experience of
disavowal that Roland Barthes describes so well and so relishes: '*I know
these are only words, but all the same . . .*'.[3] You may come away from
your reading and then return, veering back into it, rather like the mind of
Margaret, perhaps, into the house and garden, that is also a novel, called
Howards End (1910): 'her mind trembled towards a conclusion which
only the unwise have put into words. Then, veering back into warmth,
it dwelt on ruddy bricks, flowering plum-trees, and all the tangible joys
of spring.'[4] 'Veering back' is a way of describing what is said to go on in
a character's mind, but also in a reader's. E. M. Forster's novel has you
veering about in this way, and that is the pleasure of the text.

*

In the following few pages I want to consider the idea of reading a novel as an experience of veering, as well as look at some of the ways in which novels themselves invite us to think about veering. Let us start with a perhaps deceptively 'easy read': Alan Bennett's charming novel, *The Uncommon Reader* (2006).[5] This title wittily inverts a phrase, 'the common reader', perhaps now associated primarily with Virginia Woolf (though initially taken from Dr Johnson). Set in a roughly contemporary (and explicitly post-Thatcher[6]) context, Bennett's novel tells the story of the British sovereign, Her Majesty the Queen, discovering the joys of reading. The Queen proves to be an 'opsimath' (49), in other words 'a person who begins to learn or study late in life' (*OED*). *The Uncommon Reader* offers a gentle and at moments very funny account of the subversive possibilities of reading novels, especially if one is the Queen. (The play on the Queen as 'one' is among the most uncommonly entertaining aspects of the text: one is highly amused, if not at moments quite beside oneself.) There is an underlying drive towards republicanism, literary or otherwise. Reading indeed leads to her abdication. We are a party to what the Queen thinks, of course, thanks to the magical thinking or telepathy of literature: the 'one' in the literary work is never *one*, in truth. 'She thought' is third person: another knows and records what *she thought*. Being two (or more) to think is the condition of this (as of any other) third-person narrative fiction.[7] There is no sovereign or sovereignty in literature, in this respect.

> The appeal of reading, she thought, lay in its indifference: there was something lofty about literature. Books did not care who was reading them or whether one read them or not. All readers were equal, herself included. Literature, she thought, is a commonwealth; letters a republic. Actually she had heard this phrase, the republic of letters, used before, at graduation ceremonies, honorary degrees and the like, though without knowing quite what it meant. At that time talk of a republic of any sort she had thought mildly insulting and in her actual presence tactless to say the least. It was only now she understood what it meant. Books did not defer. All readers were equal, and this took her back to the beginning of her life. (30–1)

It is striking how close the Queen here seems to Maurice Blanchot, whose marvellous little essay called 'Reading' (1955) affirms precisely this sort of joyful, innocent indifference. 'Reading,' as Blanchot puts it, 'does not produce anything, does not add anything. It lets be what is. It is freedom: not the freedom that produces being or grasps it, but freedom that welcomes, consents, says yes . . .'.[8] It is a freedom that can seem to take us back, in Bennett's phrase, to the beginning of life. As Blanchot goes on to make clear, this also entails a sense of vertigo:

There is in reading, at least at reading's point of departure, something vertiginous that resembles the movement by which, going against reason, we want to open onto life eyes already closed. This movement is linked to desire which, like inspiration, is a leap, an infinite leap . . .[9]

This desire that is a 'leap' corresponds to what he elsewhere calls, after Plato, a 'veering round of the whole being'.[10]

At first the Queen is guided in what she reads by her assistant, a young man called Norman, but then he is stealthily removed from the scene. (As the narrator puts it: 'Norman of course had not died, just gone to the University of East Anglia': 71.) She takes matters into her own hands: 'In the absence of Norman her reading, though it did not falter, did change direction' (74). Her servants and staff look on with increasing unease. Previously, we are told, she had tended to order from the London Library and from booksellers,

> [b]ut more and more now the Queen began to take books out of her own libraries, particularly the one at Windsor, where, though the choice of modern books was not unlimited, the shelves were stacked with many editions of the classic texts, some of them, of course, autographed – Balzac, Turgenev, Fielding, Conrad, books which once she would have thought beyond her but which now she sailed through, pencil always in hand, and in the process, incidentally, becoming reconciled even to Henry James, whose divagations she now took in her stride: 'After all,' as she wrote in her notebook, 'novels are not necessarily written as the crow flies.' (74)

Truly a royal inscription: *novels are not necessarily written as the crow flies*. The fictional Queen's remark serves to remind us, however, that veering is a term by which we might describe the wanderings not only of plot, but also of a sentence. Divagations, Jamesian or otherwise, are veerings at the level of syntax, as well as in the sovereignless realm of storytelling.

The appeal of *veering*, as a way of talking about digression, deviation or divagation in novels, has to do with its sense of ongoing movement, an uncertainty in and of the present. The more traditional and familiar language of 'digression', 'change of direction' and so on is a kind of stilling and fixing, an anaesthetizing of precisely what is exciting, anguishing, seductive and even dangerous about reading a novel. The wavering, unfinished character of the present participle – veering – provides a means of foregrounding the experience of reading *in the uncertainty of the present*, and the encounter with what Blanchot calls 'something vertiginous'.

Are you queer? In veering, how would you know that you were not? Certain novels perhaps enact the effects of this double question more hauntingly than others.

We might first think of veering as an image, a movement that is visible or happens in space. But it is also a matter of tone, sound and silence. It involves rhythm, syncopation and interruption, music and voice. By way of an example, we could turn to the eerie and captivating, critically neglected novel *Lolly Willowes, Or The Loving Huntsman* (1926), by Sylvia Townsend Warner.[11] The eponymous Lolly (more properly, Laura), after years as a melancholy spinster, with no particular role in life other than being governess to her brother's children in the affluent comfort of his London house, suddenly announces she is leaving and going to live in a village called Great Mop, in the Chilterns. This is more than a so-called turning point in the plot: it is where the very nature of the novel veers – from the melancholic to the demonic, from (straight) social to (queer) satanic realism.

In a fine discussion of digression, primarily focusing on Virginia Woolf's *Orlando* (1928) and *A Room of One's Own* (1929), Laura Marcus comments:

> It could be argued that Woolf's most overtly and self-reflexively digressive texts – those which point to and play with narrative digression – are those in which questions of male and female identity and the troubling of boundaries between gender categories are also made most explicit.[12]

Marcus's suggestion might be extended to the consideration of works in which questions of so-called 'sexual orientation' are in play. 'Sexual orientation' (a term already suggestive of veerings) may be foregrounded or, more subtly perhaps, undergrounded: there are digressions and there are digressions. (The relation between tautology and digression is here left, parenthetically, in suspense.) We might think, for example, of the evidently devious pleasures of being – but also the ironic process of ceasing to be – a queen in Alan Bennett's novel; or of the delirious divagations of Henry-James-writing-as-a-governess in *The Turn of the Screw*; or of the queer 'veering about' of the lawyer-narrator in Herman Melville's 'Bartleby, The Scrivener'.[13] *Lolly Willowes* certainly does not 'play with narrative digression' (in Marcus's words) in the 'overt' or 'self-reflexive' manner of Woolf. What makes Warner's novel so remarkable has to do with a quite different sort of choreography. With Laura's move to Great Mop comes an extraordinary veering in plot and genre; but this is organized as a sort of experience of secrecy or undergrounding. The veering works through delayed effect or deferred sense. And most hauntingly perhaps, it is figured through an experience of sound, tone, music.

One night early on in Laura's life at Great Mop, we are told, she heard some one playing a mouth-organ. The music came from far off, it sounded almost as if it were being played out of doors. She lit a candle and looked at her watch – it was half-past three. She got out of bed and listened at the window; it was a dark night, and the hills rose up like a screen. The noise of the mouth-organ came wavering and veering on the wind. A drunk man, perhaps? Yet what drunk man would play on so steadily? She lay awake for an hour or more, half puzzled, half lulled by the strange music, that never stopped, that never varied, that seemed to have become part of the air. (126)

This passage brings together sexual longing, virginity and secrecy. As the novel goes on to make clear, this is a secrecy not only 'about the villagers' but also within Laura herself, 'her own secret, if she had one' (127).

This 'wavering and veering on the wind' that 'never stopped, that never varied, that seemed to have become part of the air', is a figure of diversion in more than one sense. 'Wavering' (wandering about without destination, floating or fluttering) is not the same as 'veering', but they are close. Their intimacy is indeed of a strangely literal or material kind. The second and final syllables of 'wavering' are picked up in the 'veering': it is as if the words were wavering or veering into one another. Correspondingly, the 'on' seems to touch on an interruption or syncopation of sense. We might expect a veering *of* or *in* the wind, but here the 'veering' comes *before* 'the wind'. The more usual figure of the wind *as* veering is discreetly blown away.

A couple of sentences after this passage we discover that the music had emanated from a man called Billy Thomas, and that he was not drinking but agonizing, playing his mouth-organ in an attempt to 'divert himself' (126) from the pain of tooth-ache. Laura learns this from the woman in whose cottage she has taken rooms, the nicely named Mrs Leak, who liked to talk, 'talked well' and 'knew a great deal about everybody' (118). But there is also diversion in a more general and structural respect, for this night of 'strange music' does not immediately lead to a revelation of the satanic goings on in Great Mop. Laura, we are told, 'left off speculating about the villagers ... she was content to remain outside the secret, whatever it was' (127). Rather, we come upon it in a delayed, dreamy way, some sixty pages later. And having been silent all this time, the veering of the mouth-organ now returns as a peculiar refrain. Here is the moment of revelation, when Laura 'guesses the truth', 'turn[ing] to her companion':

'Where are you taking me?' she said. Mrs. Leak made no answer, but in the darkness she took hold of Laura's hand. There was no need for further explanation. They were going to the Witches' Sabbath. Mrs. Leak was a witch too ... [S]he would be Laura's chaperone. The night was full of voices. Padding rustic footsteps went by them in the dark. When they had reached the brow of the hill a faint continuous sound, resembling music, was borne towards them by the light wind. Laura remembered how young Billy Thomas, suffering from tooth-ache, had played all night upon his mouth-organ. She laughed. Mrs. Leak squeezed her hand. (187)

Such is the gentle but disquieting character of Warner's novel. The tone itself seems to waver and veer – between matter-of-fact and laughing, colloquial and diabolical.

The figure of veering comes back in the evocation of the satanic dancing that follows. The 'spinning' and 'whirl[ing]' of bodies 'in a continual flux' leaves Laura 'dizzy and bewildered' (192–4). As her dance with a young red-haired girl called Emily makes Laura 'tingle from head to foot' (192), the interlinking of the satanic and erotic becomes explicit. We are drawn into a decidedly queer scene or, rather perhaps, by the process of deferred effect produced through Warner's sixty-page delay, we come to realize that that queerness was already there, the very ambience of our reading. Veering and queering go together. The music to which everyone is dancing is strange, 'as though the sound issued from the dancers themselves' (194). Laura decides to 'slip away and sit quietly in the hedge' (194). From here she watches as 'Once again the dancers veered away to the further side of the field, their music retreating with them' (197).

Lolly Willowes leads us to think about 'veering in literature' in terms of music. Warner's novel veers in genre, subject matter and sexual coding but also, and perhaps most elusively, in tone and rhythm, in the choreography of voice. It leaves us with the playful 'air' of a wavering and veering that is at once erotic and suggestive of the demonic and possessed. There is veering in the voice. Voice in a work of literary fiction is never one, never purely or simply itself. Nor does it belong to one moment, to one time alone. There is always more or other than one voice. Voices go silent, are suppressed, come back. There is doubling and interweaving, polyphony, and ghostly absence or refrain.

This relates, in turn, to how we might think differently about 'point of view' or 'focalization' in literary narrative. Standard literary critical terms such as these are indeed *terms* in the strong sense: they close off, they determine. The *point* or *focus* is definite, single, clear and unified. Terms such as 'point of view' and 'focalization' (or 'focalizer' or 'focalized') are critical fictions that seek to repress the force – and therefore also to repress the question of the effects and value – of veering. They are a part of a sort of shaggy-dog story that literary critics and theorists (in particular, narratologists) have been telling for decades. I would like to imagine that audiences for this story are, so to speak, tailing off;

but we all know how long (and unveeringly) a shaggy-dog story can go on . . .

Here are two short passages from two novels by way of illustration. Let us plunge, first of all, into the opening episode of James Joyce's *Ulysses* (1922), and try not to lose ourselves.[14] A man is thought to have drowned, they have been looking for him for more than a week:

> The boatman nodded towards the north of the bay with some disdain.
> – There's five fathoms out there, he said. It'll be swept up that way when the tide comes in about one. It's nine days today.
> The man that was drowned. A sail veering about the blank bay waiting for a swollen bundle to bob up, roll over to the sun a puffy face, saltwhite. Here I am. (18)

There are of course too many things to talk about, even with an extract as brief as this. Joyce's writing invites the reader to veer about – or drown. Or drown *and* veer about.

Many critics have remarked on how profoundly and insidiously *Ulysses* provides a sort of meta-discursive or self-reflexive machinery for its own reading and interpretation.[15] Thus you can find yourself caught up, for instance, in what the novel seems to be doing with the verb 'to veer'. Trying to respond to this little extract about the 'sail veering about the blank bay', then, can make you feel a bit like the sort of journalist evoked later in the novel: 'Funny the way those newspaper men veer about when they get wind of some new opening. Weathercocks. Hot and cold in the same breath. Wouldn't know which to believe. One story good till you hear the next' (103). Indeed it can make you feel like an entire office, a sort of miniature or internalized Joycean telegraph office with different journalists or professors veering about, each assigned to a different story – one, for example, concerned with the story of Telemachus, and another with the role and significance of the 'five fathoms', Shakespeare's *The Tempest*, the Death of the Father and the role of song ('Full fathom five thy father lies . . .'[16]), another writing about the Importance of the Death of the Mother, and another working on the Death of the Brother, and someone putting together a rather erudite piece about Joyce's compound adjectives and the poetry of Keats (the 'saltwhite' corpse that takes us back to the 'snotgreen' and 'scrotumtightening sea' [4] at the beginning of the novel and, from there, *ubique*), and another an article about Dublin Bay and the life of boatmen in the late nineteenth and early twentieth centuries, and another engaged with modernism and aestheticism, especially correspondences between Joyce's language and the Imagist movement, and another devoted to the Bible (the differences, for instance, between 'Here I am' and 'Here am

I'[17]), and another sent off to explore the 'b'-alliteration ('veering about the blank bay waiting for a swollen bundle to bob up') and its intertextual links with Wordsworth's drowned man of Esthwaite in *The Prelude* (the 'boat', the 'beauteous scene', the dead body 'bolt upright'[18]), and so on for centuries.

Indeed, Joyce's *Ulysses* might lead us to think about veering as a key to what makes a literary classic or masterpiece. The 'great work' is the kind of text that seems to escape or sidestep the erosion of time, that exceeds interpretation, that has a kind of cryptaesthetic resistance (as I have called it elsewhere), that keeps, in a word, *veering*.[19] Rather than think of the canonical or classic text primarily as being, in Frank Kermode's phrase, 'patient of interpretation', we might reflect on its capacity for veering.[20] We will return to this question again shortly, when we come to consider Proust.

Let us stick for the moment, however, simply to making a couple of remarks about point of view or focalization. 'The man that was drowned. A sail veering about the blank bay waiting for a swollen bundle to bob up, roll over to the sun a puffy face, saltwhite. Here I am.' The first sentence ('The man that was drowned') might be understood as focalized through Stephen. But it could also be in some sense 'sharing' the point of view or voice of the boatman, in an instance of what the novel has just a few sentences earlier referred to as '[i]dle mockery' (18). There is never only one voice, one point of view or one narrative perspective, at any one time, in a literary work. Even where we think we have a transcription of Stephen's thoughts or feelings, the writing (starting from the fact that this is a third-person narrative) shows us that point of view is divided, shared, double or multiple. Focalization or point of view, I want to suggest, is veering. There is always veering about in the purportedly fixed, definite and stabilized unity of these terms.

The apposition of 'The man that was drowned' and 'A sail veering about' gives wind, perhaps, of stranger identifications. In this telegraphic or telegrammatic writing everything is shifting or drifting into the next thing. The subject of veering is itself a tropological displacement, in the form of synecdoche ('sail' for 'boat'); and, in a further turn, it is anthropomorphized as 'waiting'. The so-called point of view thus becomes, in addition, that of the sail itself. It is a remarkable sentence, in which the 'sail veering' at the start rolls into the 'puffy face' of the end, just as the (unspoken) whiteness of the sail veers through the 'blank' into the 'saltwhite' of the face of the corpse. It becomes difficult, perhaps, to hear 'a sail' without the lurking violence of 'assail'.[21] And finally the prosopopoeia here, the voice of the dead man himself ('Here I am') – coming through, in or alongside the voice of Stephen and/or the Joycean narrator – might leave us speculating on the sense that 'voice' and 'point of view' in literature will always *also* be that of the dead. As we will see in greater detail later in this book, veering is also a theory of spectrality.

The second example is a brief extract from a more recent novel, Amitav Ghosh's *The Hungry Tide* (2005).[22] In particular, I want to consider a passage that appears in a chapter called 'A Hunt', relating the process by which humans are able to fish in 'symbiosis' with dolphins (the creatures whose 'fins' are here referred to).[23] The point of view seems to be that of Piya:

> Looking ahead with her binoculars, she spotted a pair of fins far out in front. By the time they had crossed the mohona, the fins were nowhere in sight. But Fokir seemed sure of the way, for he turned unhesitatingly into a wide channel and then veered off into another that was narrower. Shortly afterward he downed his oars and pointed to the shore. Veering around with her binoculars, Piya spotted three crocodiles – she had missed them because her attention had been focused on the water. (138)

Besides the beauty of the perhaps unfamiliar 'mohona' (a Bengali word meaning 'confluence'), the writing may seem quite flat and unremarkable alongside Joyce's. Yet there are intriguing subtleties, especially around the 'veering'. The 'v'-word insists, in a rather striking fashion. Fokir 'veered off into another [channel]', we are told. And then there is Piya 'veering around with her binoculars'.

As if it had a curious proclivity for generating thinking on the topic, the figure of veering brings into focus the very question of focus. It might appear, at first sight, that we are seeing this scene through Piya's eyes. But any such 'first sight' is a critical fabrication or readerly hallucination. Literature is a space of second sight. 'Point of view' or 'focalization' always involves a sort of magical or telepathic logic (a narrator or author-figure seeing or sharing the point of view, as if through magical binoculars), and the literary work always sees us coming: it is clairvoyant by nature, it is cryptaesthetic and has seen its own future. It will have seen, for example, what a character 'missed' ('she had missed them because her attention had been focused on the water'). Even if the writer or narrator claims not to know (and proceeds as if blind to) what she or he is going to say, the reader knows that the future has already been witnessed.

Second sight is part of a more general logic of duplicity. This passage from *The Hungry Tide* invites us to construe *veer* (Fokir 'veered off', Piya is 'veering around') as a descriptor of narration itself. It is and is not Piya's word. There is uncertainty concerning the source of these words. We cannot properly speak here of a single identifiable 'voice' or 'point of view'. Ghosh's writing intimates a veering *within* veering, a veering that cannot be fixed or stilled. As with Joyce, syntax has a crucial role to play. Two sentences in succession have Fokir as their subject ('But Fokir seemed sure ... he turned ... and then veered ... Shortly afterward he downed his oars and pointed ...'), and then a third sentence begins: 'Veering around ...'. In this instant, opening the sentence with this present participle, Ghosh's writing veers: 'veering' veers from Fokir to Piya or, more precisely, it veers between them, it veers from one to the other without being simply attributable to one *or* the other. This strangeness is then mimed or repeated, in effect, by Piya's binoculars: in a further sort of double vision or binocularism, we see her 'veering around' and see a 'veering around' of what she sees. 'Veering' is a fine word, indeed, for what it is like to shift around, looking through binoculars. Vision itself veers. We feel the crocodiles veering into view.

*

There is another sense of 'veering', which I have not mentioned till now. Again primarily in a nautical context, to veer is: 'To allow (a sheet or other sail-line) to run out to some extent; to let out by releasing' or 'To let *out* (any line or rope); to allow to run *out* gradually to a desired length' (*OED*, 'veer', v. 1). There is, then, a related noun-form of veering as 'The action of causing or allowing to run out' (as in a veering cable or chain) (*OED*, 'veering', vbl. n. 1). An early use of 'veer' in this sense is to be found in Edmund Spenser's *Faerie Queene*: 'Vere the maine shete, and beare vp with the land'.[24] And for an early figurative use, with reference to good writing, we may recall Ben Jonson's advice in his *Discoveries* (1641): 'As it is a great point of Art, when our matter requires it, to enlarge, and veere out all sayle; so to take it in, and contract it, is of no lesse praise when the Argument doth aske it.'[25] In addition to Jonson's charmingly expansive image for the art of writing, I would like to propose a further figurative usage for 'veering', namely in relation to what might be called the economy of desire. At issue here is the question of how to deal with the fact that veering can be disturbing, even terrifying. As with those crocodiles evoked a few moments ago, there is something dangerous about veering. And you do not, after all, want to throw yourself to the crocodiles. Everyone is veering, everybody has their own way of veering. You have to regulate an economy, otherwise you go mad, or get eaten, or both. You have to *veer* veering, in this sense.

Veering is, then, a figure for thinking about desire – at once reassuring and unsettling. Do we *choose* to fall in love with someone, or with some thing, a piece of music, a painting or work of literature? As I was suggesting a few moments ago, when we veer into a novel we let ourselves be seduced: we can find ourselves falling in love with it. But this being-led-astray (the literal sense of 'seduction') is neither simply up to us, nor up to the novel (or poem or play) we are reading. It is the effect of something like a veering between the two.

There is no desire without veering, we might suppose, and certainly no orgasm or *jouissance*. As the idea of *la petite mort* intimates: there is exercise *and* loss of control, exercise *and* loss of self – it is all part of 'the letting go' (in Emily Dickinson's phrase).[26]

This is the principal sense in which I construe the concept of clinamen in this book: it is a swerve, a veering that is yours, your desire and no one else's (everyone has their own clinamen), and yet it resists appropriation, it is never in fact yours to have or to hold.[27] It is what veers away. Veering is other.

What appeals to one reader does not necessarily appeal to another. Think of Vladimir Nabokov and his veering little girl:

> 'You remember a lot, ha-ha,' said Lucette, standing in front of them in her green pyjamas, sun-tanned chest bare, legs parted, arms akimbo.
> 'Perhaps the simplest – ' began Ada.
> 'The simplest answer,' said Lucette, 'is that you two *can't* tell me why exactly you want to get rid of me.'
> 'Perhaps the simplest answer,' continued Ada, 'is for you, Van, to give her a vigorous, resounding spanking.'
> 'I dare you!' cried Lucette, and veered invitingly.[28]

But let us not pretend to be prudish. Literature is a space of substitutability. There is perhaps always something a bit queer about veering. No one is just one, in a work of literature, any more than 'point of view' is ever simply monocular.

*

Time for Marcel Proust. As with all the other examples we have looked at so far, veering is at once what the writing is about and what the reader is drawn into experiencing in turn. Perhaps more profoundly and more obsessively than any other work of literature, *À la recherche du temps perdu* (*In Search of Lost Time*) is about veering in time. This is both the subject and the form of Proust's writing. But if veering is at the heart of what narrative theorists will later come to fix on as prolepsis (or flash-forward) and analepsis (or flashback), Proust's way is also Proust's sway. It is singularly sensuous and phenomenal, and it is constantly on the move. It does not hold still in language, especially not the language of narratology.

Time is not reversible – except in fiction. Films can show this, but literature does it through the very language of memory and, in Proust, through the veerings of that language. The reversibility of time – the subject of, say, Harold Pinter's *Betrayal* (1978) or Martin Amis's *Time's Arrow* (1991) – is ordinarily conceived in terms of a linear model (moving in reverse as opposed to moving forward), but Proust disturbs all this. In searching or researching lost time he marks and remarks a veering in the very possibility of reversing and reversibility. With Proust, as Gérard Genette has observed, 'the order of succession and the relationships of duration that make up classical temporality are from the beginning subverted or, more subtly and effectively, *perverted*'.[29]

We veer in memory or – stranger perhaps to get our heads around – memories veer in us. As George Eliot's poem 'A College Breakfast-Party' (1878) hauntingly evokes: 'The sun was hot / On southward branches of the meadow elms, / The shadows slowly farther crept and veered / Like changing memories.'[30] Eliot's 'veered' is a changing, her 'changing' a veering. This image of veering memories is, perhaps, closer to Proust (looking forward) than (looking backward) to Wordsworth and his implicitly fixed 'spots of time'.[31]

Writing about Proust is like rolling up a sleeping bag and trying to fit it in a matchbox.

Restricting ourselves simply to a couple of passages in *Swann's Way* (the first volume of *In Search of Lost Time*) in Moncrieff and Kilmartin's remarkable translation, we might see how a reading of Proust opens up through the figure of veering.[32] It is, perhaps first of all, a matter of syntax. It is what is happening with Proust's sentences, in particular with what Terence Kilmartin calls 'their spiralling subordinate clauses'.[33] In this spinning world of writing we are invited to experience the vertigo. The Proustian narrator is veering in time – between different times of past and present, but also *within* these, veering in the present time of recollection *and* veering in memory. Time is not rectilinear but a delirious zigzagging hatchwork. Samuel Beckett succinctly comments apropos the Proustian narrator: 'As though the figure of Time could be represented by an endless series of parallels, his life is switched over to another line and proceeds, without any solution of continuity.'[34] And this veering in time is – from the very opening of *Swann's Way* – complicated by another, crossing into and over the first, to wit: veerings between being awake and being asleep.

From the very first paragraphs we are drawn into this double vortex or vertigo, in a dizzyingly twirling sinuous prose that entails, in one 'rather peculiar turn' (1) after another, a commingling of the experience of reading and falling asleep, with all the perverse allure of hypnagogic or hypnopompic seduction. For why would you want to go to sleep while you are being seduced? Unless you are already dreaming ... It is nothing less than a hypnopoetics. Thus the narrator's recollections shimmy in on an imaginary figure drifting off while reading, 'doz[ing] off' in some 'abnormal and divergent position', as 'the world [goes] hurtling out of orbit', 'sitting in a magic chair [that] will carry him at full speed through time and space', so that 'when he opens his eyes again he will imagine that he went to sleep months earlier in another place' (3–4). After giving us what he calls 'these shifting and confused gusts of memory' concerning his 'waking dream' (6) of remembering the various rooms he had once slept in, the narrator starts a new paragraph:

> Certainly I was now well awake; my body had veered round for the last time and the good angel of certainty had made all the surrounding objects stand still, had set me down under my bedclothes, in my bedroom, and had fixed, approximately in their right places in the uncertain light, my chest of drawers, my writing-table, my fireplace, the window overlooking the street, and both the doors. But for all that I now knew that I was not in any of the houses of which the ignorance of the waking moment had, in a flash, if not presented me with a distinct picture, at least persuaded me of the possible presence, my memory had been set in motion ... (7–8)

As we will see later on in this study, the apparently autobiographical gesture whereby the writer figures himself as a veering body ('my body had veered round') is not new with Proust: it goes back at least as far as Wordsworth. But there is a playful and mischievous aspect to Proust that is quite different from the seriousness of Wordsworth or indeed George Eliot. Reading Proust can make you laugh out loud: such, at least, is the temptation in encountering the helter-skelter effects generated by spiralling sentences of this sort, in which what is certain is not certain and the last veering round is only a new point from which to veer off once again. We veer from certitude ('Certainly ... the good angel of certainty ...') to a wavering.[35] *There is veering in the now*: 'Certainly I was *now* well awake ... But for all that I *now* knew ...'.

In the context of Proust and memory, we may tend to think first of those 'plump little cakes' (51) called madeleines. They do indeed provide a marvellous example of that 'elusive whirling medley' (53) of colours and tastes that has the narrator's mind veering back. But there is a still more emphatic veering, viz. in the narrator's recollections and verbal reconstructions of the steeples of Martinville and Vieuxvicq.[36] And it is here, in particular, that we can elaborate a little further on the relationship between veering and aesthetics. Veering in Proust is associated with bodily pleasure, the beauties of bodies in motion. It is a moving

multiplicity of bodies – at once the body of the narrator as he is travelling through the landscape, other bodies in the world (the movements
of the horse and carriage in which he is journeying, the windings of the
road, the quasi-dreamlike shiftings of the steeples themselves), and the
body of the writing itself in which everything is veering about. We come,
then, to a bend:

> At a bend in the road I experienced, suddenly, that special pleasure which
> was unlike any other, on catching sight of the twin steeples of Martinville,
> bathed in the setting sun and constantly changing their position with the
> movement of the carriage and the windings of the road, and then of a third
> steeple, that of Vieuxvicq, which, although separated from them by a hill and
> a valley, and rising from rather higher ground in the distance, appeared none
> the less to be standing by their side. (215–16/173)

Such are the steeples or *clochers* (173), the original French word more
immediately suggestive of the measurement of time itself, chiming (as it
were) with the English word 'clocks'. They are rendered anthropomorphic and erotic, bathed in sunlight, 'constantly changing their position',
producing a 'pleasure . . . unlike any other'.

The perversity, mourning and eroticism of Proust's work is, however,
never only an immersion in the physical or phenomenal, even or especially when this seems paramount. Veering in 'lost time': it is always also
a writing and reading. Throwing out the possibility that some 'pretty
phrase' might be lying 'hidden behind the steeples of Martinville' (217),
the narrator veers into a recollection of writing, a fragment of writing
that is a recollection of veering. He offers 'the following little fragment,
which I have since rediscovered and now reproduce with only a slight
revision here and there' (217):

> We had left Martinville some little time, and the village, after accompanying
> us for a few seconds, had already disappeared, when, lingering alone on the
> horizon to watch our flight, its steeples and that of Vieuxvicq waved once
> again their sun-bathed pinnacles in token of farewell. Sometimes one would
> withdraw, so that the other two might watch us for a moment still; then the
> road changed direction, they veered in the evening light like three golden
> pivots, and vanished from my sight. (217–18)

Veering and vanishing ('veered . . . and vanished') is a double act we
shall encounter again elsewhere in this book, in particular apropos the
poetry of Coleridge.[37] Voyeuristic, valedictory and melancholy at the
same time, Proust's steeples are beautifully veering in the light, a beautiful veering of the light. Veering in the narrator's sight, they are a veering
of seeing as such.

And for all the emphasis on the sensuousness of vision, this is also a veering concerned with writing, music and song. Appearing 'at once to contain and to conceal', the 'mobility' and 'luminosity' (216) of the steeples are connected with what the narrator calls 'the illusion of a sort of fecundity', an illusion which, he says, 'distracted me ... from the sense of my own impotence whenever I had sought a philosophical theme for some great literary work' (214). It is as if the veering of the steeples were a metaphor or substitute for literary greatness. The steeples 'veered in the evening light like three golden pivots' (*ils virèrent dans la lumière comme trois pivots d'or*: 175): they are *like* pivots and, at the same time, they *are* pivots. These golden pivots veer between the metaphorical and the literal. As 'the centre on which a mechanism turns or oscillates' or the 'physical part on which another part turns' (*OED*, 'pivot', n. 1 a), the pivot is, in this singular 'little fragment ... now reproduce[d]', at once a figure of veering and a veering of figure.

The *OED* records that a pivot was, in twelfth-century French, 'in figurative use in the name of a dance'. The metaphors or tropes by which Proust's steeples are recalled keep moving, veering and vanishing. Early on in the fragment the narrator compares them to 'three birds perched upon the plain, motionless and conspicuous in the sunlight' (217), but goes on to image them as 'three flowers', or again as 'three maidens in a legend', 'gliding one behind another' (218). He tells us that he 'never thought again of this page' (on which he had written about the veering of the steeples) but, he recalls,

> at the moment when ... I had finished writing it, I was so filled with happiness, I felt that it had so entirely relieved my mind of its obsession with the steeples and the mystery which lay behind them, that, as though I myself were a hen and had just laid an egg, I began to sing at the top of my voice. (218)

These passages from Proust encourage us to reflect more deeply on a number of aspects of our topic: queerness and perversity, desire and otherness, time and memory, song and music, metaphor and poetry. They give us a veering pivot, and veering *as* a pivot. In these ways Proust's work provides an especially rich and resourceful example for drawing together what I have been attempting to sketch here, apropos reading a novel. A novel is not necessarily written as the crow flies, to recall Alan Bennett's phrase. But how does it fly? One knows what Her Royal Highness means, and in this colloquialism she is doubtless as common as the rest of us. But perhaps there is a further irony to the efficacy of this avian metaphor. For like the gulls in DeLillo's *Underworld* that we noted earlier (in Chapter 1 'Casting Off'), crows too are given to veering. Veering offers a new and different way of construing the nature of plot and storytelling: changes in subject, narrator, time and location; alterations in characterization, or in a character's perception, knowledge, belief or feelings; deviation, digression or twisting at the level of the individual sentence, syntax or word. In reading, too, we veer: our attention is not constant, our thoughts and feelings shift about. Veering might on occasion be deliberate and voluntary on our part but, even when it is (or feels to be), it is also in reaction or response to what we are reading. In this context veering is something that happens *between* the novel and the reader: as such, it is unstable, unpredictable, silent and secret (even to oneself).

Veering is at work in the structure of language, not simply something you choose to do with words. There is an aesthetics of veering. There seems to be something erotic and even demonic about it. Veering is a force or effect of forces: when you begin to read, even the title of a novel, a sense of uncertainty, promise or threat is in play. What will this novel bring? What might it do to you? How might it change what you think or feel? In this respect reading, from the beginning, is attuned to what Blanchot describes as the vertiginous leap or (following Plato) as a veering of one's entire being. It has to do with the feeling that, when you start reading a novel, you never know *what* might happen, and you are on the very verge.

As part of a critical vocabulary, veering offers new ways of thinking about literary narrative. To speak of *veering* is to invite another kind of dynamism into critical thinking, a new riskiness and uncertainty of control. It allows us to maintain a sense of the swerving, whirling, flickering, proliferating affects and possibilities that are generated in reading: there is always more than one voice in a voice; tone is always altering, divided, a sort of differential vibration; silence is always more complex or ironic, more restless or elusive than we might think; point of view, despite its name, is never a single or unified instantiation of seeing; and focalization, likewise, is a veering of or between perspectives.

How does a novel veer? To ask this question, as I have begun to sketch it in these pages, is to engage with the singularity of the literary work, its way with words, its sway, its clinamen. It is to explore such questions as: What kinds of turning, sliding and shifting are going on in this text? How is the unpredictable, abrupt strangeness of veering evident in movements of plot and characterization, tone, point of view, the secret or unspoken, and so on? How does the novel draw us in but also resist us? How does it seduce the reader while at the same time seeming to let itself be led astray? How does it give the very movement of 'leading astray' free rein? In what ways – both at the macrological level of genre, plot, character, theme, and so on, and at the micrological level of syntax, grammar and tropes (metaphor, metonymy, aposiopesis, anacoluthon, amphibology, etc.) – does the novel veer off or veer away, escape or elude us?

Literary works do not have to contain the word 'veer' in order to be veering, any more than those we might consider uncanny (such as the tales of Edgar Allan Poe) have to contain the word 'uncanny'.[38] In this chapter, nonetheless, I have highlighted specific instances of the word in a range of novels, in order to establish a sort of strategic *pivot* or nodal point for our topic. The mode of critical analysis here designated as 'veering' inevitably involves engagement with a swathe of other figures and images (twisting, spinning, sidestepping, swerving, vertigo, jumping, leaping, digressing), all of which contribute to what is shifting, uncertain and risky in the very moment and experience of reading. Finally, as I have sought to suggest in my discussion of Joyce and Proust in particular, the figure of veering opens up new lines and angles for thinking about what constitutes a classic or canonical novel. *Ulysses* and *In Search of Lost Time* are both marked by an extraordinary sense of 'veering about': we shall return to this resonant phrase later in this book, especially in the context of the writings of Herman Melville and D. H. Lawrence. The veering of the masterpiece is about its resistance to being finished with, about what is beautiful or stubborn (or both) and gets away, about its ghostly and demonic restlessness. At issue here, it would seem, are the singularity and enigma of how the classic novel *keeps veering*.

Notes

1. Miguel de Cervantes, *Don Quixote*, trans. T. Shelton (1746), III, xxvi, 183; quoted in *OED* 'transversal', 1 B. n.
2. Stephen King, 'Big Driver', in *Full Dark, No Stars* (London: Hodder and Stoughton, 2010), p. 134.
3. Roland Barthes, *The Pleasure of the Text*, trans. Richard Howard (Oxford: Basil Blackwell, 1990), p. 47.
4. E. M. Forster, *Howards End* (New York: Vintage Books, 1989), p. 214.
5. Alan Bennett, *The Uncommon Reader* (2006; London: Faber and Faber, 2008). Further page references appear parenthetically in the main body of the text.
6. At one moment the Queen reminisces about the 'show of interest' or 'show of concern' that prime ministers down the years had wanted from her: 'Men (and this included Mrs Thatcher) wanted show' (55).
7. I have explored this more fully elsewhere: see, in particular, 'The "Telepathy Effect": Notes toward a Reconsideration of Narrative Fiction', in *The Uncanny* (Manchester: Manchester University Press, 2003), pp. 256–76.
8. See Maurice Blanchot, 'Reading', in *The Space of Literature*, trans. Ann

Smock (Lincoln, NE: University of Nebraska Press, 1982), pp. 191–7: here, p. 194.

9. Blanchot, 'Reading', p. 195.

10. See Maurice Blanchot, *The Writing of the Disaster*, trans. Ann Smock (Lincoln, NE: University of Nebraska Press, 1986), p. 95. Michael Naas writes: 'Blanchot is talking about the passage in the myth of the cave where the prisoners, chained to a wall in the underground cave, must actually be turned toward the light (the fire, the sun), not simply presented with the truth of their condition but physically turned toward the light at each stage in their ascent toward the Good. The myth suggests that it is not simply a matter of giving someone (the future philosopher) knowledge but of "turning them about", con-verting them, turning their souls toward the truth and toward the Good. The Greek word is periagōgē, which means in this context a turning about or conversion of one's entire being. It is thus not a matter of implanting or imparting knowledge but of turning the soul, a matter of having one's entire being turned or converted' (personal email communication, 10 September 2010). It is striking, too, that Plato's text describes this veering in a figurative, even dramaturgic way, comparing it to 'the scene-shifting periact in the theatre' (518d). See Plato, *The Republic*, trans. Paul Shorey (London: Harvard University Press, 1935), pp. 134–5.

11. Sylvia Townsend Warner, *Lolly Willowes, Or The Loving Huntsman* (1926; London: Virago, 2000). Further page references appear parenthetically in the main body of the text.

12. See Laura Marcus, 'Virginia Woolf and Digression: Adventures in Consciousness', in Alexis Grohmann and Caragh Wells (eds), *Digressions in European Literature: From Cervantes to Sebald* (Houndmills: Palgrave Macmillan, 2011), pp. 118–29: here, p. 125.

13. I discuss James's *The Turn of the Screw* and Melville's 'Bartleby, The Scrivener' in greater detail below, in Chapters 7 'The Literary Turn' and 9 'Veerer: Reading Melville's "Bartleby"', respectively.

14. James Joyce, *Ulysses*, ed. Hans Walter Gabler with Wolfhard Steppe and Claus Melchior (New York: Vintage Books, 1986). Further page references are to this edition and are given parenthetically in the main body of the text.

15. We would doubtless have to start with Joyce himself, who remarked of *Ulysses*: 'I've put in so many enigmas and puzzles that it will keep the professors busy for centuries arguing over what I meant, and that's the only way of insuring one's immortality' (quoted in Richard Ellmann, *James Joyce*, rev. edn (Oxford: Oxford University Press, 1983), p. 573). For a particularly acute discussion of this 'programming', see Jacques Derrida, 'Ulysses Gramophone: Hear Say Yes in Joyce', trans. Tina Kendall and Shari Benstock, in Derek Attridge (ed.), *Acts of Literature* (London and New York: Routledge, 1992), pp. 256–309.

16. See William Shakespeare, *The Tempest*, ed. Stephen Orgel (Oxford: Oxford World's Classics, 1998), I, ii, 397. For a further picking up of this line in Joyce, see *Ulysses*, p. 41.

17. The phrase 'Here I am' is used by Abraham (Genesis 22: 1). As such, Joyce's 'Here I am' also operates in a chiasmatic fashion, as a cadaver-izing of Abraham. 'Here am I' is a more widespread formulation in the

Authorized Version (see Genesis 22: 11, 27: 1, 31: 11, 46: 2 and *passim*), but would run counter to the spirit of Joycean colloquialism.

18. See William Wordsworth, *The Prelude 1799, 1805, 1850*, ed. Jonathan Wordsworth, M. H. Abrams and Stephen Gill (New York: Norton, 1979), Two-Part Prelude, Part I, pp. 274–9; cf. Book 5 (1805), pp. 468–71, and Book 5 (1850), pp. 446–9.

19. For more on 'cryptaesthetic resistance', see Nicholas Royle, *Telepathy and Literature: Essays on the Reading Mind* (Oxford: Blackwell, 1990), ch. 2 ('Cryptaesthesia: The Case of *Wuthering Heights*'), pp. 28–62.

20. See Frank Kermode, *The Classic: Literary Images of Permanence and Change* (Cambridge, MA: Harvard University Press, 1983), p. 134.

21. My thanks to Isabelle Young for alerting me to this play on 'a sail' in the context of 'The Rime of the Ancient Mariner' (see Samuel Taylor Coleridge, *Poems*, ed. John Beer (London: Dent 1974), pp. 173–89). In the lines 'I bit my arm, I sucked the blood, / And cried, A sail! A sail!' (ll. 160–1), the sounding of 'assail' would constitute a nice example of what Garrett Stewart calls transegmental drifting. I discuss veering in Coleridge's poem (as well as Stewart's neologism) more fully in Chapter 6 'On Critical and Creative Writing', below.

22. Amitav Ghosh, *The Hungry Tide* (New York: Houghton Mifflin, 2005). Further page references are to this edition and are given parenthetically in the main body of the text.

23. Ghosh does not associate veering with dolphins themselves. Like other larger sea creatures such as turtles and rays, dolphins may readily be said to veer. Something of this is perhaps intimated in Christopher Marlowe's 'Hero and Leander', in the lovely phrase 'crooked dolphin' (in turn evidently indebted to Ovid's 'curvi . . . delphines'). See Christopher Marlowe, 'Hero and Leander', Sestiad II, l. 234 in *The Poems*, ed. Millar Maclure (London: Methuen, 1968), p. 36, and editorial note.

24. See Edmund Spenser, *The Faerie Queene*, ed. A. C. Hamilton (London: Longman, 1977), Book I, Canto XII, stanza 1. Cf. also Book V, Canto XII, stanza 18: 'He will not bide the daunger of such dread, / But strikes his sayles, and vereth his mainsheat'. There are of course many other examples in literature. In the context of the novel we might think, for instance, of *Robinson Crusoe*: 'It was with the utmost Hazard the Boat came near us, but it was impossible for us to get on Board, or for the Boat to lie near the Ship Side, till at last the Men rowing very heartily, and venturing their Lives to save ours, our Men cast them a Rope over the Stern with a Buoy to it, and then vered it out a great length, which they after great Labour and Hazard took hold of, and we hall'd them close under our Stern and got all into their Boat.' See Daniel Defoe, *Robinson Crusoe*, ed. Michael Shinagel, 2nd edn (New York: Norton, 1994), p. 11.

25. Ben Jonson, *Discoveries* (1641) and *Conversations with William Drummond of Hawthornden* (1619), ed. G. B. Harrison (Edinburgh: Edinburgh University Press, 1966), p. 75. It is perhaps also worth recalling here the full drift of Jonson's title: *Timber: Or, Discoveries; Made Vpon Men and Matter: As They have flow'd out of his daily Readings; or had their refluxe to his peculiar Notion of the Times.*

26. See Poem 341 ('After great pain, a formal feeling comes') in *The Complete*

Poems of Emily Dickinson, ed. Thomas H. Johnson (London: Faber and Faber, 1975), p. 162.

27. Cf. Joan Retallack's discussion of this topic in *The Poethical Wager* (Berkeley: University of California Press, 2003). As she remarks: 'The role of the clinamen is never entirely of anyone's own choosing' (4).

28. Vladimir Nabokov, *Ada or Ardor: A Family Chronicle* (London: Penguin, 2000), p. 180. The play on sound in Nabokov's title (*Ada or Ardor*) might be said to resound in the novel's dedication (to wit: 'to Véra' or 'Veerer'): a veering is at work everywhere in his v-words, starting no doubt with his name. For more on this, see Laurent Milesi, 'Towards a Cryptanalysis: Genealogies of "Lit-Crypts" from Poe to the "Posts"', in *Parallax*, 50 (January–March 2009): 100–14, and especially 103; and 'Dead on Time? Nabokov's "Post" to the Letter', in *Cycnos*, 12: 2 (1995), 14–15 and 18.

29. Gérard Genette, 'Time and Narrative in *À la recherche du temps perdu*', trans. Paul de Man, in Michael J. Hoffman and Patrick D. Murphy (eds), *Essentials of the Theory of Fiction*, 3rd edn (Durham, NC: Duke University Press, 2005), p. 137. Genette's shifting between a language of subversion and perversion neatly evokes what we are here exploring under the rubric of 'veering'. An intriguingly similar shifting is evident in Peter Brooks's reading of Freud's *Beyond the Pleasure Principle*, 'Freud's Masterplot: A Model for Narrative', when he touches on the subject of what I have been referring to here as *veering in time*. He writes: 'All we can do is subvert or, perhaps better, pervert time: which is what narrative does.' See Peter Brooks, *Reading for the Plot: Desire and Intention in Narrative* (Cambridge, MA: Harvard University Press, 1984), p. 111. Veering connects with Brooks's work in a number of respects, above all with respect to his brilliant exploration, in 'Freud's Masterplot: A Model for Narrative' (*Reading for the Plot*, pp. 90–112), of how every novel has its own way of proceeding, of digressing and holding up, of being dilatory and of ending. I discuss the importance of Freud's writing vis-à-vis veering in greater detail below, especially in Chapter 3 'Reading a Poem' and Chapter 6 'On Critical and Creative Writing'.

30. See George Eliot, 'A College Breakfast-Party', ll. 818–21, in *Collected Poems*, ed. Lucien Jenkins (London: Skoob Books, 1989), p. 184.

31. In fact, as always with Wordsworth, things are more complex than this: his 'spots of time' are hardly static or still, even in the language in which they are recalled. Rather, they comport with a singular Wordsworthian veering, as I attempt to elaborate it in greater detail in Chapter 6 'On Critical and Creative Writing', below.

32. In the original French text the verb is *virer*: see *À la recherche du temps perdu, I Du côté de chez Swann* (Paris: Gallimard, 1992), pp. 16 and 175. Further page references to the original French are to this edition and are given parenthetically in the main body of the text (where appropriate following page reference to the English translation and preceded by a slash).

33. Terence Kilmartin, 'Note on the Translation' (1981), in Marcel Proust, *In Search of Lost Time, I: Swann's Way*, trans. C. K. Scott Moncrieff and Terence Kilmartin, rev. ed. D. J. Enright (London: Chatto and Windus, 1992), p. x. Further page references to *Swann's Way* are to this edition and are given parenthetically in the main body of the text.

34. Samuel Beckett, 'Proust' (1931), in *Proust and Three Dialogues with Georges Duthuit* (London: John Calder, 1965), p. 41.
35. It is perhaps not surprising in this respect that Beckett should be one of Proust's most acute commentators. The sort of surgical unstitching of sense from one sentence or one clause to another is a body artistry we find everywhere in Beckett.
36. I am here following a well-established tradition, and in doing so am indebted to my friend and colleague, Peter Boxall. In particular we may recall once again Beckett's remarkable essay 'Proust': Beckett does not hesitate to classify these steeples as among the most important 'fetishes' (36) that illuminate Proust's work as 'a monument to involuntary memory and the epic of its action' (34).
37. See especially Chapter 6 'On Critical and Creative Writing', below.
38. Despite being regularly acclaimed as a 'master of the uncanny', Poe himself does not use the word. I discuss this issue more extensively in *The Uncanny*: see in particular p. 34, n.60.

Chapter 3

Reading a Poem

Every revolution has been born in poetry, has first of all been made with the force of poetry.[1]

It veering
   off the path
ravine
                                                   (Lisa Fishman)[2]

Speaking of eggs (Proust's song-inducing writing), one of the best-known, funniest but also most unsettling laid in literature is Humpty Dumpty, in no small spoonful on account of his theory of language: 'When *I* use a word,' he says, 'it means just what I choose it to mean – neither more nor less.'[3] He talks about how 'to be master' of words: 'They've a temper, some of them – particularly verbs: they're the proudest – adjectives you can do anything with, but not verbs – however, *I* can manage the whole lot of them! Impenetrability! That's what *I* say!' (163). It would be nice to interrupt and ask him about 'veering' – about whether it is an adjective or a verb, about how he would manage it and what he would pay when it 'come[s] round me of a Saturday night . . . for to get [its] wages' (164). Happily, Humpty's mastery is a delusion, merely eggomaniacal. One of the curious (or curiouser and curiouser) things about 'veering' is that it comports two quite distinct and even opposing senses: it can be a matter of exercising control or of loss of control. You might be veering in a controlled manner, even (so you suppose) masterfully, or you might be veering inadvertently, hopelessly, out of control. 'Veering' thus functions in the manner of what Sigmund Freud called primal words: it seems to entail antithetical meanings.[4] No more an either this or that, in fact, than a both this and that. Just as, in Freud's phrase, 'a thing in a dream can mean its opposite', so *veering* might be one thing and/or the other.[5] There is uncertainty about who or what, if anything, is in control. It is a strange thing, veering – word and thing, word-thing, and neither.

Lewis Carroll and Sigmund Freud are important to the theory of veering for reasons 'as plentiful as blackberries' (as Freud liked to say, recalling Shakespeare's Falstaff[6]), but, most of all perhaps, their writings help illuminate the strange materiality of language, the capacity that words and letters have to slip and slide and turn into something alien. Sense can veer, even within the apparent unity and punctuality of a word. This is what literature, and poetry above all, most insidiously shares with dreams and the unconscious: the play of the letter, the treatment of words as things, the veering and vanishing of one word or thing into another (homonyms, homophones, substitutions, displacements, omissions, allusions, non sequiturs, suppressed references, 'repressed meanings', metaphors becoming literal, literal language becoming metaphorical, etc.). In literature as in dreams it is a matter of getting caught up in the protean strangeness of what is true and real, *in fact* or (as the Latin has it) *vere*. Thus we might track 'veer' itself, for example, feverishly intervolved with 'reverie', 'revere', 'reave', 'reveal', 'reverberate', 'verify', 'ever', 'sever' and more than several others. 'Veering' is, among other things, a name for this strange power or weakness of words – to be slithy and elusive in essence, in a sense, inner sense and in innocence, incensing some, perhaps, incense to others. As Joan Retallack comments in *The Poethical Wager*: 'Strange and humorous swerves occur when close attention to words reveals peculiar lettristic attractions and etymological energies.'[7] No humour without veering.

You have to be balanced. That is to pick the next blackberry. Humpty Dumpty never falls, at least not in that strangely turned, inverted world of 'through the looking-glass'.

In his conversation with Alice, Humpty Dumpty goes on to remark that he 'can explain all the poems that ever were invented – and a good many that haven't been invented just yet' (164). Few literary works in English are more linguistically inventive than Lewis Carroll's *Alice* books. Indeed Carroll's work teems with talking morphs (theriomorphs, therianthropomorphs, thingamorphs and so many other strange rebus-conductors) playing in and with words, in a sort of deformed or freshly sharpened version of the adventurous that we might neologistically phrase the *inventurous*.[8] In his reflections on poetry (and in particular the poem called 'Jabberwocky'), Humpty Dumpty gives special emphasis to what he calls a portmanteau, in which 'there are two meanings packed up into one word' (164). The portmanteau, it may also be suggested, is a figure of veering, in which one word or meaning appears to veer into or out of another. It veers, too, in its inventurousness, its linguistic flair. As Derek Attridge has observed, with the portmanteau 'there is no escape from its insistence that meaning is an *effect* of language, not a presence within or behind language, and that the effect is unstable and uncontrollable.'[9] But as Carroll himself makes clear, in his later Preface to *The Hunting of the Snark* (1876), the portmanteau is no mere randomness or mental anarchy: it intimates 'the rarest of gifts, a perfectly balanced mind'.[10]

A good deal has been written about Humpty Dumpty's coining of the portmanteau, but comparatively little attention has been given to the fact that it takes place in and across dialogue.[11] If a portmanteau entails at least two meanings, it also involves at least two voices. Let us consider the 'wabe', one of the words from 'Jabberwocky' that he and Alice discuss. A wabe is, as Alice suggests ('surprised at her own ingenuity'), 'the grass-plot round a sun-dial'. This is because, as Humpty Dumpty clarifies, 'it goes a long way before it, and a long way behind it—'. The long dash in the text signifies that he has not (perhaps) finished, as Alice immediately adds: 'And a long way beyond it on each side'. 'Exactly so' (165), confirms Humpty Dumpty. 'Wabe' is inventured. Its stated meanings are generated through what is said *between* the girl and the egg. Moreover, it is a portmanteau of more than two meanings, entailing a craziness of *space in motion*. It is the area of grass around a sun-dial that *goes*, a way that goes in many ways, in wabes of ways: it 'goes a long way before' and 'a long way behind' and 'a long way beyond . . . on each side'.

This example of 'wabe' invites us to ponder the character of examples more generally. The example is a veering, it is in the nature of exemplarity to veer. An example is something singular that is literally taken out, a sample, an instance, and that at the same time refers beyond itself: it goes way before and behind and beyond. And the space of this example, let us not forget, is a space of gyring and gimbling: ''*Twas brillig, and the slithy toves / Did gyre and gimble in the wabe* . . .' (164). In addition to 'the wabe' itself, in other words, the *toves* (a chimerical spiralling out of 'badgers' and 'lizards', 'something like corkscrews') are going 'round and round like a gyroscope' while 'mak[ing] holes like a gimblet' (164–5).

Lewis Carroll and Sigmund Freud may sound like strange cabin crew for navigating the topic of 'reading a poem'. Neither is known primarily as a poet, in any conventional sense of that term. Their writings provide crucial boatyardsticks, however, for reflecting on what we might rather flamboyantly call poetry now – at the frontiers of theory.

They are constantly sailing, as it were, very close to lunacy. We are all insane in our dreams, as Freud noted in 1893.[12] 'We're all mad' (51), as the Cheshire Cat remarks in 1865, in the wonderland of literature.

Freud's descriptions and theories of who and what we are constitute a trauma in the very nature and history of reason, an enduring affront and twist to all those (that is, one likes to hope, all of us) who proceed according to the logic of non-contradiction, attentive to the practical demands and challenges of everyday life, guided by principles of common sense, and so on. Logic itself veers. Freud shows that what we feel, think, say, desire or fear is not necessarily (or even faintly) straightforward. Of course this is what makes some people afraid. As Sara Ahmed nicely observes: 'risking departures from the straight and narrow makes new futures possible, which might involve going astray, getting lost, or even becoming queer'.[13] And such straying happens every day and night. In dreams and in forgetfulness, in 'free association', in slips of the tongue or pen, in moments of misreading, in 'tunes hummed "thoughtlessly"', and in the 'irregular and twisting path' or 'zigzag line' by which memories are ordered, the human mind is veering.[14]

The writings of Lewis Carroll and Sigmund Freud are engines of poetic transformation. Perpetually on the move, borne along by the energies of reversal and displacement, deviation and substitution, they are remarkable works of veering. Which is to say, at the same time, they are astonishing balancing acts. Their explorations of the strange materiality of words, their trapeze artistry with the language of dreams and madness alert us in new and unprecedented ways to the *form* of writing, to the pervertibilities of so-called linear prose. They open up new sorts of space and direction, new apprehensions of poetic writing. As Lionel Trilling memorably put it, in 'Freud and Literature' (1947): 'The Freudian psychology makes poetry indigenous to the very constitution of the mind.'[15] Correspondingly, the *Alice* books establish a sense of childhood as radically poetic: everything, living or otherwise, speaks a kind of poetry. And they immerse us, in all innocence, in the polymorphous uncanny. Carroll and Freud give us a new poetry of thinking.

At issue here is the experience of what French philosophy calls *pensée pensante*, thought thinking or thinking-thought, thought in the very act or passion of its proceeding. We have already noted this in the dynamics of the 'Exactly so' between Alice and Humpty Dumpty. The concept of telepathy, the thought of 'an experiment in Telepathy' does not appear by name in Carroll's writing until *Sylvie and Bruno* (1889), but in the *Alice* books the experiment is already underway.[16] We are invited to hear what Alice is thinking – as well as saying – to herself. Carroll's writing is a *magical thinking aloud*, in which the reader is a party to what Alice is thinking 'to herself' as well as to what is veering between one speaker and another. 'Exactly so': thinking in Carroll is a sort of dreamy contagion, beautifully shifting. 'Speech is what the characters *do to each other*' (as Elizabeth Bowen says, apropos novel-writing and the art of dialogue), but it is also matter of what they do *to* speech and language and to the possibilities of thinking.[17] In an extraordinarily balanced fashion, the *Alice* books *think veering*: from one sentence, one word or one space between letters to the next, the text might veer off anywhere.

Something strangely akin is going in Freud, as Patrick J. Mahony shows in his fine study, *Freud as a Writer*. Few commentators on Freud catch the veering thinking of his writing with such care and clarity. He recalls Freud's remarking on his own writing practice: 'At the beginning of a paragraph I never know where I should end up.'[18] This is the sort of radical openness that Freud also describes in *Beyond the Pleasure Principle* (1920), namely the impulse 'to throw oneself into a line of thought and to follow it wherever it leads'.[19] Mahony explores 'the groping, turning, and self-correction and self-modification of Freud's thought from sentence to sentence' (83), 'the mobility of his attention', the capacity of 'the dance and play of his intellect to roam from one realm of certitude to another, to juggle an array of concepts, to train his eyes on the changing position of each one relative to all others, and resist any tempting, immediate explanation for contradictory phenomena' (84). As with Carroll on the 'balanced mind', Mahony foregrounds how 'Freud's keenly balanced intellect is hunched over, running, ever ready to swerve and veer off in pursuit of the dodging subject matter' (87).

At the heart of Mahony's account of Freudian veering is the notion of diataxis, which he borrows from François Roustang.[20] Following Roustang, he defines diataxis as 'the stylistic figure of interpretation that tips discourse over, turns it back, or makes it advance' (12). It is what happens, as Mahony puts it, '[w]hen the *pensée pensante* suddenly breaks off and veers off in a new direction' (123). As Roustang remarks: 'It is diataxis which gives parataxis its dynamism, puts it in motion, makes the difference . . .'[21] In a footnote Mahony veers in turn – back to Aristotle and off to Milton. Diataxis goes, in Lewis Carroll's word, wabe. Mahony writes:

> I cannot refrain from extending the richness of Roustang's term. *Diataxis* may be linked with the grammatical term anacoluthon, a change of syntactic construction that leaves the beginning sentence structure uncompleted, introducing a new thought in midstream . . . On a larger scale, we might associate diataxis with the pivotal dramatic concept of peripety or reversal of fortune (cf. Aristotle's *Poetics*, *passim*) and with those inner 'rousing motions' felt as decisive spiritual illuminations (Milton, *Samson Agonistes*, 1381–3). (138–9, n.9)

Diataxis is about *pensée pensante*, thinking veering, a transcription of thought as it veers. It is about dislocations of grammar and syntax, sentences sent sideways, sense deranged. Diataxis is *pivotal*, we could say (picking up Mahony's use of the word and recalling our earlier discussion of Proust's steeples), for thinking about narrative and dramatic turns – not only the major reversals or returns that characterize the plays of Sophocles or Ibsen and literary narratives from fairy tales to Philip Roth, but also the micrological deviations, digressions or divergences that occur mid-sentence. And finally, Mahony suggests, diataxis is about the veering of the 'inner' world, having to do with moments of 'decisive spiritual illumination'. It is about a sudden alteration in understanding or even a transformation of self.

*

But there is another line of diataxis waiting.

For diataxis is also a compelling figure for thinking about reading a poem. Above and beyond those characteristics we have just noted (often in more compact, intense and disruptive forms), diataxis in poetry would entail (1) a special attentiveness to the surprising or interruptive play of the letter, the twists and turns a word might take or make, the disjunctive or deviant effects of homonyms and homophones, the strangely mobilized energies of etymology, and so on and sew forth; and (2) everything that is at play in the word 'verse' as such, the force of turning that is the very veering of a line, diataxis *in and across line-endings*.

Let us recall the lines from which Mahony cites the phrase 'rousing motions'. Samson says:

> I begin to feel
> Some rousing motions in me which dispose
> To something extraordinary my thoughts.[22]

The sense of metanoia, of some great shifting or metamorphosis within, is crucially embedded in the form of Milton's words, in the turns they make and the spaces that turn them. 'My thoughts' here are strangely 'in me' and yet other, 'something extraordinary'. The verb 'dispose' has connotations of what is right or proper, as in *Paradise Lost* when Satan says of God: 'He / Who now is Sov'reign can dispose and bid / What shall be right.'[23] But here it is a twisting of disposition, a dramatization of thinking-thought inseparable from that veering in silence that is more usually known as enjambment ('dispose / To something extraordinary'), and from the rousing motions of syntax inverted ('dispose . . . my thoughts'). The 'me' in these marvellous lines, moreover, is also disposed, inveigled in the repetition of 'some' and 'something'. It is not a matter of supposing that Milton intended to play on the 'me' in 'some' and 'something', rather it has to do with the play or veering of the letter. It is like the 'appeal' that Garrett Stewart hears in Samson's 'vanquished with a peal of words' (l. 235) – and so many other instances (especially in *Paradise Lost*) of what he calls 'transegmental ghost[s]', flitting across and between Milton's words, crossing Milton's swords.[24] It is like the 'poem' in 'portmanteau'. It need be thought about as neither intentional nor unintentional. Instead we might attribute it – in a portmanteau that should perhaps be taken away by the security services and destroyed – to the inadvertention of language.

Poetry is, in John Ashbery's phrase, 'grace and linearity'.[25] Or, to say the thing perhaps more in the lingo of a rebus-inspector: *it veers*. What is poetry? It veers. Verse veers.

In a note entitled 'The Verse' added to the preliminary pages of his *Paradise Lost* in 1668, Milton defends the fact that the 'measure' of his poem is 'English heroic verse without rhyme'. Rhyme is viewed as 'trivial and of no true musical delight'. He concludes:

> This neglect then of rhyme so little is to be taken for a defect, though it may seem so perhaps to vulgar readers, that it rather is to be esteemed an example set, the first in English, of ancient liberty recovered to heroic poem from the troublesome and modern bondage of rhyming.[26]

It is tempting to link this image of bondage to Blake's celebrated remark about Milton writing 'in fetters': 'The reason Milton wrote in fetters when he wrote of Angels & God, and at liberty when of Devils & Hell, is because he was a true Poet and of the Devils party without knowing it'.[27] Everyone knows that *Paradise Lost* does not rhyme. Milton meticulously sidesteps the 'fault', as he calls it in his Note in 1668, of 'the jingling sound of like endings': such 'a fault avoided' is in a sense the very *modus vivendi* of 'the verse'.[28] As Andrew Marvell puts it, in a beautifully witty rhyming couplet, in 'On Mr. Milton's *Paradise Lost*', in 1674: 'Well mightst thou scorn thy readers to allure / With tinkling rhyme, of thine own sense secure'.[29] But what is going on with the securing of sense when signs of 'bondage' seem to impose?

Here is Satan as serpent, making his cunning approach to Eve, in Book IX:

> With tract oblique,
> At first as one who sought accéss but feared
> To interrupt, sidelong he works his way.
> As when a ship by skilful steersman wrought
> Nigh river's mouth or foreland where the wind
> Veers oft, as oft so steers and shifts her sail,
> So varied he and of his tortuous train

Curled many a wanton wreath in sight of Eve
To lure her eye. (IX, 510–18)

In what Wordsworth will later call 'the turnings intricate of verse',[30] this passage keeps up the sense of the serpent as 'a surging maze' (499), a 'pleasing' and 'lovely' (503–4) figure of metamorphosis and ongoing alteration. Inversion at the level of the phrase ('tract oblique'), and of the larger form of the sentence ('. . . he works his way'), is entwined with temporal inversion: what is 'At first' enfolds both past ('sought' and 'feared') and present ('works'). 'Tract' here is 'manner of proceeding', 'way', 'path', but the convolvement of syntax also carries a suggestion of 'The drawing out, duration, continuance, process, passing, or lapse of time' (*OED*, 'tract', n. 3, I, 1a), and even, in a figurative sense, 'The action of drawing or pulling' (*OED*, II, 4). Satan as serpent has not yet spoken, not yet begun his 'fraudulent temptation' (IX, 531) of Eve, but (in its singularly oblique way) 'tract' also implies an awareness of words and writing, the tract as 'treatment' (*OED*, 'tract', n. 1).

And then – not a case of 'like endings', to be sure – but lurking in the midst of these seductive lines is the rhyme of '[v]eers' and 'steers'. It is as if 'Veers', as it rears up at the start of the line, were some alien but irrepressible word, with a forked tongue, conjuring rhyme. Shifting back into 'feared' (511) and forward into 'varied' (516), it comes on the wind, a strange ship of the tongue. And it is so soft, so transegmentally soft ('Veers oft, as oft' > 'Veers soft, as soft') in its sidelong work, its drive 'to allure' (in Marvell's phrase).[31] What are we to make of the 'musical delight' of *veers* and *steers*? Is it not the very soundtrack of the devil's party? This rhyme – internal but still striking – reverberates the veering strangeness of Milton's verse, its wreathing syntax and intervolving metaphors (serpent, speaker, steersman, seducer), its demonic balancing act. What is the source of Satan's speech? 'He, glad / Of her attention gained, with serpent tongue / Organic or impúlse of vocal air / His fraudulent temptation thus began . . .' (IX, 528–31). It is uncertain, in suspense – 'serpent tongue' or 'impúlse of vocal air'. In his note to these lines, Gordon Teskey comments: 'Satan emits sound through the serpent either by using the serpent's tongue or by emitting pulses of air, which make sound by vibrating in the elongated tube of the serpent's body' (211n.). A veering wind seems softly, almost imperceptibly to return in this image of pulsing air.

We shall see later how a 'demonics' of veering gets staged and reworked in English Romanticism (especially the poetry of Coleridge and Wordsworth) and in post-Romantic writing (from Melville to

Lawrence and beyond). Let us for now, however, note very briefly four
directions in which veering goes, after Milton:

1. Love and desire. Milton's serpentine veering already intimates a
   luring ('To lure her eye'). It is in poetry, perhaps above all, that we
   encounter a love of veering and the veerings of desire. In love we
   veer. An emphasis on the veering character of love and desire can be
   traced back, in particular, to John Dryden. As Nigrinus remarks of
   love, in *Tyrannick Love* (1669): 'Love only does in doubts and darkness dwell. / For, like a wind, it in no quarter stays; / But points and
   veers each hour a thousand ways.'[32]
2. Imagination – that force that comes 'athwart' Wordsworth, arresting
   the 'progress of [his] song'.[33] Amoeba of fantasy, veering is a compelling figure for exploring the disjunctive, irrepressible, unpredictable inventiveness of poetic thinking. Such is, in Alfred Tennyson's
   phrase, 'ever-veering fancy'.[34]
3. Otherness. Already inferred or infernal in the demonic resonances
   of Milton's verse, veering entails an acknowledgement of something
   other, something strange in or to the self.
4. War. Poetry is necessarily at war, not only in response to the enormities going on across the world (and into the earth's atmosphere and
   beyond) every day, but also with regard to language itself. Especially
   in the context of English (or 'Anglo-American' as it is sometimes
   branded), the war is civil. *Paradise Lost* is a great war poem, of
   course, but poetry today has to address war in immeasurably more
   diffuse and insidious ways, whether in relation to the wars of global
   capital and terror, nanotechnology or ecological crisis.[35] 'The great
   poems of heaven and hell have been written,' as Wallace Stevens
   observed in 1948, 'and the great poem of the earth remains to be
   written.'[36] Needed now, for and beyond this earth, are new kinds of
   war poetry.

If the truest poetry is the most veering, it is also a matter of trapeze
artistry, queer balancings or (to give a twist to T. S. Eliot's word for
Marvell) equipoise.[37] As Eliot also reminds us (while reminding himself
of Coleridge), 'good poetry' is concerned with 'making the familiar
strange, and the strange familiar'.[38] Analysis of veering broaches an
economy of the uncanny. The relations between poetry and veering have
to do with the strange materiality of language, diataxis, elusive sense,
a thinking close to madness, rousing motions and seduction. At a time
when, more than ever perhaps, it is supposed that poetry 'makes nothing
happen' (in Auden's phrase), and when the nulling power of 'informa-

tion flows' may seem to minimize if not entirely wipe out the sense of the poetic, contemporary writing must seek out new strategies and possibilities, new energies and allergies of veering.[39]

*

It is in this context that we might think about the poetry of J. H. Prynne. With remarkable consistency and intricacy, beauty and violence, Prynne's poems affect and haunt, above all, as works of veering. Let us consider, as an example, a poem entitled 'Crown', first collected in *The White Stones* (1969). This poem invites us to think of 'the city' and of the meaning of 'crown' (both symbol of sovereignty and piece of money, as well as the spectrally coronal form on the page that this poem appears to take) in ways we have never done before. It gives us the city as 'a rising fountain / quite slim and unflowering as it / is drawn off', a place where 'cash slides / & crashes into the registers', a place which can be 'achieved as a glance – inwards, across, / the Interior Mountain with its cliffs / pale under frost.' It is a city of 'slopes' that 'burn[s] a man up'. On the one hand, it is a place of singular beauty ('the silver police / station, the golden shops, all holy'), unpleasantness ('false shouts', 'Each face a purging / of venom, an absent coin') and suffering ('the / shoulders break'). It is the city as 'market-place', as the embodiment of capital (head or 'crown'). On the other, and by the same turn, it is a city of ever-veering imagination, a city dreamed up in words, a poetic singularity. In these respects it is not a thousand miles perhaps from the dreamlike 'stuff', the 'cloud-capp'd towers' and 'insubstantial pageant' of Shakespeare's *The Tempest*.[40] But at the same time it maintains a fierce preoccupation with a sense of the relations between what Milton calls 'rousing motions' and what is here, more flatly, called 'the market-place'.

And the poem does this, it assembles and dissembles this strange and beautiful coronal, in an unprecedentedly veering form. It is, as it were, Prynne's coinage and currency, his stamp and signature: a poetry that, more than any before it, practises diataxis. It veers. From one word or image to the next, and especially in its line-endings, its silent veerings from one line into what follows, you never know which way it is going to go, what shift will have been taking place:

Thus the soul's discursive fire
veers with the wind; the love
of any man is turned
by the mere and cunning front:

No hand then but to coin, no
face further than

needs be, the sounds fall
quickly into the gutters.[41]

Everything turns on a coin, on what it is 'to coin', on the implacable ironies of what kind of crown this poem offers.[42]

Such a poetics of veering is pursued also in the remarkable work of Keston Sutherland. Let us cite here just a few lines from a recent poem entitled 'Reindeer' (2010):

> It's late Spring, and the spiralling
> sun leaves a glow across the thriving earth,
> and eight million reindeer head north
> loose through dark snow
> to mate with eight million zombies on ecstasy
> who will not hurt you because they're not hungry
> to mutter of old men's voices,
> and we waste our smart bombs on the wedding carpet
> like youth
> because the people on it explode they become civilians
> youths
> mealy-mouthing casual meaty metaphors
> you
> humans who are secondary data like dentures in porn stars.[43]

'Grace and linearity' is doubtless too anodyne a phrase to characterize Sutherland's work, in particular to convey its sense of being *at war* and *in the language of war*, at war in language with the nauseating realities of war, atrocity and injustice, and with the language in which these realities are 'captured' in the discourses of the so-called media, teletechnology and everyday speech.[44]

In its title and opening lines, 'Reindeer' recalls but rapidly swerves away from Auden's

> Altogether elsewhere, vast
> Herds of reindeer move across
> Miles and miles of golden moss
> Silently and very fast.[45]

Sutherland's poem offers no such utopic or heterotopic imaginative space. Rather it stresses, provocatively and irrecusably, the coimplications of registers, tones, discourses. This is poetry veering in the mouth – a surgical oscillation of long and short lines (the latter here attenuating, ominously, into silence: 'like youth ... youths ... you ...') – in which 'we' are designated participants. It is a spiralling verse in which any innocence of 'casual meaty metaphors' is drowned: explosions of wasted youth, smart bombs, a wedding of carpet bombing in which people become, in mealy-mouthed fashion, 'civilians', 'civilian casualties' or 'civilian deaths' when they get blown up. More markedly *in your face* than Prynne's, Sutherland's poetry operates at and beyond the limits of intelligibility, veering between the lyrical and satirical, between an inventurous intimacy and a frenetic critical twisting of the everyday languages of military, bureaucratic, consumerist, capitalist hegemonic power.

What enables us to speak of such writings as poems has to do with form, of course, and above all perhaps with what we conventionally call lines and line-endings. One of the arguments I have sought to sketch out in these pages is that the figure of veering haunts and unsettles 'enjambment' and 'line break'. (Later, to speak in the guise of a stately prolepsis, there will be talk of *veerers*.) In particular via the elaboration of diataxis, I have tried to suggest how veering offers different ways of conceiving the spaces and turns and the dynamic oddity of what happens from one line to another. If 'enjambment' shows too much leg (the tacit anthropomorphism of *les jambes*, legs that bestride), 'line break' is a different kind of misnomer (suggesting definiteness and conclusion instead of a less certain, open and unfinished turning). What J. H. Prynne has advocated regarding 'innovation and experiment' in contemporary poetry seems especially relevant for thinking about line-endings as veerings: it is a matter, he suggests, of 'discovering new reflex slants and ducts and cross-links that open inherent potentials previously unworked'.[46]

*

I have entitled these pages 'Reading a Poem', but what is the poem? Where? It might be in the turning of a word, the apparitions of thinking thought, thinking as it veers. It is a question of the unleashing of a veering in poetry, of poetry as veering, a poetic or poematic force that enables us to broach the thought of new kinds of writing that meddle with all the fronts and frontiers.

I would like to conclude by veering back in time, however, and focusing on a couple of passages from the poetry of Thomas Hardy. The first consists of the closing stanzas of his 'At Moonrise and Onwards', one of the marvellous 'queer' poems, as he calls them, in his *Late Lyrics and Earlier* (1922):

> – How many a year
> Have you kept pace with me,
> Wan Woman of the waste up there,
> Behind a hedge, or the bare
> Bough of a tree!

> No novelty are you,
> O Lady of all my time,
> Veering unbid into my view
> Whether I near Death's mew,
> Or Life's top cyme![47]

The moon, figured as a woman, is veering.[48] Construed earlier in the poem as 'a fire', then 'turn[ing] a yellow-green, / Like a large glow-worm in the sky', this 'furtive feminine shape' encapsulates the strangeness of life on earth. It is 'no novelty', yet comes 'unbid'. For the speaker, its veering seems to be the great spooky constant of 'all [his] time'. A figure of otherness, uninvited yet '[keeping] pace', it is a veering that happens in a kind of phantasmagoric iteration – regardless of whether the speaker is approaching the 'mew' (the secret place, prison or confinement) of death, or 'top cyme' (the first or greatest flowering) of his life. This 'veering' is then, retrolexically, inscribed in the peculiar temporality implied in the title, 'At Moonrise and Onwards'. And, then, perhaps the greatest strangeness in Hardy's poem resides in what might seem its most familiar gesture, namely that the poet or speaker is addressing the moon. Recalling Nathaniel Hawthorne's description of the moon 'creating, like the imaginative power, a beautiful strangeness in familiar objects', Hardy's poem evokes the eerie veering of the moon through the fiction of apostrophizing it.[49]

It is perhaps worth adding here that the 'poem of earth' (in the Stevensian phrase of 1948) would not be the special preserve of the so-called post-war (i.e. post-1945) period. Moreover some of the most powerful poetry of earth might be about the unearthly (the moon, for example) or, at any rate, about non-anthropocentric perspectives on the world and its environment. This is not to suggest that 'At Moonrise and Onwards' is not, also, a war poem of sorts. In spite or even on account of its seeming other-worldliness, Hardy's poem calls to be read in the context of the Preface ('Apology') to the volume in which it appeared, *Late Lyrics and Earlier*, dated February 1922:

> Whether owing to the barbarizing of taste in the younger minds by the dark madness of the late war, the unabashed cultivation of selfishness in all classes, the plethoric growth of knowledge simultaneously with the stunting of wisdom, 'a degrading thirst after outrageous stimulation' (to quote Wordsworth again), or from any other cause, we seem threatened with a new Dark Age.[50]

Finally, I would like to offer a very brief note, no more than a telegram, concerning what might yet some day come to be more widely regarded as the greatest long poem of the twentieth century in English,

Hardy's war poem, *The Dynasts* (1904–8).[51] Fifty years earlier than Wallace Stevens's remark about the poem or poems of earth that are still to be written, Hardy was involved in a three-volume epic about the 'vast international tragedy' of Europe in the Napoleonic Wars, a work explicitly countering and thinking otherwise the 'celestial machinery' of Milton's *Paradise Lost*.[52] In place of a God of 'anthropomorphic conception' (5), Hardy conjures a universe of spirits in the form of 'impersonated Abstractions', 'contrivances of the fancy merely' (4).[53] Hardy also seeks to dislocate an anthropocentric conception of war: one of the most frequently anthologized passages of the poem hauntingly evokes the devastation of armies from the points of view of rabbits, moles, larks, hedgehogs, snails, worms and butterflies.[54] Veering between descriptive historical prose and a dizzying array of verse forms, *The Dynasts* confused and misled many of its early readers who supposed that it could or should, as 'an epic-drama', be staged. But as Hardy points out in his Preface, it is in fact 'intended simply for mental performance' (6). If that 'simply' carries a charge of understatement, so the 'mental' veers towards madness.

We might select any one or more of dozens of extracts from the poem in order to illustrate its veering nature, but let us confine ourselves to just one example, indeed a single word. It is, so far as I have been able to determine, the earliest recorded usage of the word 'veering' in the plural. It comes in a passage in Part 2, Act III, scene ii, when Napoleon has just read the latest dispatches, observing (and, as at so many other moments in this extraordinary work, the eerily contemporary resonance is hard to miss) that 'England still is fierce for fighting on, – / Strange humour in a concord-loving land!' He then announces that he will withdraw from Spain (he is currently positioned just outside Astorga) to Paris,

> so as to stand
> More apt for couriers than I do out here
> In this far western corner, and to mark
> The veerings of these new developments,
> And blow a counter-breeze . . . (295)[55]

'Veerings' is finely suggestive of various aspects of the poem as a whole, above all its shifting historical, narrative and dramaturgic perspectives, its kaleidoscopic qualities or 'multiplied shimmerings'.[56]

These veerings are to be marked: as elsewhere in the poem, Hardy stresses the indissociable links between war and writing itself (including, here, the dispatches that these couriers will bring). 'The veerings of these new developments' are, first of all, a question of reading. And they are in the mouth of Napoleon: 'veerings' is not simply Hardy's word, but that of a dramatic, fictional, 'mental' persona, as well as an actual historical figure long dead at the time of Hardy's writing. It is a strange polyphony in which Napoleon speaks of future 'veerings' and 'blow[ing] a counter-breeze' in a kind of phastasmic past. Hardy was concerned with the exploration of what he called, in a note written in September 1889 looking ahead to the writing of this work, 'a spectral tone'.[57] Turning back – or turning for the first time – to *The Dynasts* may remind us that a poem can also be a time bomb, veering in time, awaiting its reading.

Notes

1. 'All the King's Men', in *Situationist International Anthology*, rev. and expanded edn, ed. and trans. Ken Knabb (Berkeley: Bureau of Public Secrets, 2006), pp. 150–1.
2. Lisa Fishman, 'Retrieve', in *Dear, Read* (Boise, ID: Ahsahta Press, 2002), p. 58. Elsewhere, in a poem of Shakespearean orientation entitled 'Midsummer', we read: 'you veer to the end, a side / show, a backward sleep / of all we restive in the meadow [. . .]'. See *The Happiness Experiment* (Boise, ID: Ahsahta Press, 2007), p. 3.
3. Lewis Carroll, *Through the Looking-Glass*, in *Alice in Wonderland*, ed. Donald J. Gray, 2nd edn (New York: Norton, 1992), p. 163. Gray's edition contains both *Alice's Adventures in Wonderland* (1865) and *Through the Looking-Glass* (1872). Further page references are to this edition and are given parenthetically in the main body of the text.
4. Sigmund Freud, 'The Antithetical Meaning of Primal Words' (1910), in *SE* 11: 153–61.
5. Freud, *SE* 11: 155.
6. See William Shakespeare, *Henry IV*, Part One, ed. David Bevington (Oxford: Oxford University Press, 1987), II, iv, 232; and *SE* 14: 24, 287.
7. Joan Retallack, *The Poethical Wager* (Berkeley: University of California Press, 2003), p. 139.
8. 'Inventurous' here would thus be a sort of reversal or reinventing of the sense of this word as 'not venturous'. (See *OED*, 'inventurous', adj.)
9. Derek Attridge, 'Unpacking the Portmanteau, or Who's Afraid of *Finnegans Wake*?', in Jonathan Culler (ed.), *On Puns: The Foundation of Letters* (Oxford: Basil Blackwell, 1988), p. 145.
10. Regarding the portmanteau 'frumious', Carroll writes: 'For instance, take the two words "fuming" and "furious". Make up your mind that you will say both words, but leave it unsettled which you will say first. Now open your mouth and speak. If your thoughts incline ever so little towards "fuming", you will say "fuming-furious"; if they turn, by even a hair's breadth, towards "furious", you will say "furious-fuming"; but if you have the rarest of gifts, a perfectly balanced mind, you will say "frumious".' See Preface to *The Hunting of the Snark*, in *Alice in Wonderland*, p. 220.
11. I have explored this figure in greater detail elsewhere: see 'Portmanteau', in *New Literary History*, 37: 1 (Winter 2006), 237–47.
12. See 'On the Psychical Mechanism of Hysterical Phenomena: Preliminary

Communication' (1893), in Josef Breuer and Sigmund Freud, 'Studies on Hysteria' (1893–5), *SE* 2: 13.

13. See Sara Ahmed, *Queer Phenomenology: Orientations, Objects, Others* (London: Duke University Press, 2006), p. 21.

14. See Sigmund Freud, 'Psycho-Analysis' (1923), in *SE* 18: 240, and 'Studies on Hysteria', in *SE* 2: 288–90.

15. Lionel Trilling, 'Freud and Literature', in Perry Meisel (ed.), *Freud: A Collection of Critical Essays* (Englewood Cliffs, NJ: Prentice Hall, 1981), p. 107.

16. See Lewis Carroll, *Sylvie & Bruno* (Stroud: Nonsuch Publishing, 2007), p. 30.

17. Elizabeth Bowen, 'Notes on Writing a Novel', in *The Mulberry Tree: Writings of Elizabeth Bowen*, ed. Hermione Lee (London: Virago, 1986), p. 41.

18. Patrick J. Mahony, *Freud as a Writer*, expanded edn (New Haven, CT: Yale University Press, 1987), p. 122. Further page references appear parenthetically in the main body of the text.

19. See Freud, *SE* 18: 59. The devilish or demonic is not far away. In the very same sentence, indeed, Freud goes on to compare this procedure with being 'an *advocatus diaboli*, who is not on that account himself sold to the devil' (59).

20. See François Roustang, 'Du chapitre VII', *Nouvelle Revue de Psychanalyse*, 16 (1977): 65–95.

21. Roustang, 'Du chapitre VII', p. 88 (my translation).

22. John Milton, 'Samson Agonistes', ll. 1381–3, in *Complete Shorter Poems*, ed. John Carey (London: Longman, 1971), p. 388. Further line references are to this edition and appear parenthetically in the main body of the text.

23. John Milton, *Paradise Lost*, ed. Gordon Teskey (New York: Norton, 2005), Book 1, ll. 245–7. Further references to Milton's poem (Book number, followed by line numbers) appear parenthetically in the main body of the text.

24. See Garrett Stewart, *Reading Voices: Literature and the Phonotext* (Berkeley: University of California Press, 1990), pp. 147–9.

25. John Ashbery, 'Litany', in *As We Know* (Harmondsworth: Penguin, 1979), p. 20.

26. Milton, 'The Verse', in *Paradise Lost*, p. 2.

27. William Blake, 'The Marriage of Heaven and Hell', in *The Complete Poetry and Prose of William Blake*, ed. David V. Erdman, newly rev. edn (New York: Anchor Press, 1982), p. 35.

28. See Milton, 'The Verse', *Paradise Lost*, p. 2. On writing and books as living, let us simply recall Milton's beautiful words in *Areopagitica*: 'For books are not absolutely dead things, but do contain a potency of life in them to be as active as that soul was whose progeny they are; nay, they do preserve as in a vial the purest efficacy and extraction of that living intellect that bred them' (*Paradise Lost*, p. 342).

29. Andrew Marvell, 'On Mr Milton's *Paradise Lost*', in *The Poems of Andrew Marvell*, ed. Nigel Smith (Harlow: Pearson Education, 2003), pp. 182–4: here, p. 184 (ll. 45–6).

30. William Wordsworth, *The Prelude 1799, 1805, 1850*, ed. Jonathan

Wordsworth, M. H. Abrams, and Stephen Gill (New York: Norton, 1979), Book 5 (1805 text), l. 627.

31. For further discussion of such 'sidelong' effects, to which Garrett Stewart has given the orthographically playful name *transegmental*, see in particular Chapter 6 'On Critical and Creative Writing', below.

32. John Dryden, *Tyrannick Love, Or The Royal Martyr* (1670), IV, i, 6–8, in *The Works of John Dryden*, vol. 10, ed. Maximillian E. Novak (Berkeley: University of California Press, 1970). As the officer Placidius remarks, earlier on in the play: 'How soon the Tyrant with new Love is seiz'd! / Love various minds does variously inspire' (*Tyrannick Love*, II, i, 291–2). In *An Evening's Love, Or The Mock-Astrologer* (1671), on the other hand, Dryden plays on the silence of veering when he has Beatriz say that 'a Treaty of commerce will serve our turn' and Maskall replies: 'With all my heart; and when our loves are veering, / We'll make no words, but fall to privateering' (IV, i, 786–8, in *The Works of John Dryden*, vol. 10). It is not by chance that Dryden's 'love' interest should take after Shakespeare's most veering couple, Antony and Cleopatra. As Alexas puts it to Cleopatra in *All for Love* (1678): 'You see through Love, and that deludes your sight; / As, what is strait, seems crooked through the Water.' See *All for Love; or, The World Well Lost*, II, i, 85–6, in *The Works of John Dryden*, vol. 13, ed. Maximillian E. Novak (Berkeley: University of California Press, 1984). As the *OED* suggests, Dryden is the first writer to explore the nature of veering as 'pass[ing] from one state, position, tendency etc to another' (*OED*, veer, v. 2, sense 4) and, more specifically, to identify veering with 'feelings' and 'thoughts' (sense 4b). The earliest instances given are, respectively, from *The Conquest of Granada* (1672) and *Amphitryon* (1690). In both cases it is the veering of a weathercock that provides the basis for Dryden's figurative elaboration. Thus, in the earlier play, Almanzor declares: 'The word which I have giv'n shall stand like Fate; / Not like the King's, that weathercock of State. / He stands so high, with so unfix't a mind, / Two Factions turn him with each blast of wind. / But now he shall not veer: my word is past: / I'll take his heart by th' roots, and hold it fast.' See *The Conquest of Granada*, Part I, III, i, 9–14, in *The Works of John Dryden*, vol. 11, ed. John Loftis and David Stuart Rodes (Berkeley: University of California Press, 1978). In *Amphitryon* (as we noted in Chapter 1 'Casting Off', above), it is Gripus who is likened, in his veering views and attitudes, to the 'Weather-cock of Government'. See *Amphitryon*, V, i, 13–16, in *The Works of John Dryden*, vol. 15, ed. Earl Miner (Berkeley: University of California Press, 1976).

33. See Wordsworth, *The Prelude* (1805), Book 6, ll. 529 and 526.

34. Alfred Tennyson, 'Pelleas and Ettarre', l. 483, in *The Poems of Tennyson*, ed. Christopher Ricks (London: Longmans, 1969), p. 1702. Tennyson's phrase is evidently indebted to Keats's 1820 poem, 'Fancy': 'Ever let the Fancy roam, / Pleasure never is at home . . .'. See *The Poems of John Keats*, ed. Jack Stillinger (London: Heinemann, 1978), pp. 290–3.

35. For a provoking and valuable collection of essays around contemporary questions of war and language, see *The Word of War*, ed. Peggy Kamuf, special issue of the *Oxford Literary Review*, 31: 2 (2009).

36. Wallace Stevens, 'Imagination as Value', in *The Necessary Angel: Essays on Reality and the Imagination* (New York: Vintage Books, 1951), p. 142.

37. See T. S. Eliot, 'Marvell', in *Selected Prose of T. S. Eliot*, ed. Frank Kermode (London: Faber and Faber, 1975), p. 169.
38. Eliot, 'Marvell', p. 169.
39. W. H. Auden, 'In Memory of W. B. Yeats', in *Selected Poems*, ed. Edward Mendelson (London: Faber and Faber, 1979), p. 82.
40. William Shakespeare, *The Tempest*, ed. Stephen Orgel (Oxford: Oxford University Press, 1994), IV, i, 152, pp. 155–6.
41. J. H. Prynne, 'Crown', in *Poems* (Newcastle: Bloodaxe Books, 1999), pp. 116–17.
42. In a characteristically dense and idiosyncratic essay a year earlier (in 1968), 'A Note on Metal', Prynne explores the way in which 'the history of substance (stone) shifts with complex social implication into the theory of power (metal)'. The concluding paragraph or so, summarizing his sense of the historical emergence of 'the form of *coin*' and 'a monetary system', should be quoted at length, not least in order to convey the veering nature of Prynne's critical prose, its preoccupation with shifts and turns, balance and overbalance, side-slippings and displacements: 'And Croesus, the first recorded millionaire, is also the first to devise a bimetallic currency, where even the *theoretic* properties of metal are further displaced, into the stratified functionalism of a monetary system. We are almost completely removed from presence as weight, and at this point the emergence of a complete middle class based on the technique of this removal becomes a real possibility. So that by this stage there is the possible contrast of an exilic (left-wing) history of substance. And yet the shifts are off-set and multiple, and in the earlier stages are accompanied by extensions of awareness newly sharpened by exactly that risk. The literal is *not* magic, for the most part, and it's how the power of displacement side-slipped into some entirely other interest which is difficult, not a simple decision that any one movement is towards ruin. Stone is already the abstraction of standing, of balance; and dying is still the end of a man's self-enrichment, the "reason" why he does it. The North American Indians developed no real metallurgy at all, at any stage of their history. The whole shift and turn is *not* direct (as [V. G.] Childe, too insistently, would have us believe [in "The Bronze Age", *Past and Present*, 12 (1957), 2–15]), but rather the increasing speed of displacement which culminates only later in a critical overbalance of intent. If we are confident over the more developed consequences, at the unrecognized turn we are still at a loss to say where or why.' See 'A Note on Metal', in *Poems*, pp. 128–31. Prynne's is, manifestly, an *exilic* writing, fascinated by 'the unrecognized turn'.
43. Keston Sutherland, 'Reindeer', in *The Stats on Infinity* (Brighton: Crater Press, 2010), n.p.
44. In an interview discussing recent work such as *Stress Position* (London: Barque, 2009) and *The Stats on Infinity*, Sutherland comments on the potential gratuitousness and vapidity of 'extremity' in poetry: 'Simply to conduct experiments in extremity and to confine art to producing evidence of such extremity, whether extremity of intention or of the manipulation of materials or the creation of shock value, without a dialectical turn back to illuminate the centre from which extremity is measured, is always going to be a tedious and cyclical thing to do in art. So what I hope at least is

that in its extremities and in its push towards more and more confounding and complicated and perhaps offensive and upsetting extremes of expression, that this poetry does nonetheless finally bring all of its resources into a counter-turn in which it will turn back and throw its light and its weight upon the centre from which extremity is presently judged and also try to illuminate that mobile dialectic itself.' See 'Brighton Poetry: An Interview with Keston Sutherland' (with Zoe Sutherland, Danny Hayward and Jonty Tiplady), in *Naked Punch: Engaged review of contemporary art and thought*, 14 (Autumn 2010), 41–6: here, 46. A question might be posed here concerning the relationship between what Sutherland calls the 'mobile dialectic' and veering. The force of 'veering', as I try to explore it in this book, has to do with what is not reducible or recuperable to a thinking of the dialectic.

45. W. H. Auden, 'The Fall of Rome' (1947), in *Selected Poems*, ed. Edward Mendelson (London: Faber and Faber, 1979), pp. 183–4.

46. See J. H. Prynne, 'Poetic Thought', *Textual Practice*, 24: 4 (2010), 595–606: here, 596–7. Prynne also aptly observes that 'strong poetic thought frequently originates . . . in the tension about and across line-endings': see 599.

47. See Thomas Hardy, *The Complete Poems*, ed. James Gibson (London: Macmillan, 1976), pp. 558 and 566–7.

48. Hardy's poem suggests the ways in which the moon veers into view, and we might also think of 'veering' as an apt word to describe its shifting across the night sky; but in more strictly physical, if less immediately spectacular terms, it is also now known (thanks to the mirror placed on the moon's surface in 1969) that it is literally veering away from the earth at a rate of 3.5 centimetres per year. The moon will not always be so much with us.

49. Nathaniel Hawthorne, 'My Kinsman, Major Molineux', in *Nathaniel Hawthorne's Tales*, ed. James McIntosh (New York: Norton, 1987), p. 11.

50. Hardy, *The Complete Poems*, p. 560. For the provenance of Wordsworth's phrase, see 'Preface to *Lyrical Ballads, with Pastoral and Other Poems*' (1802), in *William Wordsworth*, ed. Stephen Gill (Oxford: Oxford University Press, 1984), p. 599. Just prior to this passage about 'the late war', Hardy evokes the writing of poetry ('numbers') and other forms of '"high thinking"' in suggestively veering fashion: 'Verily the hazards and casualties surrounding the birth and setting forth of almost every modern creation in numbers are ominously like those of one of Shelley's paper-boats on a windy lake . . . So indeed of all art, literature, and "high thinking" nowadays' (560). It is also evident that Hardy is thinking, in this Preface, about history and time itself in veering terms: in the context of Comte and Einstein, among others, he evokes the figure of 'advanc[ing] never in a straight line, but in a looped orbit' (562).

51. This view is also held by the editor of Hardy's epic: see Harold Orel's Introduction to Thomas Hardy, *The Dynasts: An Epic-Drama of the War with Napoleon, in Three Parts, Nineteen Acts, and One Hundred and Thirty Scenes, The Time Covered by the Action Being About Ten Years* (London: Macmillan,1978), p. viii.

52. See Hardy's Preface, in *The Dynasts*, pp. 3–8: here, pp. 3 and 5. Further page references are given parenthetically in the main body of the text.

53. Hardy's description of Lord Nelson's 'trust in God', for example, might apply just as well to that of a certain Tony Blair and war in Iraq: 'A certain sort of bravery / Some people have – to wit, this same Lord Nelson – / Which is but fatuous faith in their own star, / Swoln to the very verge of childishness, / (Smugly disguised as putting trust in God, / A habit with these English folk) . . .'. See *The Dynasts*, p. 94.

54. See Hardy, *The Dynasts*, p. 651 (Part 3, VI, viii).

55. The ellipsis ('. . .') is Hardy's. It is a consistent grammatical feature of *The Dynasts*, and is in turn silently indicative of the veering syntax and organization of the poem.

56. The Spirit of the Years speaks of the '[m]ultiplied shimmerings of my Protean friend' in Part 3, VI, ii: see Hardy, *The Dynasts*, p. 624.

57. Again, in elliptical fashion: 'A spectral tone must be adopted . . . Royal ghosts . . .' (quoted in Orel's Introduction: see Hardy, *The Dynasts*, p. xiii).

Chapter 4

Drama: An Aside

– This *veering* thing, it's weird. I can't put my finger on it.

– Yes, indeed. As in the chase in Walter Scott's *The Lady of the Lake*, 'Lost for a space, through thickets veering': it's in transit, a space of enigma, you lose sight of it.[1]

– OK, that's a neat quotation to have up your sleeve, but I don't see how what you've been saying adds up to 'a theory of literature'.

– No? Well, with respect, perhaps you need to get your eyes examined.

– My eyes?

– Or your voice.

– My voice?

– Or your silence.

– My –?

– You're never satisfied. It doesn't matter how hard I try to provide a lucid and accessible laying out of ideas and examples, and so on, you are always looking for things to nitpick, resist, dismiss or disagree with. No wonder so-called 'intellectual life' doesn't change much.

– I'm sorry, you can't anticipate how I am going to react to what you're saying. I'm not an automaton.

– But that's just the trouble. You are, rather. What Joan Retallack says about swerving is entirely apropos for veering: 'Swerves . . . are necessary to dislodge us from reactionary allegiances and nostalgias.'[2] There's so much that's so endlessly predictable. And meddling with the programme is never easy. Your very resistance to what I have been saying, however, constitutes a certain validation –

– Oh, not that Freudian weaselling . . .

– One of the principal forms of veering is avoidance. You veer to avoid something – which might be something dangerous or unpleasant, but might also be an object of desire.

– Do you have to go on with this?

– What else am I supposed to do?

– Veer in silence, like you were saying earlier.

– Ah, you're beginning to come round.

– No, I'm being straight as a die –

– Die? Don't die.

– I'm simply saying I fail to understand how what you've been talking about amounts to a theory of literature that scholars or students could take away and apply to some text or some author that they happen to be reading.

– Well, it's a matter of acknowledging a certain riskiness and strangeness. I'm trying to do something that I would like to hope is quite new, at once conventional (respectful of academic rigour and scholarly protocols) and not. The quirkiness is already intimated in the idea of 'veering' as a title-word. Am I offering a theory of literature *about* veering? Or is it a theory *called* by that name, a title-word to be heard, then, as a sort of neologism or nonce word?

– As if it were summoned up in two voices simultaneously?

– Don't overreach yourself. I'm just saying that veering is perhaps more slippery and elusive, closer to the literary itself than what is conventionally associated with 'theory'. That's why I suggest the phrase 'theory of literature' has to be heard in two ways –

– Now you're beginning to sound like me –

– A seemingly straightforward way (it is a new theory concerning the so-called literary object, how we read literature, how we 'place' it in relation to other fields, the social and political, ethics, aesthetics, 'animal studies', the environment, etc.) and a quirky way (it's irreducibly a swerving into the object, it is perhaps a failed veering in that sense, but a necessary failing, or a success perhaps insofar as it fails, insofar as it is a theory *of* literature, a sort of analytical entangling *within* the literary).

– I don't have time for that. Really, I just like reading books. You know, stories and poems and stuff.

– I am with you there. The text's a fine and private place. I'm just trying to elucidate that extraordinary solitude, the space in which each one of us in his or her own fashion reads and veers. It's all about how you read veering.

– So thinking about veering is a way of thinking about singularity?

– Exactly.

– But what about those texts in which the figure of veering doesn't appear? And how does the theory work in relation to other languages?

– Give me a break. The job I've set myself is necessarily limited and, I hope you'd agree, quite modest: to confine myself to the workings and effects of a single English word (and its cognates), along with a small cluster of others with which it seems to be closely associated. Obviously there's a certain passage – even if it's a sort of cryptic or condemned passageway – between English ('to veer', 'verse', etc.) and other European languages (*virer* in French, *virar* in Spanish, *virare* in Italian, and so on), but what's at issue here is doubtless something to do with the untranslatable, something beautiful and strange about the word 'veering' in English that has to be reckoned with, every time afresh, depending on the text and context. Nonetheless, I think that another account could be elaborated – similar but different – as regards literature in another language.

– That would be some task for a translator.

– Yes, I'm sorry. I don't suppose it will ever happen.

– Anyhow, I'm still not clear about the sort of privilege you're giving to the word 'veering'. It's not the same, surely, as 'swirling', 'swerving' and so on? How do you deal with a writer who doesn't use the word 'veer' or 'veers' or 'veering' or whatever? What about Shakespeare, for example?

– Yes, he is a fascinating case. The v-word doesn't appear anywhere in his work. I think that's understandable in historical terms: in Shakespeare's time the verb 'veer' is principally confined to a nautical context.[3] It's not until later in the seventeenth century that the word comes to be used with reference to changes of state in things, or alterations of feelings or thoughts and so on. The closest Shakespeare gets to 'veer' is a reference to 'Lord Aubrey Vere', eldest son of John de Vere, twelfth Earl of Oxford, being 'done to death' in *The Third Part of King Henry VI*.[4]

– Perhaps the absence of the v-word in Shakespeare is fodder for the paranoiac anti-Stratfordians: you know, Shakespeare's works were really written by de Vere, the seventeenth Earl of Oxford, and the predominant absence of the v-word is merely a . . .

– Oh no, please, don't go there. It's true my main focus is on specific instances of 'veering' in literature (and elsewhere) and that tends to be an organizing principle of the theoretical exposition. At some level indeed it is a theory of the literary example, of how literary language veers, of how an example (which, in order to be what it is, has to go beyond itself, has to be an example *of* something larger or other) is itself a veering. But that is also a further reason why veering cannot be a merely 'literalist' or philological enterprise. Analysis of veering necessarily veers – into 'thickets', into other times and spaces, into silence, into other figures and images, such as the literary turn.

– The what?

– The *literary turn*: we come to it later, I promise.

– So you're suggesting that actually you could have called what you are doing 'The Literary Turn'? Or 'Swerving: A Theory of Literature'? Or 'Clinamen in Literature'?

– Sure, if that makes you feel better. While there's no veering, in a literal sense, in Shakespeare's writings, I hope what I'm doing might provoke new perspectives on thinking about his work. Shakespeare is, if I may put it like this, the greatest turner in the English language. Remember what Ben Jonson said about Shakespeare's 'well-turned' lines: 'he / Who casts to write a living line must sweat, / Such as thine are, and strike the second heat / Upon the muses' anvil, turn the same, / And himself with it that he thinks to frame'.[5] Jonson registers here how intensely Shakespeare turned himself *with and within* the turning of his lines: it's a superbly physical, toiling, sweaty image. It would be perfectly plausible, in other words, to elaborate a reading of Shakespeare in terms of veering, even if that word isn't to be found in his poems or plays.

– Nor is 'turner', since you mention it.

– But there are hundreds of instances of 'turn'.

– Nor is 'trope', if I can say that without you getting touchy.

– *Touché*. But there's a wonderful 'tropically' (that comes out as 'trapically' in the First Quarto of *Hamlet*): 'What do you call the play?' asks Claudius; 'The Mousetrap. Marry how? Tropically', replies Hamlet.[6]

– Where are we anyway?

– Ah, I thought you'd never ask. Eyes closed. Feel the gentle breeze. The warmth on your face.

– Don't tell me: we're on a tropical island. What are we doing here?

– We're having a conversation.

– For how much longer?

– Just a couple more minutes. Three at most.

– Then what?

– Relax. Stop asking questions. Soak up the atmosphere. Take in your surroundings.

– What, with my eyes closed? I'm not enjoying this. Tell me what's happening. I like things to be orderly and straightforward.

– I was just in the middle of telling you that I could quite readily imagine a book about Shakespeare and veering, and I was going to suggest an example – *Measure for Measure*.[7] While there is, literally, no 'veer' in this play, there are many figures, images and instances of movement going astray or out of control, of perverse, unexpected or unpredictable movement – from 'warp' (I, i, 14) or 'warpèd' (III, i, 142) to 'bend[ing] . . . speech' (I, i, 40), from 'advertise' (I, i, 41) or 'advertising' (V, i, 376) to 'wrinkled' (I, iii, 5) and 'athwart' (I, iii, 31), from 'sway' (I, iii, 44) to 'swerve' (IV, ii, 90), from 'blench' (IV, v, 5) to 'glance' (V, i, 305), from 'turn' as orgasm to 'turn' as execution (IV, ii, 45–6). It's all about 'pervert[ing] . . . course[s]' (IV, iii, 148). *Measure for Measure* is a deeply perverse play, a veritable perverformance, at every turn – of plot and character, desire and faith, prose and verse.[8] It veers.

– I don't like this. I can feel stirrings in 'dark corners' (IV, iii, 148). Can I open my eyes? What are we doing here anyway?

– I brought you here because I thought it would make you happy. The whole thing has been arranged so that people like you don't have to feel unduly anxious and put off. I can hardly begin to say how hard I've tried to establish and maintain a sense of clarity and reasonableness. I thought that if there were a chapter about 'Reading a Novel', followed by a chapter about 'Reading a Poem' . . .

– And then, you thought, best have something on drama, did you? Where would it stop? What about the short story? What about the critical essay itself? I'm sorry. I see where all this is going. You'll say that you've already been talking about drama, with all that stuff about character, voice, point of view, silence, dialogue, metanoia, 'mental performance' and so on, in the context of the novel and poetry. After all, it's not as if you haven't referred to dramatic examples (Sophocles, Shakespeare, Dryden, Ibsen, Hardy, Pinter) . . . I expect you'll add some clever further remark about directing, acting and performing, about how the spectacle of theatre gives a space for the theory of veering . . .

– For a physical actualization, a literal enactment of veering, unlike any other literary form . . .

– That's it. I've had enough. I'm off. [*Exit*]

– OK, it's your life. Hope you can swim. You were wrong though. I only wanted to offer an aside, an aside on the aside. It seems as if something extraordinary happened in a secret corner of London in 1599. At least that is how James Shapiro invites us to think about it, in his book *1599: A Year in the Life of William Shakespeare.*[9] It's to do with a breakthrough in the nature of the soliloquy, between the time of composition of *Julius Caesar* and *Hamlet*. We are prompted, as it were, to imagine the most remarkable aside in history. Shapiro observes that Hamlet speaks to us, in soliloquy, 'in a way that no character in literature had done before' (327). He goes on:

> One of the mysteries of *Hamlet* is how Shakespeare, who a half-year earlier hadn't quite been able to manage it in *Julius Caesar*, discovered how to write such compelling soliloquies . . . The sense of inwardness that Shakespeare creates by allowing us to hear a character as intelligent as Hamlet wrestle with his thoughts is something that no dramatist had yet achieved. (327–8)

Soliloquy as a noun does not yet exist: its sense as 'An instance of talking to or conversing with oneself, or of uttering one's thoughts aloud without addressing any person' (*OED*, soliloquy, n.) is not recorded prior to 1604. The closest term in use is the *aside*. The *OED* gives:

> Apart from the general company; in privacy. *to speak aside*, i.e. apart, so as to be inaudible to the general company. Used as a stage direction in plays, to indicate that certain words are to be spoken out of the hearing of other characters on the stage. (*OED*, aside, adv., III, 9)

Rather oddly, the dictionary illustrates this with a reference to *The Taming of the Shrew*, to the moment when Petruchio confides: 'Prithee, Kate, let's stand aside and see the end of this controversy.'[10] A more appropriate example might be Marlowe's 'Hero and Leander': 'Yet she this rashness suddenly repented, / And turn'd aside, and to herself lamented.'[11] In any case, when Shakespeare writes 'To be, or not to be . . .' (*Hamlet*, III, i, 56), there is no established term to describe what he is doing. To speak aside (with or without others on stage) is, I would suggest, to veer. It is a remarkable example of speech, apostrophe or address as veering. With such speeches from Hamlet Shakespeare gives us *pensée pensante*. It changes the nature of literature. It opens up a space of magical thinking, a mental transparency or telepathic exposure, in which we as spectators and audience are able to discover and share what a character is thinking and feeling. The novel, and indeed literary narrative in a more general way, would be unthinkable without it. James Shapiro brilliantly speculates, apropos this new 'sense of inwardness' dramatized in *Hamlet*: 'The breakthrough is one that Shakespeare might have arrived at sooner or later, but it was given tremendous impetus at the time he was writing *Hamlet* by his interest in a new literary form: the essay' (328). The unprecedented flourishing of the aside and soliloquy in drama is inspired by *the essay*, above all the essays of Montaigne. I'll fall silent now. It is time to veer again.

Notes

1. Sir Walter Scott, 'The Chase' (Canto I, stanza xiii), in *The Lady of the Lake* (London: Adam and Charles Black, 1891), p. 42.
2. See Joan Retallack, *The Poethical Wager* (Berkeley: University of California Press, 2003), p. 3.
3. While not to be found in Shakespeare, 'veer' does appear in the writings of his friend Ben Jonson, not only in his *Discoveries* (see Chapter 2 'Reading a Novel', above), but also in *The Devil is an Ass*, a play first performed in the year of Shakespeare's death (1616). Merecraft makes a figurative use of 'veer' in the sense of letting out a line or rope (*OED*, 'veer', v. 1): 'every cable / Is to be veered. We must employ out all / Our emissaries now.' See

Ben Jonson, *The Devil is an Ass*, ed. Peter Happé (Manchester: Manchester University Press, 1994), V, v, 46–7.

4. See William Shakespeare, *The Third Part of King Henry VI* , ed. Michael Hattaway (Cambridge: Cambridge University Press, 1993), III, iii, 102–3.

5. See Ben Jonson, 'To the memory of my beloved, the AUTHOR Master William Shakespeare and what he hath left us', in The RSC Shakespeare, *Complete Works*, ed. Jonathan Bate and Eric Rasmussen (London: Macmillan, 2007), pp. 61–2.

6. See William Shakespeare, *Hamlet, Prince of Denmark*, ed. Philip Edwards, updated edn (Cambridge: Cambridge University Press, 2003), III, ii, 215–6, and Edwards's charmingly anachronistic note on this 'Joycean pun' (175n.). Further quotations from *Hamlet* are from this edition.

7. William Shakespeare, *Measure for Measure*, ed. Brian Gibbons, updated edn (Cambridge: Cambridge University Press, 2006). All references are to this edition, given parenthetically in the main body of the text.

8. This notion of drama as perverformance is indebted to Jacques Derrida who, at one moment in his 'Envois', in *The Post Card*, rewrites the word 'performative' as 'perverformative' in an attempt to suggest the role of the perverse and unpredictable, the necessary possibility that any speech act (promise, declaration of love or war, act of naming, founding of an institution, etc.) can go off course, drift, deviate. See *The Post Card: From Socrates to Freud and Beyond*, trans. Alan Bass (Chicago: Chicago University Press, 1987), p. 136.

9. James Shapiro, *1599: A Year in the Life of William Shakespeare* (London: Faber and Faber, 2005). Further page references are given parenthetically in the main body of the text.

10. William Shakespeare, *The Taming of the Shrew*, ed. H. J. Oliver (Oxford: Oxford World's Classics, 1982), V, i, 54–5. A similar usage occurs in the Folio (1623) text of *Hamlet*, when Hamlet says to Horatio, in the graveyard: 'But soft, but soft! Aside – here comes the king' (V, i, 184). The Second Quarto gives 'awhile' instead of 'aside'.

11. Christopher Marlowe, 'Hero and Leander', Sestiad II, ll. 33–4 in *The Poems*, ed. Millar Maclure (London: Methuen, 1968), p. 28.

Chapter 5

The Essay: A Note (On Being Late)

The animal that I am. (D. H. Lawrence)[1]

Nobody in the world can write and live at the same time; there is always a discrepancy. But one can write as closely as possible to the living. One has to learn to live in slow motion. (Hélène Cixous)[2]

More urgently than ever, perhaps, it is to the essay we should turn, in an attempt to engage critically and inventively with what is happening, with the question of writing and literature now. Despite the remonstrances and pontifications of a certain academic journalism, the 'essay in literary criticism' has been extinct for several decades. As Sarah Wood observes, in a commentary on Jacques Derrida's *Writing and Difference* (1967): 'Criticism must learn to be writing and not the contemplation of writing as form.'[3] And the same is true of the 'theoretical essay'. We need to let ourselves be traversed, as ever, by the energies of Montaigne, by his astonishing practice of 'scattering . . . a word here, a word there, examples ripped from their contexts, unusual ones, with no plan and no promises', by his veering perspectives on a given topic guided by the inclination 'to catch it from some unusual angle'.[4]

We need to keep discovering and learning from the extraordinary essays of Theodor Adorno, the title of whose 'The Essay as Form' (1958) may mislead.[5] In truth it scatters like Montaigne, affirming the value of the genre of the essay as *writing that goes off*, as a work of 'discontinuity' (16) and 'mobility' (20).[6] The essay 'suspends the traditional concept of method' (11), Adorno declares; it proceeds 'as though it could always break off at any point' (16). The essay is impelled by an acknowledgement that 'thought does not progress in a single direction' (13). Thinking, for him, is of a singular and perverse kind: there is 'an emancipation from the compulsion of identity' and this 'gives the essay something that eludes official thought' (17).

If the analysis of veering has anything to teach, this would have to do with a practice of critical thinking and writing newly attuned to the strangeness of literature (including its relation to law and democracy); the animal that you are; spectrality; and the environment. As Adorno and Derrida make clear, the essay is untimely, anachronistic, never on time.[7] In this respect the essay today finds itself, as never before perhaps, crossing over with what is happening in literary practice. It thus corresponds with what Peter Boxall has described as 'a very wide sweep of contemporary writing which registers a kind of late untimeliness'. Focusing in particular on the late short novels of Don DeLillo, Boxall comments:

> *Cosmopolis* [2003] explores the possibility that the globalization of finance capital has produced a kind of weightless temporality which has 'lost its narrative quality', and *Point Omega* [2010] and *The Body Artist* [2001] are set in this peculiarly slowed, stalled time.[8]

We may be reminded here that the word 'late' itself comes to us from the Old English *læt*, meaning 'slow'.

This is not to advocate some new dilatoriness in the essay but, on the contrary, new ways of apprehending speed in slow motion, new dodges and accelerations, new turns and rhythms, other velocities and untimelinesses. The 'globalization of finance capital' is inextricably bound up with war and terror (and with all the forces and counter-forces of the pursuit of democracy, the establishment of human rights in a worldwide context, and an indestructible passion for justice), but also with questions of the earth, the place of non-human animals, the sense and value of the environment. Lateness need not be construed only in human terms. As Timothy Clark puts it: 'the speed with which the world happens for a human being need not be a norm.'[9] If literature has a singular power in enabling us to think about veering and time, veering *in* time, it is a matter of linking this not only with the astonishing rapidities of technoscience and 'the computer age' but also with the more obviously non-anthropocentric challenges of 'deep time' – whether prehistoric or futural.

We have as yet hardly begun to reckon with what Derrida calls the trace, with that strange interweaving of traces that enables us to perceive time and space in the everyday way we do. More particularly perhaps, we have scarcely started to acknowledge its non-anthropocentric implications and effects (the logic of the trace as pointedly not confined only to the human) and its essentially veering character or, in Derrida's phrase, its 'destinerrant indirection'.[10] It is in this context, perhaps, that we may most productively elucidate Timothy Clark's recent proposition that 'in some ways "originary environmentality" might seem a stronger term of deconstruction than "originary trace".'[11] As Clark's own work admirably shows, nowhere is the need for rigour and inventiveness more urgently demanded than in the experimentations of 'environmental writing'.[12]

To link the question of the essay with veering is to observe first of all, perhaps, that it is not a matter of simply following the thinking of another writer. When it comes to the theory and practice of the essay, veering is the art of the singular and perverse. As Montaigne says (in effect, with every sentence he writes or cites): 'To follow another is to follow nothing.'[13] We might illustrate this by way of a brief consideration of Edward Said's reading of Adorno, in a haunting essay called 'Timeliness and Lateness'.[14] Said meditates on the question of what constitutes 'late style', focusing on the music of Beethoven and recalling Adorno's words: 'the maturity of [Beethoven's] late works does not resemble the kind one finds in fruit'; they are 'devoid of sweetness', he goes on, 'bitter and spiny' (12). 'Late style', Said then suggests, 'involves a nonharmonious, nonserene tension, and above all, a sort of deliberately unproductive productiveness going *against . . .*' (7). The drift into elliptical silence ('. . .') is Said's. 'Timeliness and Lateness' offers compelling perspectives on Beethoven and Adorno, but also on the question of critical writing today – not just on aspects of form or style, but on what we might call the environment and inventive possibilities of the essay and 'late writing'.

Said explores Adorno's interest in what is 'wayward and eccentric' (10) in Beethoven's late works, noting that 'for Adorno, *lateness* is the idea of surviving beyond what is acceptable and normal' (13). 'Late style', in Said's phrase, 'is *in*, but oddly *apart* from the present' (24). It is weirdly future-oriented. As Stathis Gourgouris has put it:

> late style is precisely the form that defies the infirmities of the present, as well as the palliatives of the past, in order to seek out [the] future, to posit it and perform it even if in words and images, gestures and representations, that now seem puzzling, untimely, or impossible.[15]

'Timeliness and Lateness' is at once attuned to Adorno's critical writing and a gracious veering away. Adorno's own thinking was, in Said's phrase, 'always to one side' (21).[16] He considers Adorno's work to be 'amazingly peculiar and inimitable' (22); his prose is 'slow, unjournalistic, unpackageable, unskimmable' (14–15). And yet they are also very close. Thus Said identifies Adorno with Beethoven in terms it is difficult not to extend to himself: 'Adorno, like Beethoven, becomes therefore a figure of lateness itself, an untimely, scandalous, even catastrophic commentator on the present' (14).

At an especially densely textured moment in the essay Said quotes Adorno as saying that 'thinking has the momentum of the general', then adds in square brackets: 'Here Adorno means both that individual thought is part of the general culture of the age and that, because it is individual, it generates its own momentum yet veers or swerves off from the general' (15). Following the insertion of this sentence, he picks up Adorno's own words once again: 'What once was thought cogently must be thought elsewhere, by others' (15–16). Said's interpolated statement is striking in a number of respects. It has a dynamic and generative character: it is thinking *with* Adorno, in some sense, while adding something distinctive of its own. It is also suggestive as an apparent example of the 'late style' with which Said is concerned. It veers or swerves off, breaking up Adorno's prose, and does so in the form of a sort of anacoluthon. In particular, the 'yet' ('because it is individual, it generates its own momentum *yet* veers or swerves off from the general') doesn't quite seem to follow. An 'and' might have seemed more apt. The 'yet' has the unexpected effect of making the 'individual' a bit strange to itself.[17] As Said reads Adorno (beside himself), he lets us see that any essay worthy of the name is engaged in the art of veering.

Notes

1. In what transpires to be his last letter to John Middleton Murry, on 20 May 1929, Lawrence comments: 'The animal that I am you instinctively dislike ...' (and he goes on, in this context, to compare Murry with T. S. Eliot, among others). See *The Letters of D. H. Lawrence, Volume 7, November 1928–February 1930*, ed. Keith Sagar and James T. Boulton (Cambridge: Cambridge University Press, 1993), p. 294. Lawrence's formulation appears, rather cruelly perhaps, to recall Murry's own earlier characterization of him as (in Lawrence's words) 'a sort of animal with a sixth sense': see *Letters*, 7, p. 166 and n.1. The phrase 'the animal that I am' has of course more recently been associated with Jacques Derrida, especially on account of his remarkable, posthumously published book *The Animal That Therefore I Am*, ed. Marie-Louise Mallet, trans. David Wills (New York: Fordham University Press, 2008); *L'animal que donc je suis* (Paris: Galilée, 2006).
2. Hélène Cixous, *Reading with Clarice Lispector*, trans. Verena Conley (Minneapolis: University of Minnesota Press, 1990), p. 162.
3. Sarah Wood, *Derrida's Writing and Difference: A Reader's Guide* (London: Continuum, 2009), p. 45. Wood's remark is specifically oriented by a sense of what readers are invited to discover through Derrida's early essay 'Force and Signification' (1963).

4. Michel de Montaigne, 'On Democritus and Heraclitus', in *The Complete Essays*, trans. and ed. M. A. Screech (London: Penguin, 2003), p. 338.

5. Theodor W. Adorno, 'The Essay as Form', in *Notes to Literature*, vol. 1, ed. Rolf Tiedemann, trans. Shierry Weber Nicholsen (New York: Columbia University Press, 1991), pp. 2–23. Further page references to this essay are given parenthetically in the main body of the text.

6. Closely corresponding to Montaigne's practice of 'examples ripped from their contexts', Adorno notes: 'The essay cunningly anchors itself in texts as though they were simply there and had authority' (20).

7. As Adorno observes at the end of 'The Essay as Form': 'The contemporary relevance of the essay is that of anachronism' (22). For Derrida on the 'untimely' and 'never on time', see, for example, 'Aphorism Countertime', trans. Nicholas Royle, in *Psyche: Inventions of the Other*, vol. 2, ed. Peggy Kamuf and Elizabeth Rottenberg (Stanford: Stanford University Press, 2007), p. 141; and 'I Have a Taste for the Secret', Jacques Derrida in conversation with Maurizio Ferraris and Giorgio Vattimo, in Derrida and Ferraris, *A Taste for the Secret*, trans. Giacomo Donis (Cambridge: Polity, 2001), pp. 6–7, 12 and 15–16.

8. Peter Boxall, 'Late: Fictional Time in the Twenty-First Century', in *Contemporary Literature*, 53: 4 (2012, forthcoming). The phrase 'lost its narrative quality' comes from *Cosmopolis* (London: Picador, 2004), p. 77, and refers not to temporality, in fact, but to 'money'. Boxall goes on to suggest that, 'in their sculpting of a vivid but brief and fragile duration', these 'late novels' by DeLillo 'give expression to a wider cultural historical condition', in particular 'to the extent that the culture has itself become historically disoriented, uncertain of its bearings or its sense of direction'. I am grateful to Peter Boxall for letting me read his essay prior to its publication, as well as for many stimulating conversations about 'veering'. I would like to dedicate these brief remarks about lateness to my friend and colleague, in whose name I cannot help but hear 'box-haul', a verb meaning 'To veer a ship round on her heel, when it is impracticable to tack or make a great sweep' (*OED*, 'box-haul', v.).

9. Timothy Clark, *The Cambridge Introduction to Literature and the Environment* (Cambridge: Cambridge University Press, 2011), p. 197. For more on this, especially in terms of ecology and time-lapse photography, see Timothy Morton, *The Ecological Thought* (Cambridge, MA: Harvard University Press, 2010), pp. 43ff. and 68.

10. See Jacques Derrida, 'Passions: "An Oblique Offering"', trans. David Wood, in *On the Name*, ed. Thomas Dutoit (Stanford: Stanford University Press, 1995), p. 30.

11. See Timothy Clark, 'Climate and Catastrophe – A Missed Opening?', in Sean Gaston and Ian Maclachlan (eds), *Reading Derrida's Of Grammatology* (London: Continuum, 2011), p. 162.

12. On experimentation and the essay, in particular, see Clark's chapter on 'Genre and the question of non-fiction', in *The Cambridge Introduction to Literature and the Environment*, pp. 35–45.

13. Montaigne, 'On Educating Children', in *The Complete Essays*, p. 170.

14. Edward Said, 'Timeliness and Lateness', in *On Late Style: Music and Literature Against the Grain* (London: Bloomsbury, 2006), pp. 3–24.

Further page references to this essay are given parenthetically in the main body of the text.

15. Stathis Gourgouris, 'The Late Style of Edward Said', in *Alif: Journal of Comparative Poetics*, 25 (2005): 168. Quoted by Michael Wood in his Introduction to *On Late Style*, p. xv.

16. Intriguingly, Said here compares Adorno with Proust: 'Adorno, like Proust, lived and worked his entire life next to, and even as a part of, the great underlying continuities of Western society: families, intellectual associations, musical and concert life, and philosophical traditions, as well as any number of academic institutions. But he was always to one side, never fully a part of any' (21).

17. There is a correspondence here perhaps with what Said recalls Adorno saying of 'late-style Beethoven': 'music is transformed more and more from something significant into something obscure – even to itself.' See 'Timeliness and Lateness', p. 13.

Chapter 6

On Critical and Creative Writing

It could only be the symphonies coming from the whirling worlds above me . . . (Knut Hamsun)[1]

Faced with these charged events, prepackaged emotions already in place, we can only stitch together a set of emergency scenarios, just as our sleeping minds extemporize a narrative from the unrelated memories that veer through the cortical night. (J. G. Ballard)[2]

'The thing about you is never knowing', my mother once said, 'which way you're going to jump.' My mother is no longer alive. She spent the last decade of her life *with Alzheimer's* (strange phrase), its sloping abyss or abyssal slope, so that when I now evoke her, or when she evocates or is evoked in me, I do not know whether I am hearing her voice in madness or in sanity, if in sanity is not insanity. I can be sure, you might suppose, that I am calling up within myself a voice of the dead. But nothing in truth is assured here, in the identity of this voice within me, whether coming from me or from the other in me, in the survival of that voice, in 'the goodness' (as Wallace Stevens calls it in 'An Ordinary Evening in New Haven') of 'lying in a maternal sound', in the mother's ghost and the time of madness. As Stevens goes on to suggest, a few lines further on in the same poem: 'In this identity, disembodiments / Still keep occurring'.[3] No writing (critical or creative) without jumping: jump start, jumping off, jumping ship.

*

How should we respond to one of the most important shifts in literary studies in recent years, namely the perceived demise or end of 'theory' and rise of so-called 'creative writing'? In what ways are critical and creative writing in tension, at odds with one another, necessarily distinct from one another? And conversely perhaps, in what ways do they correspond, traverse or interlink?

Of course it will already be evident from the foregoing pages, and from the fact that the present book is part of a series called 'Frontiers of Theory', that we are not at the end of theory.[4] On the contrary, my concern in this book is to re-inflect the question of 'theory' in the wake of a new attentiveness to the literary. The following few pages, in particular, explore the possibilities of a critical writing that veers into the literary or, perhaps, *vice versa*. It is a question of the essay, then, in literal as well as literary mode – as essaying, experiment, trying out, expedition. And there is every chance of getting wrecked or lost at sea, especially as I attempt to navigate around what appear to be three tiny fictional islands. This is no 'exercise in creative writing', but rather an attempt to reflect on the environment in which writing (critical or creative) happens, and on how the figure of veering conditions the very idea and experience of *environment*.

*

Veering is a strange word, at once suggestive of a certain grace and beauty, and perhaps also a bit unnerving, even frightening. It engages weird brakes. Uncertainty breaks out between control and lack of control. As we have seen, 'veering' has a curious capacity for antithetical meaning: it can be intentional (an exercise of or in control, as in veering to avoid something) but it can also be unintentional (a failure to control, a lack or loss of control). 'The vehicle veered out of control,' someone says of a car or plane, for example, prior to a crash. Who or what controls the veering? 'Veering' can turn strange, as if its meaning were veering within. There is something ghostly about veering. It has connotations of unexpected force, uncertain and unfinished movement, secrecy and silence. It entails an unsettling of distinctions between the internal and external: you are not certain where seeing or thinking ends and hallucinating or imagining begins. In the case of the crash, for instance, did the driver's mind veer prior to the vehicle's veering? Where is this veering? What happens to locus or location?

From the very opening of this book (indeed from the startling photograph of the Galapagos green turtle on the cover), we have been concerned with non-human animals. Veering is not human or, in any event, not only or not exclusively human. Man is not the only veering animal. If, in Akira Mizuta Lippit's memorable phrase, animals 'exist in a state of *perpetual vanishing*', the ghostly character of veering might help us to think about our own positions or places in the world.[5] As the name of a theory, 'veering' is inextricably linked to a critical and deconstructive questioning of anthropocentrism. The pivot for all of these issues is the question of the environment – what an environment is, what is understood by the 'the' when we say '*the* environment', how writing relates to the experience and concept of environment, and so on.

Environment is a strange word, too. The 'environs' (without wanting to start sounding overly like Jane Austen) are the places that environ; to environ is to surround or encircle. There is something formidably centric going on here. Wherever there is 'environment', it seems, certain kinds of centrism – logocentrism, anthropocentrism, egocentrism – are at work. We doubtless too easily assume that the environment, environs or environments are what surround or encircle, and that what they surround or encircle is *us*. The word 'environment' *turns*, it may be noted, on its second syllable, the three-letter 'vir'. It is the same as 'veer' (orthographic variations on 'veer' include 'vear', 'vere' and 'vire'): it comes from the French *virer*, to turn. There is no 'environment' without veering. But the place of veering in the word and concept 'environment' may seem odd, even eerie. Veering is at once inscribed and apparently effaced.[6] There is a powerful desire or even compulsion (this has to do with the logocentrism I just mentioned) to construe veering as a shifting or turning *around*, in other words to impose order, structure and centre on the thought of veering. The word 'veer' is thus often associated with the figure of the circle, or at any rate with a turning that is smooth, orderly, as if fortuitously yet naturally systematic, neat as clockwork.[7] But the sense of a haphazard or unpredictable, non-teleological de-centring nonetheless haunts this little word, keeps it going, makes it veer. Nowhere is this haphazard and disruptive strangeness of veering perhaps more evident than in the space of literature. Indeed, as I have been trying to suggest, in a sense this is what literature *is*. It is in literary or creative writing that we might most effectively track and think critically about the veering that haunts writing, 'you' and 'me', and 'the environment'.

The concern here, then, is to try to think about veering in ways that question – and veer away from – the sorts of anthropocentric, logocentric, egocentric or subject-centred motifs just evoked. 'Veering', in this context, would refer to the swerving, interweaving, sudden turning between/within one register or tone and another, between/within one genre or discourse and another. It would be a sort of creative and critical, literary and theoretical figure in motion, a dream-shifter.

Here is 'The Etymologist':

*

Everybody was sick of him, the Etymologist.

In the early years people had been baffled, intrigued, amused. They'd never known anyone like him. He came to live among them when he was a young man, still in his twenties. He took a job first as a hotel waiter, then later he worked in the post office. Even from the beginning he was known simply as the Etymologist. He was brilliantly clever and exerted great charm. Not a few of the young women were swept off their feet.

'So clever,' sighed Elizabeth.

'So handsome,' said Jennifer.

Amanda mused for a while in silence before confiding:

'Most of all, I like the way he smells. Have you smelt him?'

But even those who were not romantically attracted were struck. He was handsome, yes, but he seemed to conceal his looks. He was like some strange reticent animal; it was as though he had burrowed in beneath his dark, heavy eyebrows and quick brown eyes. People couldn't make him out. But when he laughed people liked him. He had a delightful, soft way of laughing, often at the most unexpected moments.

'Etymologist,' he explains to a group of young boys who have been playing in the park and dusk is falling and they know their parents will be expecting them to come home. 'Yes, let me tell you. *Etymon* is the true origin of a word; the genuine or literal sense of a word. It's from the Greek *etymos* meaning true. And the *-ologist* bit means to do with the science or investigation of. So you see,' he laughs, 'I'm an etymologist.' The little boys, Mark, Henry, Richard, Rufus and the others, all think he is very funny indeed and they squeal with laughter and lisp as they try to imitate him:

'Epimologist!' 'Epimolops!' 'Epimeringue!' 'Ettispaghetti!'

The Etymologist is very much the same way with the adults. You cannot have a conversation without him sooner or later interrupting or altering the flow of things by explaining the etymological background to some of the words you are using. Even if you happen to be passing as he is posting a letter through a neighbour's door and you remark, without thinking,

'Nice day!'

—even then he is liable to stop and say:

'Peculiar word *nice*, from Old French *nice* meaning foolish, simple, from the Latin *nescius* ignorant, from *ne* not, and *scire* to know. Day, from Old English *daeg*, linked with German *Tag* and not, as you might suppose, Latin *dies*. Nice day, yes!'

But people became sick of him, the Etymologist. He always held back. He was like an animal, shielding something, forever concealing something behind his quick brown eyes. He never really made friends with anyone. In his careful, furtive way he always resisted the advances of his female admirers and always managed to leave the men feeling that the conversation, insofar as there was any, was forever conducted on his own terms.

The years went by. Amanda, Jennifer and Elizabeth all got married. The little boys who played in the park all grew up and forged families of their own. Mark, Henry, Richard, Rufus and the others, over the years, all became sick of the Etymologist, sick of the sight of him, sick of the sound and smell of him. They grew to hate him. His handsome looks had fallen away. His voice had become muffled and indistinct – it was infuriating trying to make out what he was saying. He was old and becoming decrepit. No longer capable of delivery-work on foot or bicycle, he was obliged to spend the final few years of his working-life in the sorting-room at the back of the post office. And he smelt. So that even the once-admiring, now equally aging Amanda declared:

'Pah! I can't bear him. He smells dreadfully. Have you smelt him?'

Whatever the reason, it was true. The young man she had once found so pleasing was now disgusting, a windbag whose speech nobody any longer had the patience or power of hearing to understand and who went about smelling like Jonah must have smelt on returning from the whale. Yes, people came positively to hate him, he was so offensive, such a stinking paltry insignificant old thing. A hatred of the Etymologist became a focus for the community's sense of itself. Everyone was together, it seemed, in their sense of being sick and tired of the old man.

And then, one night, matters got out of hand. Mark and Henry and some of the other men were in the pub and had been drinking more than usual and the discussion turned to the Etymologist and they became incensed. There was a momentary stony silence after Mark announced in a fierce whisper:

'So let's kill him!'

But the silence didn't last long. They were united, out of control. They knew that the old man took a walk at the end of the evening, from his house down to the park. They finished up their drinks and went out. They waited for him, hiding in some bushes at the edge of the park. And sure enough, after a few minutes, they could make out his silhouette, shambling slowly towards them.

'Attack!' yelled Mark, as the old man finally came within pouncing reach.

And Henry, Rufus and Richard lurched out of their crouching positions in the bushes and set about their task.

'We're going to kill you, you pathetic old bastard!'

'You never belonged to this place anyway!'

'You're stinking dead meat, old man!'

Mark proceeded to give orders and, as he did so, the men became increasingly vicious, goaded on by the indistinctly moaned words they could hear the Etymologist struggling to utter.

'Crush his face!'

'Crush, from Old French *croissir*, perhaps cognate with Middle High German *krosen* to crunch; face from the French *face*, coming down from the Latin *faciēs*, form or face, perhaps from *facere* to make.'

'Smash his legs!'

'Smash, one presumes imitative: compare the Swedish dialect verb *smaske*, to smack; legs, Old English, *leggr*, a leg ...'

'Stop analysing!'

But the old man was becoming more and more incoherent.

'Analyse, yes, quite, from the Greek verb *analyein*, to untie . . . Pathetic, old, yes, um . . .'

The four men, in their inebriated frenzy, finally beat and kicked the Etymologist to death, thus at last ridding themselves and the community of a thoroughly nauseating, insignificant, useless old man. It was only, however, after applying the ultimate deadly cracks to the face, back and chest that Mark, the initiator of the deed, for the first time reflected on the fact that, through all these years, none of them had any idea of the Etymologist's real name.

*

The environment of critical and creative writing is indissociably bound up with violence, even (or especially) when a writer seeks to affirm or produce a work of non-violence. To recall and transpose a pivotal proposition from our discussion of 'reading a poem' (in Chapter 3, above), critical and creative writing is necessarily at war, writing in the midst of war, first of all perhaps as a warring in and over language. There is a responsibility (which can include a certain irresponsibility) to make language veer, show it veering and be faithful to its veering, to attend to spectral strangeness, the divisibility of words, the foreignnesses within a language, the limits of a language and what is beyond. What would it mean to be a real, true etymologist? What is the true meaning of a name? What is a 'real name'?

In his *Aids to Reflection* (1825), S. T. Coleridge makes a provoking link between etymology and military campaigns. He writes about 'the use of etymology in disciplining the youthful mind to thoughtful habits', conjuring the value of knowledge of etymology in specifically military terms:

> In a language like ours, where so many words are derived from other languages, there are few modes of instruction more useful or more amusing than that of accustoming young people to seek for the etymology, or primary meaning, of the words they use. There are cases, in which more knowledge of more value may be conveyed by the history of a *word* than by the history of a campaign.[8]

The murderous men in 'The Etymologist' are clearly not Coleridgean. They do not seem to have had much in the way of that 'wild pleasure' evoked in 'Frost at Midnight', which falls upon the ear 'Most like articulate sounds of things to come' and which derives from the figure of 'the *stranger*'.[9] They seem a long way from any intimations or recollections of early childhood concerning what William Watkin terms a child's 'main means of environmental dominance: language'.[10] You would not exactly say that these men have developed 'thoughtful habits'. But the story itself is Coleridgean, perhaps, in terms of its engagement with the question of *war in and over language*. At the same time, it may also offer an aid to reflection on the delusions of mastery and domination that accompany language-use and on whether one can really speak at all of 'a language like ours'. In language we are veering; no one owns it.

'The Etymologist' was written in the autumn of 1995.[11] I scarcely remember the thing. (For example, just now, rereading in order to navigate its appearance here, I am struck, really for the first time, by the etymologist's mole-like character, this 'strange reticent animal' that has 'burrowed in': the taupological element appears to me only years after the fact. And then: what to make of this mole?) I was staying in Finland at the time, in the red light district of Helsinki, a grim place of prostitution (mostly Estonian or Russian prostitutes) and drugs, poverty and shootings, the overflow effects of the collapse of the Soviet Union and the spread of the sort of 'phantom state' of drug cartels detailed by Jacques Derrida in *Spectres of Marx*.[12] That was, at least in part, the 'writing environment'. But 'The Etymologist' is not to be located in this way: set in an apparently anglophone environment, it foregrounds a sense of estrangement of place.

No writing environment without the veering logic and effects of intertextuality. Kafka doubtless veers out a spectral line to 'The Etymologist'. Perhaps more than any other novelist or fiction-writer of the past century or so, his work has challenged the sense of place, of what a writing or reading environment might be. When you read a story by Kafka you are not encouraged to think, 'Ah! Prague!' or, 'Oh yes, so true of Berlin!' On the contrary, the singularity of Kafka's work has to do with a certain resisting or avoidance of location. As in many of Samuel Beckett's later writings, there is a shifting dreaminess, an insistent focus on the putative or potential importance of place, context and environment, yet at the same time an overwhelming sense of dislocation and the unlocatable. 'The Etymologist' also seems to bear curious traces of D. H. Lawrence: there is something perhaps of the intermingling of fairy tale and psychic drama that characterizes his stories.

Intertextuality is heterophony. One cannot hope to analyse the notion of a writing environment without reckoning with the effects, for example, of what Coleridge's 'Kubla Khan' calls 'ancestral voices'.[13] In reading or listening to a literary work there is always another voice, in the wings or already centre stage, beside oneself, beside the voice of the speaker or character, narrator or reader. What kind of text is 'The Etymologist'? I suppose it is, in part, a satire on people's indifference to language, to the words that they use, where words come from, what hidden possibilities they carry. A violent satire on a violent indifference, it may be said, for it is also about the ways in which the letter killeth. And at the same time it is deeply interested in questions of psychoanalysis and in particular the possibilities for fiction of thinking about what I call cryptaesthesia, about the ways in which literature can see us coming and traps us, even as it sends us off course.[14] 'The Etymologist' is a text about what René Girard calls the scapegoat, about Freud's *Totem and Taboo*, about my father of course and my mother (no 'writing environments' without their spectral vigilance, their voices and language), but also about the borders or shores, the links or limits of etymology. It is about veering, above and beyond what linguists call 'folk etymology' – the energetic *versatilities* of language.[15]

It is not a matter of authorial control: this is one reason why the phrases 'creative writing' and 'creative writer' are so deadeningly inept.[16] It is as much a question of losing as of trying to keep control, for the versatilities of language are never one's own. Shifting alongside this is the notion of a kind of veering ethical imperative, a respect for and responsibility to the spirit and impishness of words as summoned in, for example, Freud's *The Psychopathology of Everyday Life* (1901): ideas, feelings, phantasms suggest themselves, out of the veering waywardness of words. In its meticulous, if also in some ways clearly crazy sketches of the semic, scenic, seismic versatilities of words (omissions, substitutions, distortions, non sequiturs, inadvertent or advertent slips of tongue or writing fingers, anagrams, homophones and other sorts of paronomasia), 'verbal bridges' and nodal points, not to mention forms of 'negative hallucination' and 'delusions of reference', *The Psychopathology of Everyday Life* constitutes a first draft of regulations for veering in sanity and literature. It is all there, for instance, in the extraordinary final chapter, 'Determinism, Belief in Chance and Superstition – Some Points of View', with its lovely pluralized subtitle – so many 'points of view' according to which one can veer about, playing the child and the professor, analyst and analysand, poet and philosopher, normal and abnormal, superstitious and rational, as and when.[17] It is not, of course, a matter here of 'following Freud' in a simply dutiful or merely deferential manner. It is up to you to veer *with* what he says. You have to veer in your own way. You have to veer *uncanonically*, as H. D. might say.[18] Perhaps more sharply and succinctly than any

other of Freud's books, *The Psychopathology* lays out a basis for thinking, reading and writing in terms of what Derrida calls '"literatures" and
"revolutions" that as yet have no model': it lets us see how 'everything
becomes possible against the language-police'.[19] It is a legacy taken up by
Lacan and by Abraham and Torok, as well as Derrida, Cixous and others;
but we are still perhaps only at the infancy of a critical writing attuned to
the strangeness of words operating by themselves within us, beyond the
grave, veering.

One might be haunted by a word one has never heard. There are
what Abraham and Torok call 'words that hide', 'cryptonyms', words
with allosemic force, alluding 'to a foreign and arcane meaning'.[20]
'Epimologist! Epimolops! Epimeringue! Ettispaghetti!': in this string of
neologistic hypocorisms (the young boys trying to say 'etymologist'), we
can perhaps hear and follow the contours of a certain 'molest'. What to
make of this apparent hyperbole, the *most* 'mole' (recalling Kafka's 'giant
mole')?[21] For what person, figure or name would this mole be a substitute? Who stole the mole? Or is it the mole itself that 'steals away'?[22]
(Everything here goes by way of the necessity of chance, the veering
of a *mole* as unforeseeability: I have just happened upon a moment in
Freud where he reads or misreads 'molestation'. In a brief text entitled
'A Seventeenth-Century Demonological Neurosis' (1923), Freud remarks
that when, in May 1678, the painter Christopher Haizmann 'returned to
Mariazell [a place of pilgrimage some eighty miles south-west of Vienna],
he complained of *maligni Spiritûs manifestationes* ["manifestations of
the Evil Spirit"]'. Freud's English editor then provides a footnote, detailing Freud's misreading: 'The manuscript reads: "*de maligni Spiritûs
infestatione* (of . . . molestation by the Evil Spirit)".'[23]) If molestation,
then, shows up in 'The Etymologist' as a sort of authorial mole-station or
mole-hill, what does this conceal? Where does it lead? How many moles
are there (*Hamlet*, Kafka again, E. M. Forster, Lawrence's 'Second Best',
Coleridge's 'Limbo' . . .)? This protean figure of the mole (a writing-mole,
the silent and improper *mole* in 'etymology', among others), may suggest
something of the force of veering that, after Freud, necessarily characterizes any rigorous critical reflection on the nature of literary or creative
writing.[24]

Here is something, hardly bigger than a tooth cavity, about going to the
dentist's. It is called 'Today the Dentist's':

*

Today the dentist's. Tist's. Say, *tist's*. My dentist frightens me. Marathon
Man meets Wittgenstein. The silent type. *Ent, ist*. He arrived a year or
so ago, the latest act at my local NHS pay-as-you-go circus. My dentist

is not young. He has big glasses like a snooker player. His hands tremble and he has a speech impediment. *Ment*. Hence perhaps the air of post-Tractatus. He hails from up north. I am convinced he was struck off and has been rehabilitated, incomprehensibly. Hensibly, he *ti*culates erely *its* of words, when he does peak. Alcohol-illum, Parkinshun, ental break done? I can't help imagining he killed someone. *Man's law. Accidentist*. I have never had any treatment from him, only check-ups, till today. But now two cavities, *tiz*, tizzy, *viz*: both upper right. No mask. He operates as if there is no tomorrow. In goes the injection, like a knife in the street. Blue rubber gloves. I don't know whether to open or shut my eyes. Out of the picture, the indifferent young assistant listens to the radio, looks at her nails. I car peak any more, anaesthetic impacts, in *pax*, hunting in, fingers crossing, tighten, tightest, impacted, *im*-prac-*tist*. And he says nothing, no falsely reassuring *that-should-be-numbing-up-nicely-by-now*, no time for words, he is in like a feeding frenzy in reverse. I keep feeling, as in a dream. Perhaps hallucinatory his halitosis. *Tosis*. Fingers shaking, perspiration beading inside the aquarium spectacles, he lunges, invades, retreats, returns, wielding who knows what, a drill then something else, eels, feels, files, patient eyes closed now for business, long pause as if in exhaustion. Then assault recommences, flailing, thrashing, splay in my mouth, then falls back abruptly with a single word, strangularly tittled out: *done*, he says. He turns as from the scene of a crime and puts down his instruments, like a car mechanic, on the side, still juddering.

*

This might read like a piece of fiction: in truth it is what I would call reality literature.[25] It is written from the most real experience imaginable. I could if required specify the place, as well as the date and time of the appointment. No doubt everyone who has spent time in a dental surgery will have had some anxiety, however faint or haunting, about the dentist's hand slipping, the drill or other instrument veering. The dentist of 'Today' is, alas, just that worrying sort of dentist. He is reminiscent of the dentist in the Alice Cooper song who gleefully declares of his patient that the teeth are fine but the gums have got to go. But there is also a sense of the poet in this figure who 'operates as if there is no tomorrow'. Wallace Stevens's 'An Ordinary Evening in New Haven' returns: 'The poem is the cry of its occasion, / Part of the res itself and not about it.' The poet 'speaks / By sight and insight as they are. There is no / Tomorrow for him.'[26] It is in a sense the dentist who is writing here, producing his signature or work in the mouth of the narrator.

One of the ironies of this quick fiction is that, for all its *in*-sist-*ence* on an immediacy of narrating what is going on, for all the emphasis on description *in situ*, the reader knows that the narrator cannot be either speaking ('*I car peak*') or writing at the moment of what is happening. Correspondingly, 'Today the Dentist's' is highly specific in its sense of location and yet it could, fearfully, be set in a dentist's surgery more or less anywhere. On the one hand, the text testifies to a presentation of the immediacy of the present as necessarily derived, dislocated.[27] On the other, there is a sort of cry of the occasion, a preoccupation with a sense of writing now, *writing today* as 'part of the res itself', an experience of veering, operating through shifts and turns, slippages and slidings, anagrams or partial anagrams, homophones tacit or interrupted, transegmental breakdowns, stoppings in action, dental and accidental, images evoked from other places, felt or filed eelsware.

Veering is the diversion of the one. It is divisibility itself, divisibility of word, direction and address. As we have noted earlier, even at the most dictionarcotically elementary level (*OED*, 'veer', v. 1 and 'veer', v. 2), one 'veer' can appear to veer out or into another (change, shift course, turn round or about, alter, let out, slacken, set loose, tack). Thus, we are inclined to think, there is always some 'play', some slackening, tacking or veering in *veering*, shifting between *and* within one 'veering' and the other. There is a striking instance of this in the 'strange power of speech' of Coleridge's 'The Rime of the Ancient Mariner', at that moment when 'the ancient Mariner beholdeth' what the marginalia cryptically terms 'a sign in the element afar off'.[28] There is 'A something in the sky' (l. 148), shifting and turning. It will shortly transpire that this 'something' is the 'spectre-bark' (l. 202) whose crew comprises 'the Night-mare LIFE-IN-DEATH' (l. 193) playing dice with 'DEATH that woman's mate' (l. 189).

But before becoming 'spectre-bark' it is merely a 'speck' (l. 149). Of course, nothing in Coleridge's poem remains the same – from the division of addressees at the start ('It is an ancient Mariner, / And he stoppeth one of three') to the waywardly im/pertinent marginalia that keep the reader's eyes turning away from the main text and back again.[29] Among the most demonic and haunted poems in English, 'The Rime of the Ancient Mariner' is also perhaps the most relentlessly veering. It veers from one nightmarish experience to the next, imperilled and impelled by disconnection, a twisted overturning of cause and effect. It veers along or within the strange border between what is apparently in the world and what is phantasmagory. And it veers in time – between that of its initial rendition and the uncanny, deferred revelation of the Mariner's passing 'from land to land' and his need interminably to maintain his 'strange power of speech' by 'teach[ing]' his 'tale' once again, from the beginning. The wedding-guest's '[t]urn[ing]' from the bridegroom's door' thus marks the twisted ending that is a turning round once more to start all over. If Coleridge's poem conforms to the logic of the ouroboros, this is not a static figure.[30] As in Milton, we might say, the serpent veers. (And so too, of course, does the albatross.[31])

Above all, perhaps, the demonic and haunted nature of Coleridge's poem has to do with veerings in and out of the sound of words. There is derangement and dread to be read in the whirlings of sound: 'The boat came close beneath the ship, / And straight a sound was heard. / Under the water it rumbled on, / Still louder and more dread: / It reached the ship, it split the bay; / The ship went down like lead. /. . ./ Upon the whirl, where sank the ship, / The boat spun round and round; / And all was still, save that the hill / Was telling of the sound' (ll. 544–9 and 556–9). Veering about in verse: in these lines, perhaps more explicitly than anywhere else in 'The Rime', the reader is alerted to the sort of force or forces of sound that drive the poem. This spinning 'round and round' is, eerily, 'still', even as that 'still' still echoes with the '[s]till louder' (l. 547) of a few lines earlier. There is something maddening in this deferred 'telling of the sound' – a sense of subterranean or submarine disruption ('It reached the ship, it split the bay') that is characteristic of Coleridge's language throughout. 'The Rime' is a mire of strange sound from the start. The word 'rime' itself veers, rhymes with itself in the strangeness of homophony while spinning away: it is an old spelling of 'rhyme' that also means 'frost' or 'mist', as well as 'crack, chink, fissure' (*OED*, 'rime' n. 1 and n. 3). Coleridge's poem figures as a sort of deranged whirligig, a phantom music machine that plays by itself: 'Around, around, flew each sweet sound, / Then darted to the Sun; / Slowly the sounds came back again, / Now mixed, now one by one' (ll. 354–7).

Manifestly, manifestively, a considerable measure (or 'rime') of 'The Rime' is a deliberate, superbly wrought exercise in veering. At the sort of level of detail noted by Susan Eilenberg, for example, we might think of the deconstitution of the letters of the word 'mariner' into 'manner' into 'man' – 'What manner of man art thou?' (l. 577) – or the anagrammatic play of 'name' in this provocatively anonymous storyteller.[32] But alongside and beyond this there is a more radical veering, akin to what Garrett Stewart calls 'an irresolute and disruptive drifting that destabilizes any given constraint upon the bonding of phonemes into words'.[33]

In order to track this more closely, let us return to the split moment at which (according to the marginalia) the mariner sees 'a sign in the element afar off', when the strange spectacle of the 'speck' is still approaching:

At first it seemed a little speck,
And then it seemed a mist;
It moved and moved, and took at last
A certain shape, I wist.

A speck, a mist, a shape, I wist!
And still it neared and neared:
As if it dodged a water-sprite,
It plunged and tacked and veered. (ll. 149–56)

It begins with veering and veering begins with *it*: 'It is an ancient Mariner', 'it seemed', 'it seemed . . .'. In these eight lines 'it' will have 'moved and moved', 'neared and neared', and is still, finally, veering. 'It' (the letters of the word 'it' and *its* or *it's* uncertain referent) veers into 'mist' and 'wist'. The reiteration of 'I wist' comes with a twist: the claim to knowledge or certitude ('A certain shape, I wist') is loosened ('A speck, a mist, a shape, I wist!'). 'Wist' is in a mist. 'Moved' is not the same as 'moved', nor 'neared' 'neared'. Sounds and letters dodge and turn: just as 'speck' shifts through 'sprite' towards 'spectre-bark', so 'it' tilts into 'sprite' and 'still'. What is 'still' (it goes without saying) is not still: 'still it neared and neared'. And 'and' is in a spin. The 'sign' veers. However near it nears it still 'plunge[s] and tack[s] and veer[s]'.

It is difficult not to read Wordsworth when one reads Coleridge, or *vice versa*. (*Vice versa* is itself a veering figure, the turning of position, a turning from one place to the other, turning in the other.[34]) The figure of veering appears in Wordsworth's poetry on numerous occasions. In 'Hart-Leap Well' (written in 1800), for instance, we encounter 'Sir Walter, restless as a veering wind'.[35] In more nautical fashion, the sonnet 'With Ships the sea was sprinkled far and nigh' (written May 1802–March 1804) opens with a strikingly uncertain veering ('one knew not why'):

With Ships the sea was sprinkled far and nigh,
Like stars in heaven, and joyously it showed;
Some lying fast at anchor in the road,
Some veering up and down, one knew not why.[36]

But the most remarkable example of veering in Wordsworth – at once the most idiomatic, we might say, and the most spookily Coleridgean – comes in *The Prelude*, at the beginning of Book 4, where he describes the summer vacation when he returns from Cambridge to the Lake District, and more precisely to Hawkshead, where he had gone to school:

> Thence right forth
> I took my way, now drawing towards home,
> To that sweet valley where I had been reared;
> 'Twas but a short hour's walk ere, veering round,
> I saw the snow-white church upon its hill . . .[37]

The Norton editors note that the poet would be making this approach along Esthwaite Water, and that from here 'the church does seem to sit above the roofs of the village'.[38] We could wander and wonder in these apparently simple lines for a long time. The 'sweet valley' may not be Wordsworth's 'sweet birthplace', which was at Cockermouth (and here we will already have veered into Coleridge: when Wordsworth writes of his 'sweet birthplace', early on in *The Prelude* (Part 1, l. 8 of the 1799 text; Book 1, l. 278 in the 1805 text), he is citing his friend's great poem 'Frost at Midnight'), but there is nonetheless a strong sense of homecoming here. 'Home' would be, as it were, the effort, expectation and desire of 'veering'.

There are complex and curious correspondences between these lines and the passage in 'The Rime of the Ancient Mariner'.[39] But then the very idea of passage becomes disoriented: we speak of 'a passage of prose' or 'passage of poetry' as if to assure ourselves that we can and will pass, we have a reader's right of passage, the passage is what passes and we pass over the passage. A passage is 'a continuous but indefinite portion of a book' (*Chambers Dictionary*), from the Latin *passus*, a step. Might there not be other ways of construing the movement of writing than in a smooth and seemingly assured anthropomorphism of walking? What if the step were a veering? Certainly we do not think of Coleridge's Mariner as a *walking* narrator. His passages are enigmatic, in the dark: 'I pass, like night, from land to land' (l. 586).

Just as Coleridge's poem feminizes the veering ghost-ship ('How fast she nears and nears! / Are those *her* sails that glance in the Sun, / Like restless gossamers?' (ll. 182–4)), and just as this 'she' shifts into the figure of 'that Woman' who at first seems to be 'all her crew' (l. 187), the figure of the nightmarish woman 'Who thicks man's blood with cold' (l. 194), so Wordsworth feminizes 'the snow-white church' (sitting 'like a thronèd lady') and has the 'gracious look' of this lady shift into the figure of the 'old dame' perusing the poet:

> 'Twas but a short hour's walk ere, veering round,
> I saw the snow-white church upon its hill
> Sit like a thronèd lady, sending out
> A gracious look all over its domain.
> Glad tidings had I, and some tears perhaps,

From my old dame, so motherly and good,
While she perused me with a parent's pride. (Bk 4: 14–20)

The 'dame' is of course not Wordsworth's mother, but a surrogate mother, his landlady Ann Tyson, who died at the age of 83 in 1796. If, as Mary Jacobus has suggested, 'autobiography comes into play on the basis of a missing mother',[40] there is always surrogacy, there are always spectral mothers, and spectral figures (mariners or poets) being read or perused by a surrogate mother. The very invocation and possibility of autobiographical writing is a work of surrogation. Everything here is veering, I confess, in the wake of the voice of my mother. And veering from one mother to another, from Coleridge's nightmarish 'mate' of death ('the Spectre-Woman and her Death-mate', as the marginalia has it) to the gracious, 'motherly and good' woman in Wordsworth. It is as if Wordsworth were rewriting, *vice-versing* the ghost-ship in Coleridge. It is perhaps always a matter of a ghost-vessel, when it comes to veering.

What is the time of this veering? Wordsworth effectively introduces this question with the evocation of 'but a short hour's walk'. In this blithe figuring of time as 'short', the adjective has jumped back or jumped off to join the 'hour' not the 'walk'. (How to talk about this? 'Transferred epithet' would be dead-in-the-water.) The hour is or was a short hour, the walk no one else's, a singular homecoming evoked above all in the place of 'veering'. Wordsworth is unsure about how to punctuate what is going on here. In the 1805 text we have ''Twas but a short hour's walk ere', then a comma, then 'veering round', followed by another comma. Environed by commas, 'veering round' intimates a kind of enclosure or activity in itself, rather like what Wallace Stevens calls 'the pleasures of merely circulating', becoming giddy.[41] In the 1850 version Wordsworth has moved the first comma to before the 'ere'. 'Ere' the 'ere': ''Twas but a short hour's walk, ere veering round . . .'. The later version might suggest a dissatisfaction at the oddity or impropriety of a clause that had begun ''twas' and ended 'ere', as if one might misread the line as non-narrative or non-progressive, as talking about an earlier time and event (a walk before). Correspondingly, the 1850 text omits the comma at the end of the line and thus strengthens the link between the 'veering' and the 'I', the one rounding into the other: '. . . ere veering round / I saw . . .'.

In truth one wants both versions, to be responsive and responsible to the literality of *turning* that the word 'version' itself inscribes. One wants to veer between them (1805 and 1850), or to see and hear them veering – to see not only the eye-rhyme in the 'ere' and 'veer', but also the jumping about of commas between versions, and to hear not only the 'veering' pick up the 'reared' of the previous line (the assonantal, internal rhyming of 'rear' and 'veer' intimating a further secretive correspondence between 'veering' and 'home', as well as between these lines and the 'neared'/'veered' of 'The Rime of the Ancient Mariner'), but also the different pauses dictated by those bobbing or drowned commas across the 1805 and 1850 texts. "Twas but a short hour's walk ere, veering round / I saw . . .'. The flickering or double gesture of the comma – in one version *between* 'ere' and 'veering', and in the other *before* 'ere veering' – underscores the sense that the 'ere' and the 'veering' interfere with one another: time, already strangely foreshortened ('a short hour's walk'), is veering about.

In the Wordsworthian turn of the line (enjambed in the 1850 text: 'veering round / I saw'), the subject of the sentence is suspended. Is it the walk or the I that is veering?[42] There is a simplicity and beauty in this roundness, this implicit circling around that is at once an apparent homecoming and a turning round of the verse. But, as always in Wordsworth, we are left also with residual strangenesses of language, syntax and sense. In the most ghostly closeness of its phonemes we might note, for example, the transegmental drifting that allows a scarcely audible sense of the *ground* shifting, a veering of the earth as well as 'I' ('veering round' > 'veering ground'), and even a whiffling of mortality in the intricate turning of the verse ('round / I' > 'round die').[43] At least in part phantasmatic boat or ship, the 'I' of these lines comes after the 'veering', at once subject *of* and *to* it. Whether isolated as a separate clause (the 1805 version) or allowed to drift, enjamb or turn into the 'I' itself (the 1850 version), 'veering round' figures as a peculiar event unto itself, an uncertainly subjected veering in language, orientation and direction.

Wordsworth's lines entail a striking instance of what Garrett Stewart has called 'the micro-grammar of narrative', as well as its chiasmatic counterpart, a micro-narrative of grammar.[44] Wordsworth's wavering but meticulous attention to questions of syntax, punctuation and enjambment in these versions of 'veering round' comports with the suggestion explored earlier (in Chapter 3 'Reading a Poem') that we might think not so much of 'line-breaks' in poetry, as of lines *veering*, 'veering[s] round'. Finally, let us note what is, after all, perhaps the most enduring and provoking detail concerning these lines from Wordsworth: they offer what is (so far as I have been able to discover) the earliest example in English of an autobiographical 'veering'. Wordsworth speaks of himself veering. Here, at the start of the nineteenth century, begins the story and the history of the veering 'I', the 'I' itself as veering.

*

The last thing on the horizon here is the slide. It appeared in a dream: there was nothing to do but note it down. Where is literature born, where does it belong, if not in the dream, and *vice versa*? No dream, no condensation or displacement, no distinction between 'latent' and 'manifest content', no 'secondary revision' without veering. In the fascinating fragmentary work entitled *The Prose of the World*, Maurice Merleau-Ponty writes of what is 'hazardous' in literature. He characterizes this as a matter of being open, or opening oneself up, to the unknown:

> Literary language can say new things only with the condition that we make common cause with it, that we stop examining its origins in order to follow where it is going, that we allow the words and means of expression in a book to be enveloped in that haze of signification that they derive from their particular arrangement, and finally, that we let the whole work veer toward a second-order tacit value where it almost rejoins the mute radiance of painting.[45]

In this respect, Merleau-Ponty goes on to say, 'the essential meaning of the work of art is perceptible at first only as a *coherent deformation* imposed on the visible'.[46] Literature entails the 'coherent deformation' of the known. One must veer in the haze, in the haze of the hazardous.

'The Slide' is dedicated to Harold Bloom.[47] It seems curious how little critical attention has been given to his theory of 'influence anxiety' in the context of fictional narrative or indeed critical prose. Bloom's is, among other things, a theory based on veering. This is perhaps especially evident in the revisionary ratio he specifies as clinamen (a Latin word usually translated as 'inclination' or 'leaning'): it is Bloom's term for how a younger poet (or 'ephebe') swerves away from the precursor. He contends that the '*clinamen* or "swerve" is the trope-as-misreading', in other words that it constitutes the decisive, ironic opening gambit or defence (the first 'revisionary ratio', as he calls it) in which a poet consciously or unconsciously tropes on or misreads an earlier poet or poem. Bloom derives the notion of clinamen from Epicurus and Lucretius, but also, in more recent critical usage, from Coleridge's *Aids to Reflection*.[48] Part of the appeal of Bloom's characterization of clinamen is that it poses as a (fittingly ironic) figure of itself: *his* reading is itself a trope or misreading, a singular swerve or veering.[49] Bloom thus invites us to think about the ways in which clinamen, bias, swerve or veering is figured in any literary or critical writing. But where or when would veering end? Or begin?

We might here set Bloom's work alongside the reading of clinamen in Lucretius and Epicurus that Jacques Derrida sketches in his remarkable essay, 'My Chances/*Mes Chances*: A Rendezvous with Some Epicurean Stereophonies'.[50] Veering, in this context, would entail reckoning with the thought that there is no atom, that there is what Derrida calls 'a certain divisibility or internal difference of the so-called ultimate element (*stoikheion*, trait, letter, seminal mark)'.[51] At issue is what he calls 'a diversion of atomism' (*un détournement de l'atomisme*).[52] On this he claims to stake everything: 'My *clinamen*, my luck or my chances, that is what inclines me to think the *clinamen* beginning with the divisibility of the mark.'[53] You do not create or own your clinamen, indeed you can never properly see or experience it as such. Yet there is a singularity about the clinamen, about what we may provisionally designate as Bloom's clinamen, for example, or Derrida's.[54] At the same time, the 'divisibility of the mark' is something that can be traced in the proper name itself, in what might appear to gather together or give unity to a text or to an oeuvre. As Derrida puts it: 'Why do we refrain from applying the *clinamen* to Epicurus's name, and in his name itself?'[55] There is veering in the name, of the name – from Lucretius to Derrida and beyond.

If we turn back – or, today, turn for the first time – to that great, unfinished poem, *De Rerum Natura*, it is hardly for a scientifically accurate account of the nature of things. It is above all, perhaps, for an encounter with the uncanny veering of the environment. It gives us a thinking of veering as beautiful and strange, as an experience of uncertainty of time and place, a universe of swerving atoms, from the swirling movements of what passes through water and air and goes rippling through our limbs to the sways of fear and pleasure in the mind: sheer veering.[56]

*

There is this slide, just as you might find in a park for children. The only difference is that it is bigger and not in a park. You do not trouble to reflect upon such matters as you start clambering up. You are not alone. There is an 'almost festival atmosphere', the sun is shining and people are enjoying themselves enormously. You join in, laughing and making witty remarks as you go. But the climbing is tricky. The rungs of the ladder are wooden and, trodden by so many feet, prove at moments treacherously smooth. Every so often someone slips and falls. This happens, however, without any great commotion. Indeed there is, almost straightaway, no indication that the incident even occurred. You begin to sense that the laughter of those around is not altogether genuine, but rather conceals a pervasive edginess concerning the demands of the ascent. The distance between rungs has increased. You feel you have to launch yourself up and forwards, as if very slowly and clumsily pole-vaulting, from one rung to the next. Each rung is wide and deep enough to give standing room for three or four people. For what feels like the first time, you stop. You pause to take in the view and see with a start how high you have climbed. You feel dwarfed. You gaze out over a tremendous vista of river, fringed with thick jungle. You are so preoccupied with the climb that you scarcely think about how long you have been at it. You find you have to rest more frequently. The river over which you are perched is so wide now that you can no longer make out any of the jungle observed earlier, not even at the farthest horizons. You know that the end is approaching. You are so near the top that you can see where the steel railings curve inwards and the rungs narrow, restricting the passage of climbers to just one person per step. The atmosphere becomes sombre. For the first time it dawns on you that you have not actually seen the chute itself, and that the amazing, endlessly sparkling silver slipway rushing downwards is a thing that exists only in your imagination. You cast your mind back and realize that all your impressions of the slide are based on what you have heard from others and pictured to yourself. You do not look down any more, you are so filled with trepidation. You haul your exhausted body, by now practically useless, quivering, on to the brink. You are at the top now and, immeasurably elevated, on the very verge, can finally see that there is no slide, glittering and swaying, stretching away down before you. There is only a sheer drop. 'At last,' you tell yourself, as you inch into your final position, 'I can start living.'

*

Notes

An earlier version of this essay was first presented at the 'Contemporary Writing Environments' conference, Brunel University, 8 July 2004, and published as 'On Creative and Critical Writing, Environments and Dreaming: Veering (1)', *Textual Practice*, 23: 6 (2009), 913–33. I would like to record my gratitude here to William Watkin for inviting me to address this topic.

1. Knut Hamsun, *Hunger*, trans. Sverre Lyngstad (Edinburgh: Canongate, 1996), p. 38.
2. J. G. Ballard, *The Atrocity Exhibition*, new rev. edn (San Francisco: RE/Search, 1990), p. 89.
3. Wallace Stevens, 'An Ordinary Evening in New Haven', in *Collected Poems* (New York: Alfred Knopf, 1954), p. 482.
4. In her timely and probing book *Ugly Feelings* (London: Harvard University Press, 2005), Sianne Ngai recalls Fredric Jameson's view that 'Ours is an antitheoretical time, which is to say an anti-intellectual time.' She then asks: 'Why is it that at the "same time" capital grows more virtual and abstract in its daily operations, cultural critique grows increasingly positivistic and empirical, veering away from the methods best suited for the analysis of its

proliferation?' (See pp. 299–300.) The present study is an attempt to veer *otherwise* – to veer in more effective, if also more elliptical ways, vis-à-vis precisely such 'daily operations'.

5. Akira Mizuta Lippit, *Electric Animal: Toward a Rhetoric of Wildlife* (Minneapolis: University of Minnesota Press, 2000), p. 1. The sense of ghostliness in this observation is linked to the statement from John Berger, with which Lippit begins his book: 'Everywhere animals disappear.' See John Berger, *About Looking* (New York: Vintage, 1980), p. 26.

6. We might think about 'climate change' in a corresponding way: there is something absurd about this phrase, as if the 'change' were something simply going on apart from – at a distance from – ourselves, as if our hallucinatory place at the centre of the world were left entirely intact and unaffected by what is going on outside, over there, somewhere else. There is something laughable also about the pacifying use of 'change' rather than, say, 'disintegration' or 'transformation', and about the calm insistence on this noun in the singular. The very 'change' or *changes* in 'climate change' entail veering, veering perhaps in its most terrifying forms.

7. On veering in terms of the 'fundamental circling mechanism in all animals', see Ian P. Howard and William B. Templeton, *Human Spatial Orientation* (New York: John Wiley, 1966), p. 258. On the fact that humans may veer to the right or the left, see C. Mohr, P. Brugger, H. S. Bracha, T. Landis and I. Viaud-Delmon, 'Human side preferences in three different whole-body movement tasks', *Behavioural Brain Research*, 151 (2004): 321–6.

8. S. T. Coleridge, *Aids to Reflection in the Formation of a Manly Character: On the Several Grounds of Prudence, Morality and Religion*, rev. edn, ed. Thomas Fenby (London: Routledge, 1905), pp. 15, 5.

9. See Samuel Taylor Coleridge, 'Frost at Midnight', in *Poems*, ed. John Beer (London: Dent, 1974), pp. 137–9.

10. William Watkin, *On Mourning: Theories of Loss in Modern Literature* (Edinburgh: Edinburgh University Press, 2004), p. 183.

11. 'The Etymologist' was originally published in Finnish, as 'Etymologi', trans. Asko Kauppinen and Arto Schroderus, in *Kulttuurivihkot*, 12 (1996), 39–40. It appears here in English for the first time.

12. See Jacques Derrida, *Spectres of Marx: The State of the Debt, the Work of Mourning, and the New International*, trans. Peggy Kamuf (London: Routledge, 1994), p. 83.

13. See Coleridge, 'Kubla Khan', in *Poems*, p. 167.

14. For more on cryptaesthesia, see Nicholas Royle, *Telepathy and Literature: Essays on the Reading Mind* (Oxford: Blackwell, 1990), pp. 60–2 (apropos Emily Brontë's *Wuthering Heights*) and *passim*.

15. On the veering beauty of 'versatility' (*versatilité*), turn to Hélène Cixous, 'The Unforeseeable', trans. Beverley Bie Brahic, *Oxford Literary Review*, 26 (2004), 190. It is a word which she doubtless hears in French but also turning between French and English and I first heard her pronounce in English (at an 'Inventive English' lecture at the University of Sussex in June 2004). It is a word that, again, comes from the Latin *vertere*, to turn, and in French has more of a sense of 'fickle', 'capricious', 'changeable', than in English where the primary signification is of 'turning easily or freely from one thing to another' (though it can also mean 'changeable', 'unsteady').

She remarks: '*versatility* . . . is a word which rings pleasingly in my ears and mind. I could write a book on versatility. Naturally I would call it *Versatilities*. Those I love the most are versatile' (190).

16. Cf. Maurice Blanchot's comment that 'writing is nothing if it does not involve the writer in a movement full of risks that will change him [or her] in one way or another': see Blanchot, *The Work of Fire*, trans. Charlotte Mandell (Stanford: Stanford University Press, 1995), p. 244. For a further discussion of critical and creative writing in this context, see Andrew Bennett and Nicholas Royle, *Introduction to Literature, Criticism and Theory*, 4th edn (Harlow: Pearson, 2009), pp. 88–95.

17. Sigmund Freud, *The Psychopathology of Everyday Life* (1901), *SE* 6.

18. H. D. (Hilda Doolittle) was analysed by Freud in Vienna, in 1933–4. She documents this in her *Tribute to Freud: Writing on the Wall; Advent* (Manchester: Carcanet, 1985), first published in 1956. In two short passages early on (see pp. 14–16), detailing the experience of being on the analyst's couch, the image of veering appears in a striking and insistent fashion. In a prose intricately responsive to what she calls 'the science of the unravelling of the tangled skeins of the unconscious mind' (16), H. D. records the moment at which 'I veered round off the couch, my feet on the floor. I do not know exactly what I had said' (14). And then again, this time in the present tense: 'For myself, I veer round, uncanonically seated stark upright with my feet on the floor' (15). (It is part of H. D.'s 'uncanonicity' here, perhaps, to evoke being naked through this 'upright'.) And finally, repeating it a third time, when she reveals what it is that apparently triggered the veering: '*Consciously*, I was not aware of having said anything that might account for the Professor's [i.e. Freud's] outburst. And even as I veered around, facing him, my mind was detached enough to wonder if this was some idea of *his* for speeding up the analytic content or redirecting the flow of associated images. The Professor said, "The trouble is – I am an old man – *you do not think it worth your while to love me*"' (16). Such is H. D.'s position, somewhere between veering off the couch (away from psychoanalysis in what we might call its most clinical sense) and veering round to encounter Freud.

19. Jacques Derrida, 'Limited Inc a, b, c . . .', trans. Samuel Weber and Jeffrey Mehlman, in *Limited Inc* (Evanston, IL: Northwestern University Press, 1988), p. 100.

20. Nicolas Abraham and Maria Torok, *The Wolf Man's Magic Word: A Cryptonymy*, trans. Nicholas Rand (Minneapolis: University of Minnesota Press, 1986), pp. 18–19.

21. See *The Complete Short Stories of Franz Kafka*, ed. Nahum N. Glatzer (London: Minerva, 1996), p. 470.

22. William Shakespeare, *Hamlet, Prince of Denmark*, ed. Philip Edwards, updated edn (Cambridge: Cambridge University Press, 2003), III, iv, 135.

23. Sigmund Freud, 'A Seventeenth-Century Demonological Neurosis', in *SE* 19: 78.

24. For more on the mole in this context, see Nicholas Royle, 'Mole', in *The Uncanny* (Manchester: Manchester University Press, 2003), pp. 241–55, and *E. M. Forster* (Plymouth: Northcote House, 1999), p. 6 and *passim*.

25. See Nicholas Royle, 'Reality Literature', Afterword to *Quilt* (Brighton:

Myriad Editions, 2010), pp. 152–9. 'Today the Dentist's' was first published in Susanna Jones and Lawrence Zeegen (eds), *The Illustrated Brighton Moment: True Stories* (Brighton: Unmadeup Arts, 2008), p. 139.

26. Wallace Stevens, 'An Ordinary Evening in New Haven', in *Collected Poems*, p. 473.

27. Cf. Jacques Derrida: 'Immediacy is derived (*L'immédiateté est dérivée*)', in *Of Grammatology*, trans. Gayatri Chakravorty Spivak (Baltimore: Johns Hopkins University Press, 1976), p. 157; *De la grammatologie* (Paris: Éditions de Minuit, 1967) p. 226.

28. Coleridge, 'The Rime of the Ancient Mariner', in *Poems*, pp. 173–89: see marginalia at ll. 146–8. Further line references are to this version of the text.

29. There is also, of course, the rich and intractably complex question of which text of Coleridge's poem we are talking about: 'The Rime' was first published anonymously in *Lyrical Ballads* in 1798 but appeared in numerous altered and revised versions right up to 1834. The marginal glosses, for example, did not appear until 1817. For a detailed discussion, see Jack Stillinger, *Coleridge and Textual Instability: The Multiple Versions of the Major Poems* (Oxford: Oxford University Press, 1994), pp. 60–73.

30. On Coleridge and the ouroboros, see H. B. de Groot, 'The Ouroboros and the Romantic Poets: A Renaissance Emblem in Blake, Coleridge and Shelley', in *English Studies*, 50 (1969): 553–64, especially 562–3.

31. See, for example, http://www.arkive.org/black-browed-albatross/thalas-sarche-melanophrys/video-06b.html.

32. See Susan Eilenberg's admirable essay, 'Voice and Ventriloquy in *The Rime of the Ancient Mariner*', in *Strange Power of Speech: Wordsworth, Coleridge and Literary Possession* (New York: Oxford University Press, 1992), pp. 31–59.

33. See Garrett Stewart, *Reading Voices: Literature and the Phonotext* (Berkeley: University of California Press, 1990), p. 48. Stewart's brilliant study offers a multitude of examples of the veering character of Coleridge's writing: see especially pp. 150ff. In the process he considers this poet-philosopher's account of what is 'unfixed and wavering' regarding Shakespearean oxymoron and also recalls Coleridge's dizzy and dazing formulation of authorial intention and inadvertency of meaning: 'Anymadversions of an Author's meaning now a days pass for animadversions' (see Stewart, *Reading Voices*, p. 151).

34. For further discussion of the figure of '*vice versa*', see in particular Chapter 8 'Veerer: Where Ghosts Live', below.

35. See 'Hart-Leap Well', in *William Wordsworth*, ed. Stephen Gill (Oxford: Oxford University Press, 1984), pp. 168–73: here, p. 168, l. 17.

36. 'With Ships the sea was sprinkled far and nigh', in *William Wordsworth*, p. 272, ll. 1–4.

37. William Wordsworth, *The Prelude 1799, 1805, 1850*, ed. Jonathan Wordsworth, M. H. Abrams and Stephen Gill (New York: Norton, 1979), Book 4 (1805 text), ll. 9–15. Further references are to this edition, based on the 1805 text unless specified otherwise.

38. See *The Prelude*, p. 126, n.3.

39. For veering between Wordsworth and Coleridge, it would also be necessary

to engage here with the latter's astonishing short lyric 'Constancy to an Ideal Object' (*Poems*, pp. 311–12). In John Beer's edition the poem is printed immediately before the section of poems entitled 'Work Without Hope' in which, the editor tells us, 'self-dramatization, veering towards self-pity, is a dominant trait' (313). One wonders whether Beer picks up this word (rhyming of course with his own name) from 'Constancy to an Ideal Object', which begins: 'Since all that beat about in Nature's range, / Or veer or vanish; why should'st thou remain / The only constant in a world of change, / O yearning Thought! That liv'st in the brain?' Everything veers or vanishes, Coleridge's poem suggests, except 'yearning Thought'. Or rather, everything '*or* veer[s] *or* vanish[es]': the repetition of the 'or' functions at once as an 'either veer or vanish', and as a ranging *between* 'veer' and 'vanish'. While the 'only constant in a world of change' (the 'you', the 'loveliest friend', the 'Home' that is the addressee of the poem) is threatened by the ancient mariner-like image of a 'Helmsman on an ocean waste and wide', who 'Sits mute and pale his mouldering helm beside', there is (as so often in Coleridge) a peculiar recourse or looping back whereby what is initially negated haunts and mingles, as in 'a glist'ning haze', with what is ostensibly opposed to it: no 'yearning' without veering, no haunting ('Yet still thou haunt'st me') without what 'veers or vanishes'.

40. See Mary Jacobus, *Romanticism, Writing and Sexual Difference* (Oxford: Clarendon Press, 1989), p. 242.

41. See 'The Pleasures of Merely Circulating', in *Collected Poems*, pp. 149–50.

42. Elsewhere, in the much later poem 'The Triad' (1828), Wordsworth deploys the wonderful phrase 'veering gait' to describe the movement of a peacock, 'the bird of Juno':

> –She comes!–behold
> That Figure, like a ship with silver sail!
> Nearer she draws–a breeze uplifts her veil–
> Upon her coming wait
> As pure a sunshine and as soft a gale
> As e'er, on herbage covering earthly mould,
> Tempted the bird of Juno to unfold
> His richest splendour, when his veering gait
> And every motion of his starry train
> Seem governed by a strain
> Of music, audible to him alone.–

See 'The Triad', ll. 41–51, *Last Poems 1821–1850*, ed. Jared Curtis (Ithaca, NY: Cornell University Press, 1999), p. 106. Here too, it may be noted, the inflection of the 'veering' is more complex than might at first appear. Wordsworth's lines describe the movement of a peacock but at the same time also a ship, in terms of a cryptic or even cryptaesthetic strain of music, in order to evoke the approach of 'Lucida', in other words a quasi-idealized figuration of Edith May Southey, one of the triad (along with Sara Coleridge and his daughter, Dora Wordsworth) of the poem's title.

43. For more on transegmental drifting, see Stewart, *Reading Voices*, especially pp. 25 and 293–4, n.4.

44. See Stewart, *Reading Voices*, p. 198.
45. Maurice Merleau-Ponty, *The Prose of the World*, ed. Claude Lefort, trans. John O'Neill (Evanston, IL: Northwestern University Press, 1973), p. 90. (*The Prose of the World* was never completed and was first published post-humously, in French, in 1969.)
46. Merleau-Ponty, *The Prose of the World*, pp. 90–1.
47. 'The Slide' was first published in Roy Sellars and Graham Allen (eds), *The Salt Companion to Harold Bloom* (Cambridge: Salt, 2007), pp. 33–4.
48. See Harold Bloom, *Poetry and Repression: Revisionism from Blake to Stevens* (New Haven, CT: Yale University Press, 1976), p. 16. Coleridge writes of the '*lene clinamen*' or 'the gentle Bias' in *Aids to Reflection*, p. 136.
49. For an early and perhaps still the most provoking reading of Bloom from this perspective, see Paul de Man, 'Review of Harold Bloom's *Anxiety of Influence*', in *Blindness and Insight: Essays in the Rhetoric of Contemporary Criticism*, 2nd edn (London: Methuen, 1983), pp. 267–76.
50. Jacques Derrida, 'My Chances/*Mes Chances*: A Rendezvous with Some Epicurean Stereophonies', trans. Irene Harvey and Avital Ronell, in Joseph H. Smith and William Kerrigan (eds), *Taking Chances: Derrida, Psychoanalysis, and Literature* (Baltimore: Johns Hopkins University Press, 1984), pp. 1–32. Further page references appear parenthetically in the main body of the text.
51. Derrida, 'My Chances', p. 10.
52. Derrida, 'My Chances', p. 10; the original French text, 'Mes chances: Au rendez-vous de quelques stéréophonies épicuriennes' (1982), can be found in *Psyché: Inventions de l'autre* (Paris: Galilée, 1998), pp. 353–84: here, p. 363. It is in the context of this more radical 'veering' or *détournement* that we should read Derrida's remarks on veering (*virer de bord*) and the so-called 'ethical turn' or 'political turn' of deconstruction in the 1990s: see *Rogues: Two Essays on Reason*, trans. Pascale-Anne Brault and Michael Naas (Stanford: Stanford University Press, 2005), p. 39; *Voyous: Deux essais sur la raison* (Paris: Galilée, 2003), p. 64.
53. Derrida, 'My Chances', p. 16, trans. modified. The original French here reads: 'Mon *clinamen*, ma chance ou mes chances, voilà ce qui m'incline à penser le *clinamen* depuis la divisibilité de la marque' (369).
54. Cf. here Jean-Luc Nancy's remarks about clinamen: 'Singularity never takes place at the level of atoms, those identifiable if not identical identities; rather it takes place at the level of the *clinamen*, which is unidentifiable. It is linked to ecstasy: one could not properly say that the singular being is the subject of ecstasy, for ecstasy has no "subject" – but one must say that ecstasy (com-munity) happens *to* the singular being.' Jean-Luc Nancy, *The Inoperative Community*, ed. Peter Connor, trans. Peter Connor, Lisa Garbus, Michael Holland and Simona Sawhney (Minneapolis: University of Minnesota Press, 1991), pp. 6–7.
55. Derrida, 'My Chances', p. 10.
56. See Lucretius, *De Rerum Natura*, with an English translation (*On the Nature of Things*) by W. H. D. Rouse, rev. Martin F. Smith (London: Harvard University Press, 1992), Book 2, pp. 216–93. My very condensed and doubtless rather twisted evocation of this extraordinary passage of the poem is indebted both to Rouse's translation and to A. E. Stallings's recent

verse translation in Lucretius, *The Nature of Things* (London: Penguin, 2007). While Rouse's translation (first published in 1924) gives us a perhaps more traditional version of Lucretian swerving, along with images of 'los[ing] the . . . path' and 'travel[ling] obliquely', at the corresponding moments in her translation Stallings deploys the word 'veer': see respectively, in *On the Nature of Things* and *The Nature of Things*, Book 1, p. 659, and Book 2, p. 247.

Chapter 7

The Literary Turn

The Bat is dun, with wrinkled Wings—
Like fallow article—
(Emily Dickinson)[1]

To turn *about* or screw in order to adjust; to cause to revolve or whirl. *Obs.* (*OED*, veer v. 2, sense 7)

You are not there. You veer about for a fold in the painting that would at last apprise you of the partition you play in a piece of theatre that was acting itself out before you were born and sings imperceptibly in your body like a bat. It is the snatch of music you are harking after, song like a raft of architecture. 'Writing in a post-Derridean era'?[2]

*

So many turns you sigh, the linguistic turn, the political, the ethical and so on et cetera, enough to make you turn in your grave, prematurely, you think, no need for another, especially not a literary turn, you have to be joking. You always considered the phrase 'linguistic turn' to be a sort of joke, a somewhat comical but also delusory gesture apparently intended to refer to a new attentiveness to the importance of language in thinking, in philosophy and culture more generally, as if there were something before the turn, as if it thus confirmed that there were writings (Shakespeare's, for example) that weren't turned and already turning from the beginning, and as if the words 'linguistic turn' could be written, read, spoken or thought about without any need to register or try to reckon with the metalinguistic logic thereby inscribed. For, to put it very quickly, the phrase 'linguistic turn' cannot simply be outside or apart from the turn to which it refers: its distinctiveness (conceptual and historical) would have to do with the way in which it engages with what Heidegger, Lacan and others refer to as the impossibility of metalanguage. In short, it is what Jacques Derrida is talking about when he evokes the necessity of 'a radical metalinguistics, which, however, integrates within itself, in its very jetty, the impossibility of metalanguage'.[3] With this radical metalinguistics, the literary turn will already have begun.

But you keep back a laugh, or at least a smile here, as well, for the way in which Derrida, thinker of the trace, of a non-alphabetic, non-linearized writing, of a non-anthropocentric conception of language, marranic conveyor of deconstruction as 'what happens' or 'what arrives', so speedily and so confidently came to be categorized as a 'linguistic philosopher'. How ridiculous can people get, you think to yourself, why don't they go and try to read something he wrote or even said, for instance in the discussion published as 'I Have a Taste for the Secret', in 1994, where in retrospective mode he emphasizes that deconstruction was all about 'a putting into question of the authority of linguistics'; it was, precisely, 'a protest against the "linguistic turn"'. Some people interpreted his elaboration of the trace 'as a thought of language' whereas 'it is exactly the opposite', he says. Don't get him wrong, language and rhetoric 'deserve enormous consideration', he stresses; 'but there is a point where the authority of final jurisdiction is neither rhetorical nor linguistic, nor even discursive. The notion of trace or of text [or of 'writing', in Derrida's elaboration of it] is introduced to mark the limits of the linguistic turn.'[4]

You saw why people talked, especially in the 1990s, about an ethical or political turn in Derrida's work (associated in particular with the 1989 essay 'Force of Law', *The Other Heading* in 1991, *Spectres of Marx* in 1993 and *Politics of Friendship* in 1994) and in so-called 'theory' more generally, the turn in one crucially linked to the turn in the other, even if you also had good reasons for not getting carried away by such generalities, necessarily mindful of the ways in which Derrida's work was engaged with political and ethical questions, with a politicizing of concepts in general, with a questioning of all forms of ethnocentrism and with a catastrophically new version of difference, from the start. You surmise that a similar argument and demonstration could readily be envisaged with regard to other turns directly or indirectly associated with Derrida's work, such as the 'performative turn', the 'pictorial turn' and the 'animal turn'.

The notion of a literary turn, on the other hand, might sound implausible in a different way. Have we not over the past twenty years or so been witnessing, or indeed participating in encouraging or bringing about, the disappearance of literary studies, the decline and even death of literature itself? As J. Hillis Miller suggests, at the beginning of his book *On Literature* (2002): 'The end of literature is at hand. Literature's time is almost up.'[5] And he goes on to clarify this by reference to what has been going on in universities:

> One of the strongest symptoms of the imminent death of literature is the way younger faculty members, in departments of literature all over the world, are turning in droves from literary study to theory, cultural studies, postcolonial studies, media studies (film, television, etc), popular culture studies, Women's studies, African-American studies, and so on. They often write and teach in ways that are closer to the social sciences than to the humanities as traditionally conceived. Their writing and teaching often marginalizes or ignores literature. This is so even though many of them were trained in old-fashioned literary history and the close reading of canonical texts. (10)

You could easily get caught up in that image of turning that Miller evokes: people are *turning in droves* from literary study.[6] It sounds as if any literary turn here would have to entail a turning *away* from the literary. Miller's account of the decline of literary studies hardly seems controversial. Indeed in Britain there are very few 'departments of literature' at all: 'literature' dropped out of most departmental denominations a while ago now.

All the instruments agree (in W. H. Auden's phrase), and especially all those technological instruments that have long since ceased to be (if they ever were) instruments but rather have infiltrated and enmeshed themselves in the very texture of our being, all the instruments agree that literature is under threat, and under threat not least thanks to the instruments. To recall a haunting assertion from one of the 'Envois' (dated 23 June 1979) in Derrida's *The Post Card*: 'an entire epoch of so-called literature, if not all of it, cannot survive a certain technological regime of telecommunications (in this respect the political regime is secondary)'.[7] Not only have universities, in their teaching, research and associated publications, significantly moved away from focusing on literature as such, but literature is necessarily imperilled by the explosion of other kinds of telecommunication and teletechnologies. As Derrida makes clear in *Archive Fever* and elsewhere, television, the internet, email and mobile phones, for example, are not merely add-ons for literature, any more than they are for psychoanalysis or philosophy. They generate a space of what he calls 'retrospective science fiction' that necessarily defines 'where we are [*nous y sommes*]' – whether we are thinking about the history of literature or philosophy or psychoanalysis.[8]

You should try to make it clear, then, that by 'literary turn' you're thinking about something quite singular. Trying to gauge what the so-called literary establishment understands by the phrase 'literary turn', you can't help noticing the way Salman Rushdie uses it when, in a discussion with Stuart Jeffries about his recent twenty-nine-city tour of the US to promote his novel *The Enchantress of Florence* (2008), he remarks: 'After J. K. Rowling, I guess I'm the biggest literary turn from the UK.'[9] That, certainly, is some way off from the literary turn you have in mind, though you remain vaguely intrigued by what has happened, in the programming of contemporary literature publishing and the quasi-pornographic industry of 'celebrity culture' (some oxymorons are more moronic than others), to enable Rushdie to use the phrase in this fashion. You may imagine some literature publishing industry spokesperson coming up and saying: 'Your particular sense of the *literary turn* presumably refers to the remarkable expansion, over the past ten or fifteen years especially, of what goes on under the auspices of the term "creative writing".' You look at her, you want to cry, you hardly know where to begin. You weigh up the likelihood of getting somewhere by replying: 'First of all, nobody said "particular", it was "singular". If you can be patient, it may become clear: it has to do with the singular and singularity.' And then follow that with what here follows. Some chance.

More germane is what Jonathan Culler talks about as 'the literary in theory', in a book of that title published in 2007.[10] Culler argues that 'the apparent eclipse of the literary is something of an illusion' (5). 'There is evidence', he suggests, 'of a new centrality of the literary, both in a return to questions of aesthetics, which for a time were regarded as retrograde and elitist, and in the use of literary works to advance theoretical arguments and to question theoretical assumptions' (14). With regard to the latter, Culler names Jacques Derrida and Giorgio Agamben as two cases in point. You like the spectral intimations of this reference to Derrida: he is dead, but Culler's phrasing implies that he isn't, he is still active, a bit like in Will Self's 'North London Book of the Dead', where people don't die, they just move to another part of London. 'There is evidence of a new centrality of the literary,' Culler says, '. . . as in the work of Derrida on writers such as Celan . . .'. He seems here to be (how ever tacitly) drawing on some of the most insistent motifs of Derrida's writing: living on; writing as structured by the necessary possibility of death; the dead can be more powerful than the living; there is no '*post-*' for deconstruction. But you also feel uneasy about Culler's claim that what Derrida is up to – in the writings on Celan and poetry (such as *Beliers*) posthumously gathered in English translation in the book *Sovereignties in Question* – is 'the use of literary works to advance theoretical arguments and to question theoretical assumptions'.[11]

You baulk, you cannot help it, at the word 'use'. This notion of the *use* of literary texts carries with it instrumentalist associations (language as something a writer *uses*, the mastery and self-identity of the writer thus figuring here as what would appear to be precisely a theoretical assumption) that are radically displaced in Derrida's writings. You know this and you know Culler knows. You know he knows in part because, as you are happy to recall, you enjoy something of a telepathic rapport, not least apropos the question of literature and telepathy (how could you maintain an instrumentalist vocabulary, you ask, in the light of the literary telepathic scenario of 'being-two-to-speak-or-think-or-feel' and so on?),[12] but more specifically you know from Culler's earlier work, such as *On Deconstruction* (1983), in which he offers a painstaking and lucid exposition of how Derrida's work interferes with notions of instrumentality or use: deconstruction, Culler stresses, 'prevents concepts and methods from being taken for granted and treated as simply reliable instruments. Critical categories are not just tools to be employed in producing sound interpretations but problems to be explored through the interaction of text and concept.'[13] Perhaps first and foremost among these concepts or categories would be literature itself, of which Culler succinctly remarks: 'The essence of literature is to have no essence, to be protean, undefinable, to encompass whatever might be situated outside it.'[14] This characterization of literature is necessarily linked to Derrida's more general conception of language, as formulated for example in *Mémoires: for Paul de Man* (1986): 'language is not the governable instrument of a speaking being (or subject)'.[15] The idea of *using* literary works, you think, is profoundly un-Derridean.

It may be a sign of the so-called post-Derridean times, however, because something similar is being proposed, in more explicit and sustained mode, in a recent book by Rita Felski entitled *Uses of Literature* (2008).[16] Felski's discussion of these 'uses' entails foregrounding the values of 'recognition', 'enchantment', 'knowledge' and 'shock' in reading and thinking about literature. But she goes about this in a curiously anaesthetizing fashion, steering between what she calls making 'strong claims for literary otherness' and a 'whittling down of texts to the bare bones of political and ideological function'. Felski wants to argue for 'an expanded understanding of "use"' which would allow us 'to engage the worldly aspects of literature in a way that is respectful rather than reductive, dialogic rather than high-handed' (7). As she goes on, in defence of the title-word and governing concept of her book: '"Use" is not always strategic or purposeful, manipulative or grasping; it does not have to involve the sway of instrumental rationality or a wilful blindness to complex form' (7–8). Suffice to say that Felski offers very little critical reflection on the utilitarian, humanist and anthropocentric conceptions of 'use' that inform and structure her account. The limits of 'recognition', 'enchantment', 'knowledge' and 'shock' in literature – and therefore of their *uses*, in her terms – are marked off in advance by the avoidance of anything that smacks too heavily of 'literary otherness', especially insofar as such otherness might also be bound up with questions of the political, starting perhaps with the profound meditations to be found in Derrida's work on literature and democracy (you recall the meticulously analysed chiasmus: 'No democracy without literature, no literature without democracy'[17]), as well as on the place of fiction and the 'as if' in the concept of the university and in relation to the future of the humanities.[18] The scale of Felski's task and, in a sense, her achievement in this book is perhaps most resonantly evoked by the fact that she manages to avoid making a single reference to Derrida. *Uses of Literature* thus poses as an intellectually progressive, non-reductive book about the contemporary value and importance of literature, in which Derrida has apparently been airbrushed out of the picture and out of history.[19] Critical writing and thinking after Derrida or 'after deconstruction' here seems to have become, at least in part, a sort of painful exercise in suppression, a strange negotiation with he who must not be named: *writing in a post-[shtumm, shtumm] era*. It makes you think of where you wanted to begin: Henry James's *The Turn of the Screw*.

The literary turn would be at once about the 'literary in theory' (as Culler calls it) and more specifically about new ways of registering the place of literature in the light of Derrida's work. Like you, Culler is interested in 'a return to ground the literary in literature' (42). Like you, and like Derrida, he is fascinated by the fact that, as he puts it, 'literary works ... have the ability to resist or to outplay what they are supposed to be saying' (42). But the literary turn isn't about *using* literary works to advance a theoretical argument or understanding: if anything, it's about the inverse logic of how we find ourselves being used – structured, haunted, played with – by literature. Culler seeks to operate in a more formalist, clinical and ostensibly extraneous manner. You are summoned by something else, more akin to the apparitions of vertigo in Derrida, the possibilities of twisting genres, the necessity of chance, the role and effects of the logic of the foreign body and crypt, a spectral hyperrealism, the provocations of magical thinking, telepathy and clairvoyance as strangely literary phenomena that call for a response or counter-signature in the form of kinds of writing that could not purport to be straightforwardly extraneous to the literary work but would, in a word, *veer*.

It remains crucial that we see Derrida as a philosopher and as a deconstructive thinker of politics and ethics. The legacies of his work are no doubt most urgently in operation, most demanding of continuing conversation and negotiation in these domains – that is to say, with regard to the spirit of what he called 'a new enlightenment', the 'democracy to come', the question and the activation of new forms of responsibility, and the pursuit of justice in the context of worldwide-ization (*mondialization*).[20] But turning about in all of this, shifting and looping, is the question of literature. Less visibly then, less urgently, perhaps, Derrida's work has also bequeathed us with the demands and provocations of a literary turn. Of course, he doesn't do this all by himself: the literary turn is evident in all sorts of places, going back, as just intimated, to Henry James and beyond, and turning through the writings of Maurice Blanchot, Paul de Man, Gilles Deleuze, Hélène Cixous and others in ways that would merit at least a bookshelf of further studies, but it is in Derrida's work, it may be said, that this turn is articulated in the most lucid, extended and sustained fashion.

*

The literary turn can be tracked according to three interrelated modes or registers:

1. It is a matter of how Derrida describes and, if you like, theorizes literature or lets literature theorize, in accordance with a concept of literature that is quite traditional and recognizable. (The notion of letting literature theorize here would correspond with his suggestion that 'deconstruction . . . is a coming-to-terms with literature'.[21]) Under this rubric we might think of how Derrida has elaborated new ways of thinking about the concept of literature, the nature of literary or poetic writing, the reading of specific authors and texts (canonical and non-canonical), the history of literature as an institution, and so on. At issue would be, for example: the elucidation of the proposition that 'there is no literature without a suspended relation to meaning and reference'; the emphasis on the interdependence of literature and democracy vis-à-vis the principle of freedom of speech and the right to say anything (or not to say anything); a history of the concept and practice of literature which entails (especially after Mallarmé) an increasing explicitness concerning the nature and effects of literarity in and of the work; the specification of literature as 'the altogether bare device of being two-to-speak'; and the exploration of literature as constitutively bound up with the secret.[22]
2. It is a matter of literature in a more ghostly and disruptive mode, in other words of literature or literary effects showing up where you might think they shouldn't or where they don't seem to belong. Here

it is rather a question of attending to the spectral and haunting effects of literature as that which has no essence, as that which is not. To recall Derrida's phrasing in *Demeure*: 'There is no essence or substance of literature: literature is not. It does not exist.'[23] This notness is nonetheless not nothing. Thus there is what he calls a 'mark of fictive narrativity' at the heart of law, for example, as well as at the basis of the founding of institutions, whether it be the American Declaration of Independence or the charter that establishes a university.[24] In a similarly haunting fashion, literature is at issue in the notion of testimony and bearing witness. As he remarks in *Demeure*:

> If the testimonial is by law irreducible to the fictional, there is no testimony that does not structurally imply in itself the possibility of fiction, simulacra, dissimulation, lie and perjury – that is to say, the possibility of literature, of the innocent or perverse literature that innocently plays at perverting all of these distinctions.[25]

Literature here acquires a kind of neologistic force, a spooking form undecidably innocent and perverse, innocently playing at the heart of the law and the reality of testimony, veering within the promise to *make truth* (as Derrida recalls Augustine's phrase) that guides autobiography and testimony alike.[26]

3. It is a question of literature as regards the 'poetico-literary performativity' and inventive character of the critical response or countersignature. As Derrida puts it in 'This Strange Institution Called Literature', it is a matter of critical or theoretical writing as 'an inventive experience of language, *in* language', of '"critical" inventions which belong to literature while deforming its limits'.[27] It is a sort of 'duel of singularities' in which 'a countersignature comes both to confirm, repeat and respect the signature of the other, of the "original" work, and to *lead it off* elsewhere' – in other words, to make or let veer.[28] There is in this respect a kind of 'imperative' at work, Derrida suggests, namely

> to give space for singular events, to invent something new in the form of acts of writing which no longer consist in a theoretical knowledge, in new constative statements, to give oneself to a poetico-literary performativity at least analogous to that of promises, orders, or acts of constitution or legislation which do not only change language, or which, in changing language, change more than language.[29]

This is what is at issue in the figure of a 'radical metalinguistics' evoked earlier, and in the emphasis that Derrida gives, in his discussion with Elisabeth Roudinesco in *For What Tomorrow*, to the value and power of 'theoretical fictions', this last formulation arising from an acknowledgement of what he calls 'the debt of all theoretical (but also all juridical, ethical and political) *positing*, to a performative power structured by *fiction*, by a figural invention'.[30]

The notion of the literary turn thus entails a quite different sense of post-1960s intellectual and cultural history, a period marked by (1) a new and unprecedented attention to the 'strange institution called literature' (in Derrida's phrase), including the academic flourishing of creative writing; (2) the emergence of deconstruction (construed here, in particular, as 'a coming-to-terms with literature'); (3) a new and unprecedented attention to the indissociable links between witnessing and fiction, as well as, rather differently, between law, institutions and performative language; and (4) a deepened awareness and ongoing elaboration of the interdependence of literature and democracy (freedom of expression, non-censorship, etc.). And that's scarcely to mention notions of literature and the ghostly – let alone the question of animals and animality ('man is not the only political animal', as Derrida stresses), and the deconstruction of anthropocentrism, especially in the context of poetry . . .'[31]

*

You are such a weyward creature. One never knows if you are alive or dead, or whether one ever hears your voice, whether it is you or the effect of some other ventriloquy, one doesn't know who makes you up, same difference, you say, you have no name, you turn, you veer, you call

*

The thing about Derrida, you have to recall, is that people think he is difficult. That's the point of departure for an interview with Catherine David that appeared in *Le Nouvel Observateur* in September 1983. She begins by noting that people say '[his] texts are difficult, on the limit of readability' and asks him about this reputation he has for being difficult: 'How do you live with that? Is it an effect you are seeking to produce or, on the contrary, do you suffer from it?' To which Derrida responds: 'I suffer from it, yes, don't laugh, and I do everything I think possible or acceptable to escape from this trap. But someone in me must get some benefit from it: a certain *relation*.'[32] He notes that people don't get angry with physicists or mathematicians for being difficult, any more than they would with someone who speaks a foreign language. What gets people's backs up is how someone (and now Derrida is no longer speaking of himself in particular but of the philosopher or writer more generally) 'tampers with your own language, with this "relation", precisely, which is yours . . .' (115). In this brief passage Derrida has shifted the term 'relation' (or, in the original French, *rapport*: 124) from something ostensibly to do with him ('a certain *relation*', as he emphatically puts it) to something to do with *you* ('this "relation", precisely, which is yours . . .'). Meddling with relation or relations: that's what Derrida is about. And he goes on to suggest, in fact, that this is what is happening whenever a writer seeks to 'invent' and 'break new paths' (116). It is always a "writer",' he says, 'who is accused of being "unreadable" . . . [It is someone] who speaks neither in a purely academic milieu, with the language, rhetoric and customs that are in force there, nor in that "language of everyone" which we all know does not exist' (116). This can even make for 'a writing that sometimes can be read with an *apparent* facility' (the interviewer, perhaps helpfully, adduces the 'Envois' in *The Post Card* as an example) but, Derrida goes on to clarify, it's a matter of 'a writing whose status, in a certain way, is impossible to assign', and he then sketches three questions that such a writing poses: 'Is it or is it not a theoretical utterance? Are the signatories and addressees identifiable in advance or produced and divided by the text? Do the sentences describe something or are they doing something?' (117). The example he gives of such an utterance is the two-word sentence: 'You come [*Tu viens*]' (117/126).

A virtual library erupts here, in testimony to everything Derrida says about the word 'come' – from the Christian orgasm at the end of the Bible, the apocalyptic tone of 'come' in theology, philosophy and literature, to the jouissance of deconstruction, the experience of the promise and the democracy to come. But what you are trying to talk about here entails another version, namely what it is to veer, veering, you veer, to come to veer to veer you come, it's you.

Derrida talks about his 'first' desire, in scare quotes, in quotes that indicate the feeling of precariousness that perhaps marks everything he says, his 'first' desire, he says, in this interview in 1983, in a backward glance that goes at least as far as the 1963 essay 'Force and Signification':

> my 'first' desire did not lead me toward philosophy, but rather toward literature, no, toward something that literature makes room for better than philosophy. I feel myself to be engaged, for the last twenty years, in a long detour [*un long détour*] that will lead me back to this thing, this idiomatic writing whose purity, I realize, is inaccessible, but about which I continue to dream. (118/127)

Strange image of the long detour. He has been busy for years, sidetracked with writing more classically 'philosophical' works, it might seem: the essays that make up *Writing and Difference, Of Grammatology, Speech and Phenomena* and *Margins of Philosophy*, for example. He appears to be talking in terms of the figure of a detour in its more comforting guise, according to which it's known what the detour was a detour *from*, the destination is inscribed in advance, and this thing (*cette chose*), as he calls it, is something to get back to or rejoin (*rejoindre*). You wonder how clear or clarifying that narrative is, the story evoked here by the writer who, let's not forget, repeatedly claimed that he never knew how to tell a story.[33]

We will get things quite wrong if we suppose that there was some literary turn in Derrida's work, traceable for instance to the writing of *Glas* or *The Truth in Painting* or *The Post Card*. It is not a question of seeing him (as he might seem to want to see himself or have his interviewer see him in 1983) as a writer who went off on a twenty-year detour towards or into the region of philosophy in order, finally, to get back to that *thing* which literature better makes room for, that 'idiomatic writing' of which he continues to dream. This would be to ignore or disavow the force of destinerrance and deferred effects, as well as the depths and intricacies of the literary at play in his writing from the beginning.

It's there, for instance, in the Introduction to Husserl's *The Origin of Geometry* (1962), most strikingly perhaps in the celebrated passage about equivocity and univocity apropos James Joyce, in the process of which Derrida remarks that 'equivocity is the congenital mark of every culture' and goes on to argue that: 'If, in fact, equivocity is always irreducible, that is because words and language in general are not and can never be absolute *objects*.'[34] But, of course, on precisely the same account, it is also everywhere in the Introduction: you turn the page, for example, and note the circumspection or circumscription Derrida implies regarding the desire or perceived need to destroy a certain 'tower of Babel' in the services of 'scholarly language' – something that emerges more explicitly in the meditations on the twists and turns, the towers, tours and detours, the tourism and detourism of Babel in 'Des tours de Babel', in 1985, and in the conjunction of the scholar and spectrality in the context of Shakespeare's *Hamlet*, in *Spectres of Marx*, some thirty years after the Introduction to Husserl.[35]

The literary turn involves phantom voices, the return or even 'first' coming of the dead, anachronicity and mourning, apparitional magical thinking-writing, the ghosts, the vertigo and vertighosting that *only happen to you*.

Thus the question of that 'idiomatic writing' of which Derrida continues to dream. Catherine David asks him what he means by 'idiomatic'. He replies:

A property that one cannot appropriate: it signs you without belonging to you; it only appears to the other and it never comes back to you except in flashes of madness that bring together life and death [*elle ne vous revient jamais sauf en des éclairs de folie qui rassemblent la vie et la mort*], that bring you together dead and alive at the same time. You dream, it's una-voidable, about the invention of a language or of a song [*Vous rêvez, c'est fatal, l'invention d'une langue ou d'un chant*] that would be yours, not the attributes of a 'self' [*un 'moi'*], rather the accentuated paraph, that is, the musical signature, of your most unreadable history. I'm not talking about a *style* but an intersection [*un croisement*] of singularities, habitat, voices, graphism, what moves with you and what your body never leaves [*ce qui se déplace avec vous et que votre corps ne quitte jamais*].[36]

This turning to 'you' is strangely intriguing, you have to confess, here in the non-intimate form of 'vous', elsewhere it's 'tu' – for instance in 'Che cos'è la poesia?' – and of course in the 'Envois': you never know who you are in these texts, do you? For instance on 28 September 1978: 'You speak and I write to you as in a dream everything that you are willing to let me say. You will have resoundingly stifled all my words.'[37] Or, apparently conversely, a postcard from May 1979:

You are the only one to understand why it really was necessary that I write exactly the opposite, as concerns axiomatics, of what I desire, what I know my desire to be, in other words you: living speech, presence itself, proximity, the proper, the guard, etc. I have necessarily written upside down – and in order to surrender to Necessity.[38]

It's the poematic you, the wound of you, you dream: *rêve*, circumflex-ively veer. And it is here in this interview of 1983, the interview on this intersection, in the place of an intersection that is moving and displacing itself with you.

This might indeed be the most succinct description anywhere in his work of 'writing in a post-Derridean era'. The writing Derrida evokes is to come, it's a madness, a musical signature. Dead and alive, a fatal dreaming, dreaming the invention of a language or a song that would be yours. You hear, however fleetingly, something of Walter Pater's voice. When Pater declares, in 'The School of Giorgione', that '*All art constantly aspires towards the condition of music*', he goes on to illustrate this, you recall, by reference to the notion of a poem (without specifying any in particular), in which matter and form would become indistinguishable. Pater admits that this is 'abstract language' and seeks to provide some 'actual examples', as he puts it: 'In an actual landscape we see a long, white road, lost suddenly on the hill-verge'.[39] It is a fas-cinatingly ghostly 'actual example', disorienting, constitutively double (an 'actual example', an 'actual landscape' that is actually a picture of a landscape): Pater indicates that he has an etching by Alphonse Legros in mind, but of course we cannot *actually* see. It is something, Pater says, 'seen' or 'half-seen', the veering moment of 'a long, white road, lost suddenly on the hill-verge'.[40]

In response to Derrida's evocation of the dream of a writing that would 'bring you together dead and alive at the same moment', 'the invention of a language or a song that would be yours', Catherine David asks: 'Are you going to write it?' Derrida at first replies: 'You must be joking,' or, more literally perhaps, 'What do you think? [*Pensez-vous*]'. But then he changes tack:

> But the accumulation of dreams, projects, or notes no doubt weighs on what is written in the present. One day, some piece of book may fall out like a stone that keeps the memory of a hallucinatory architecture to which it might have belonged ... The stone still resonates and vibrates, it emits a kind of painful and indecipherable bliss, one no longer knows whose or for whom ...[41]

This haunting and beautiful passage stutters (as Gilles Deleuze might say), it shifts and turns and *interruptifies* as much as it identifies, drifting off in a refrain of ellipses.[42] It has to do with what Derrida calls the 'old new language', something at once more ancient than knowledge and absolutely new and unheard-of. It is music one moment, memory of hallucinatory architecture another.[43]

The movement of this passage resonates, for you, with a sense of the strange placelessness, the incessant displacing of the place of literature as Derrida talks about it in so many texts. It is a question, as he has said, of something that 'literature makes room for better than philosophy [*quelque chose que la littérature accueille mieux que la philosophie*]'.[44] It has to do with the secret. This is what he says he likes most about literature, an experience of literature as being '*in place of the secret*'.[45]

You should be clear about this: there would be no literary turn without vertigo. The literary turn cannot be situated or measured, like turning a corner or accomplishing a neat three-point turn. You have to imagine, rather, something happening at unthinkable speed, spinning, tilting. That's veering for you. You cannot decide, for a start, whether what is under consideration is a literary *turn* or a *literary* turn, whether the turn would be itself literary or else the turn would be somehow beside the literary, referring to it from a non-literary place, literature beside itself. In 1997, in the context of a discussion of the notion of 'pure belief' (which, as he says, 'is possible only by *believing in the impossible*'), Derrida is prompted to reflect on the celebrated proposition in *Of Grammatology* (1967) that 'we must begin wherever we are', that is to say, 'in a text where we already believe ourselves to be'.[46] He writes:

> the 'text where we believe ourselves to be', another name for this place, place in general, interests me only where the impossible, that is to say the incredible, encircles and harries it, making my head turn, leaving an illegible trace within the taking-place, there, in the vertigo, 'where we believe ourselves to be'. . . . [*sic*] Place is always unbelievable to me, as is orientation.[47]

It is a question about what literature welcomes or makes room for apropos this 'miracle' (as he also calls it) of place, in place of the secret. It's the dream of an idiomatic writing in the context of an orientation beyond belief, what he elsewhere calls the 'destinerrant indirection' – or veering – of the trace.[48]

*

To finish off, you want to return, or turn as if for the first time, to where you began. After a twenty-year detour, you turn to the point of departure for the first book you published, *Telepathy and Literature*, in other words Henry James's short novel *The Turn of the Screw* (1898).[49] At that time this novel was going to be your subject, you even announced it as such, but then it vanished. You began by suggesting that it would operate 'like a ghost-text' and sure enough it disappeared from view.[50] You are not going to pretend to read it now either, to read it or reread it, to pretend or pretend to pretend. You simply want to remark on a couple of words. Two words for Henry James, two words *from* Henry James, in place of a conclusion apropos the literary turn.

*

The first word is 'turn' – *turn* itself, if you can say that. Something happens to *turn* in *The Turn of the Screw*: something is strangely inaugurated, unprecedented perhaps in the history or 'use' of this seemingly simple English word, this turn as trope and trope as turn. You are tempted to date 'the literary turn' (as you've been trying to evoke it, in the context of literature in English) to this little text by Henry James, just as a decisive shift in the sense of 'veering' might be traced back to Wordsworth in *The Prelude*. You would like to begin by recalling, in order to pay homage to, Shoshana Felman's essay, 'Turning the Screw of Interpretation' (1977).[51] It is a *tour de force*, in your view, a critical *pièce de résistance* in turn meriting the most exhaustive and detailed commentary. And with such little turns of phrase (the *tour de force, in turn*) the madness is perhaps already intimated. Very few critical texts manage to conspire, as hers does, to trace themselves *within* the 'madness of literature', showing how this madness is (as she puts it) 'uncanny, *unheimlich*, to the precise extent that it *cannot be situated*, coinciding, as it does, with the very space of reading' (201). One hundred and ten pages long, Felman's essay holds back, shifts and turns about in ways that are eerily and singularly responsive to the character of James's text. It is thus part of the digressive but peculiar power of her essay that it is only after eighty-five pages or so that she finally turns to focus in an explicit way on the turns of the word 'turn' in *The Turn of the Screw*, even if you could hardly fail to have noticed how she drops the word into her text, at numerous moments, from the title of her essay onwards.[52]

You talk about the return of the dead, it's one of the funniest phrases you can think of, or so it now occurs to you, for the first time, this is what Henry James's text suggests. The phrase 'return of the dead' pops up with such apparent facility but why, you think to yourself, why do people say 'return'? It's not a *return* – however 'revoltingly ... against nature' (TS: 111) this may appear – it's the dead *coming for the first time*, it's an altogether other *turn* in the return, the undoing of all sense of return. There is a turn in the return that James's text brings out, gives a turn to, sets spinning, something small and easy to miss perhaps, but something new nonetheless in the history of literature. After what James does with and to the 'turn', in the torture and bliss of *The Turn of the Screw*, there is no return.

How the text works over 'turn', makes 'turn' work overtime, and how the 'turn' works over the text, over time ... You could spend days, weeks or years turning over what happens with all the versions of *turn* that turn up in James's text, through 'the quick *turns* of simple folk' (20), the experience of what it is to *turn* and see someone (20), 'tak[ing] a *turn* into the grounds' (25), imagining that someone might appear 'at the *turn* of a path' (26), the governess feeling that her 'imagination' has, 'in a flash, *turned* real' (26), the sight of what transpires to be Peter Quint, a dead man seen (as clearly as 'the letters ... on this page') '*turn[ing] away*' (28), the experience of '*turn[ing] over*' the question of the nature of the existence of this deathly figure (28, 29), the supposition that the mystery of what happened to young Miles at school has to do with the perception of 'differences' and 'superiorities of quality' '*turn[ing] to* the vindictive' (30), the governess '*turn[ing] in*' to the so-called '"grown-up" dining-room' to 'recover' her dropped gloves (32), then a sight of the dead man again that makes her 'catch [her] breath and *turn* cold' (32), rushing out of the house, '*turn[ing]* a corner and [coming] full in sight' – of nothing, for the 'visitor [has] vanished' (32), and then when Mrs Grose sees the governess 'she *turn[s]* white' (33), '*turn[ing]* to [her] with abrupt inconsequence' (35), *turning* away, *turning* round (36), *turning* her back (44), *turning* 'right and left' (46), '*turn[ing]* pale' (47), *turning* round, *turning* it over (48), 'the *turn* of a page' and 'the great *turn* of the staircase' (58), watching the figure of the dead man disappearing into 'the silence itself', it '*turn[s]*', writes the governess, 'as [she] might have seen the low wretch to which it had once belonged *turn* on receipt of an order' (59–60), she proceeds to '[take] noiseless *turns* in the passage' (62), then is compelled to '*[turn]* away' from the hideousness (63), Mrs Grose then '*turn[ing]* to take from [her] a view of the back of the tapestry' (65), the governess says something and Mrs Grose '[does] *turn*' (70), the governess can see her 'visibly *turn[ing]* things over' (70), it is as if the governess, in her dealings with '[her] pupils', were 'perpetually coming into sight of subjects before which [she] must stop short, *turning* suddenly out of alleys that [she perceives] to be blind' (71–2), her 'manners' have now taken a '*turn*' (73), 'the summer [has] *turned*' (73), a 'lovely upward look' from the boy Miles is '*turned*' on her (74), and when he wants to know when he is able to return to school she wears her 'most responsible air' while '*turn[ing* the question] over' (79), when Miles is in church with the others she thinks about 'getting away altogether', of what it would be simply to 'give the whole thing up – *turn* [her] back and retreat' (82), she says something possibly accusatory to Mrs Grose who has '*turned* quite pale' (86), she tells Miles something and observes how he '*turn[s]* it over' (89), she asks him if there is anything he wants to tell her and he '*turn[s] off* a little, facing round towards the wall' like a sick child, and the governess feels that 'to *turn* [her] back on him' is 'to lose him' (90), when she finally puts her most appalling question to the little girl Flora, sounding the name for the first time with the words 'Where, my pet, is Miss Jessel?', and the dead woman then suddenly appears, Mrs Grose utters 'the shriek of a creature scared, or rather wounded, which, *in turn*, within a few seconds, was completed', recalls the governess, 'by a gasp of [her] own' (98), and then the little girl, instead of looking at the ghost of Miss Jessel, '*turn[s]* at [*the governess*] an expression of hard, still gravity', in 'a stroke' that 'somehow *convert[s]* the little girl herself into the very presence that [makes the governess] quail' (99), and then the governess's speculation, or stated hope, that if she left, just 'went away', Miles wouldn't '*turn* on [her]' (105), even if, shortly afterwards, the disclosure that 'he stole', and above all that '[h]e stole *letters*', has her '*turn[ing]* it over', trying to be 'more judicial' (108), and once Mrs Grose has herself gone away from the house with Flora, it leaves the governess alone with Miles 'in a tighter place still than [she] had yet *turned round in*' (109), and later at dinner it is Miles who '*turn[s]* round' after the waiter has left and declares 'Well – so we're alone!' (112), and then again when her 'insistence' is said to have '*turned* him from [her]' and keeps him silent at the window (116), and the veritable fever of turns in the concluding couple of pages where the governess queries Miles once more about why he was '*turn[ed] out*' of school, and he '*turn[s] away*' (119), and she '*turn[s] it over*' and finally he '*turn[s] to [her] again his beautiful fevered face*' (120).

And none of these turns of the *turn* can be read outside the question of the so-called 'frame narrative', or rather the turn-taking in which its fantastical form is projected (fantastical insofar as the frame turns out not to exist, since the novel ends merely with a turning into the abyss), in other words the opening scene of the story in which various characters (Douglas, the anonymous narrator and another anonymous character referred to simply as 'somebody') turn over the phrase 'turn of the screw'.[53] You recall that Douglas, the owner of the manuscript of the governess's text, reflects on the fact that, if in a ghost story it is a *child* who is subject to a ghostly visitation, this 'gives the effect another turn of the screw' (7). Already, you could say, James's language is up to something screwy: already we are in the realm of queer repetition, for we know that the title of the text is *The Turn of the Screw* – and so the word 'another' here is marked by a supplementary oddness. And the 'effect' to which Douglas refers is correspondingly peculiar, since it can hardly be envisaged without the turn invoked. The turn is already the effect, in effect – as if 'turn' here were operating as a substitute for 'cause', as if the logic of cause and effect, and of first and second, had already been quietly but irrevocably screwed up. Here is the exchange, picking up with what Douglas says:

> '. . . But it's not the first occurrence of its charming kind that I know to have involved a child. If the child gives the effect another turn of the screw, what do you say to *two* children – ?'
> 'We say, of course,' somebody exclaimed, 'that they give two turns! Also that we want to hear about them.' (7)

Between the first and second sentence, the child has shifted from object ('involved a child') to subject ('the child gives'); at the same time it is not the child but the *involvement* of a child that 'gives' (we begin, perhaps, to sense the turn already inscribed in the *volve* of 'involved'); and it is not the *effect* that this child's involvement gives, but the *turn* that involvement gives *to the effect*.

The often unnoticed little turns, you want to say, that James gives to conversational language put you in mind of Elizabeth Bowen's fine axiom about novel writing: 'Dialogue must appear realistic without being so.'[54] Singularly, perversely veristic, James's apparently realistic dialogue is, in truth, bound to double business of various kinds. 'To *two*': Douglas is not asking his listeners what they say *to* two children but rather what they say, or would say, to the idea or involvement of two children. Correspondingly, an anonymous 'somebody' takes Douglas at his word and turns it back to him: 'We say, of course . . .' (7). This royal we is already, of course, a further doubling of the narrator who is and is not James, the 'we' and the 'I' announced in the very opening words of the text: 'The story had held *us*, round the fire, sufficiently breathless . . . *I* remember . . .' (7, emphasis added). 'We say, of course, that they give two turns! Also that we want to hear about them': this response gives a further turn or two of its own – it appropriates the plural, multiplying itself in one voice ('we say', not 'I say'), and then assimilates speech to desire ('we say' becomes 'we want'). This brief assertion of being two (or more) to speak – and subsuming a knowledge of the desire of another or others within itself – is a sort of miniature or condensed illustration of what Jacques Derrida has identified as a defining characteristic of literary fiction, namely 'the altogether bare device of being-two-to-speak'.[55] And in James, you have to stress, there are *always more* than two: even when there are two, there are three. It is a matter of how, in Maurice Blanchot's words, James 'manages to make *the third party* in conversation that obscure element that is the centre and the stake of each of his books and to make it not only the cause of misunderstandings but the reason for anxious and profound understandings'.[56]

The very title of the novel, then, is to be heard in a veristic delirium of multiple voices. Among these is the voice of the governess herself. The title-phrase is a quotation from her, in effect, but queerly, *without the narrator's knowledge*, without his knowledge at least within the space of linear unfolding which the magical thinking, telepathy, clairvoyance and clairaudience of literary narrative will by the same turn have sent veering from the start. As the governess notes, near the end: what her 'monstrous ordeal' amounts to, however 'unpleasant' and however demanding of going 'in an unusual direction', is 'only another turn of the screw of ordinary human virtue' (TS: 111). It is as if the very title were a ghost, coming in or coming back, too late, anachronistic, veering in time. In the process of casting off, as you might call it, the narrator declares that he has a title, but Douglas takes no notice: '"Oh, *I* have [a title]!" I said. But Douglas, without heeding me, had begun to read with a fine clearness that was like a rendering to the ear of the beauty of the author's hand' (14). What follows, the zigzag weirdness of the start of the governess's narrative ('I remember the whole beginning as a succession of flights and drops, a little see-saw of the right throbs and the wrong' (14)), has *already* begun.

Eighty-five pages into the essay, you were saying, Felman finally gets to the turn, proposing that James's novel is 'organized as a veritable *topography of turns*' (179), a labyrinth in which we are faced with 'the *loss* of all *sense of direction*' (180). She singles out a passage in chapter 6 in which the governess reports the account given her by Mrs Grose of the death of Peter Quint. Here the governess describes the *mistaken turn* or rather (to cite the governess's own syntactical inversion) the 'turn mistaken' by which Peter Quint, leaving the pub in the dark, drunk, taking the 'wrong path altogether', slips fatally on an 'icy slope' (TS: 42). Felman proposes that this turn accounts, in the end, *for* the end – of the novel and of that 'other accident' of 'death' (that of the young boy Miles). It gives rise, at the same time, she suggests, to 'a fatal, deadly *reading mistake*' (180) on the part of the governess. Felman here focuses on the 'semantic charge' of the word *turn* as 'connoting the possible resonance of "an attack of madness" (cf. "turn of hysteria")' (180) and goes on to quote, from chapter 20 of the novel, what she considers to be 'the crucial moment when the governess is furiously accusing Flora of *seeing* Miss Jessel and of refusing to admit it, [and when] Mrs Grose who, like the girl, sees nothing, protests against the governess's accusation' (180). Mrs Grose exclaims: 'What a dreadful turn, to be sure, Miss! Where on earth do you see anything?' (TS: 100). (Felman italicizes '*What a dreadful turn*': you imagine for a moment here a wild and whirling digression on the turn given to words in or through italics, the feverish, almost mesmerizing *effects of italicization* that play over Felman's text and Henry James's in turn.)

It is this moment that prompts Felman's most extensive meditation on the word *turn*. She writes:

> Does the word 'turn' here mean 'a turning point', 'a change of meaning', 'a turn of events' or 'a turn of hysteria', 'an attack of nervousness', 'a fit', 'a spell'? And if it means a turning point (a change of meaning), does it designate a simple *reorientation* or a radical *disorientation*, i.e., a delirious twist and *deviation*? Or does the 'turn' name, precisely, the textual ironic figure of its own capacity to *reverse itself*, to turn meaning into madness, to 'project the possible other case' or other turn? Whatever the case, the metaphor of the 'turn of the screw', in referring to a *turn* – or a twist – of sense, establishes an ironical equivalence between direction and deviation, between a turn of sense and a turn of madness, between the turn of an interpretation and the turning point beyond which interpretation becomes delirious. (181)

This delirious accumulation of questions appears to pose the meaning of 'turn' in terms of alternatives (either this or that) and equivalences (between this and that), concluding with the '*ironical* equivalence' between 'the turn of an interpretation and the turning point beyond which interpretation becomes delirious'. You italicize the 'ironical' in order to suggest that the very notions of *equivalence* and of *interpretation* are here being given a sort of funny turn, and you wonder what is perhaps missed by Felman's decision to frame her analysis in terms of 'interpretation' in the first place. The *trope* of 'interpretation', announced in her title ('Turning the Screw of Interpretation'), signals a concern with hermeneutics that is at work throughout her essay. This appears to be bound up with a reliance on the language of volition and implied freedom of choice, as when she asks, in declarative mode: 'But what, in fact, is the significance of a *turn*, if not that of a *change*, precisely, of *direction*, the modification of an orientation, that is, both a *displacement* and a *choice of sense*, of meaning?' (179). The literary turn, you feel compelled to point out, would be no more a matter of 'choice' than of 'interpretation'.

You sense that what makes *The Turn of the Screw* a masterpiece has to do with its turns and what it does with the 'turn'. It shows up a veering within the figure or trope of the turn. It lets 'turn' *veer* in a singular yet delirious, even unheard-of fashion. It presents a classic case of the great literary work as a work of veering in its double and apparently antithetical sense – at once an extraordinary exercise of control and an amazing release. Everyone has an impression of James as the Master – and of how canny and knowing, controlling and calculating he was in his writing. You propose as indicative a comment in one of his Notebook entries, from April 1894, apropos an unwritten story: 'I see that my leaps and elisions, my flying bridges and great comprehensive loops (in a vivid, admirable sentence or two), must be absolutely bold and masterly.'[57] He knows all about the leaps and loops, the twists and screws. But this art of veering, as you call it, is also what allows or opens to the other. It is a question of the ways in which such control is inseparable from the precipitate, the plunging, the delirious turns of the literary – veerings away beyond any anchoring in notions of authorial intention, consciousness or unconscious. You can pick it up, above all perhaps, in the silences, in the sense of words abandoned, verbal orphans, left to play by themselves, for better or for worse, in an orphantasmatic world of their own.

We are 'in the same boat as the governess' (182), Shoshana Felman remarks. The trope of navigation, of being in a boat, and being in the same boat as the governess, is perhaps surprisingly central to James's work. *The Turn of the Screw* might seem very much a land-text, a novel told in a house, about a house, and about what haunts so-called home-territory. But a boat glides through it. It is 'a great drifting ship' and the governess is 'strangely at the helm' (TS: 18), as she puts it quite early on in her narrative. The governess keeps veering, and we veer with her. We are – in a transegmental drift – part of the governess's crew (her screw). You are inclined to suppose that James makes deliberate play on the etymology of 'govern', from the Latin *gubernare*, and originally Greek *kybernaein*, to steer (a vessel), just as he plays on the name of Mrs Grose apropos the adjectival 'gross', the adverb 'grossly' and the uneasy intimation of something that *grows*. But how far do you suppose this goes? While writing the novel in his flat in London, at 34 De Vere Gardens, does James intend to let the 'veer' embedded in 'governess' take a turn, or want us to see the letters of 'grose' anagrammatically embedded in 'governess'? Does he have an eye for the letters of the word 'turn' in 'Peter Quint'? This sort of orphantasy is, you would say, a side-effect, a *reading-side-effect*. Such play is not something anyone chooses. It is no more a question of authorial intention, than of some putative unconscious. It is what is happening in the literary turn. It is a matter of attending to the subatomic fevering of language, to the infected-infectious activities and passivities of a writing machine which, when it is operating at full tilt (as in Shakespeare, Wordsworth, Dickinson, James, Freud, Bowen, Cixous), nonetheless lays out what it is that psychoanalysis and literature share: 'a kind of magic' in motion, the poetico-performative effects of veering.[58]

You return, then, to the strangeness of location, to a sense of orientation beyond belief. 'What a dreadful turn, to be sure, Miss! Where on earth do you see anything?' This question recalls and replays another, coming a little earlier, again from the mouth of Mrs Grose, with reference to Flora after she has made off across the lake in a little boat: 'But if the boat's there, where on earth's *she*?' (96). The interrogative 'where', to be sure, is one of the great verbal resonators, a sinister insister in James's text. It is after all, literally, Miles's last word, the word that, perhaps as sharply as any other, invites an apprehension of the literary turn, the vertigo of an orientation beyond belief. The governess sees the dead man at the window and the boy, 'bewildered, glaring vainly over the place and missing wholly . . . the wide, overwhelming presence', says to her: 'It's *he*?' She turns it over:

> I was so determined to have all my proof that I flashed into ice to challenge him. 'Whom do you mean by "he"?'
> 'Peter Quint – you devil!' His face gave again, round the room, its convulsed supplication. '*Where*?'
> They are in my ears still, his supreme surrender of the name and his tribute to my devotion. 'What does he matter now, my own? – what will he *ever* matter? *I* have you,' I launched at the beast, 'but he has lost you for ever!' (TS: 121)

It is virtually the end – the dropping of the narrative into the abyss, as Felman and others have emphasized, in which we are left with the governess narrator, in turn left with the beautiful dead boy in her arms, the final '*Where?*' still there, in the ear, a strange tableau in which any so-called frame narrative has been irrevocably cut off, non-returnable, ever to veer: '. . . lost you for ever . . .'.

*

The second word, which is also the last here, is 'you'. If, as Shoshana Felman argues, *The Turn of the Screw* is exemplary in showing the 'uncanny trapping power' of a literary work 'as an inescapable reading-effect' (102), it would be about *you*, the you that you find you become, the addressee of the letter called *The Turn of the Screw*. There's a strange and singular play of the 'you', all the way through the *Screw*, starting with the seemingly blithe bandying about of the question of what '*you* will judge' (TS: 9) as regards the writing that follows, and ending most shockingly, perhaps, in the little boy's convulsed words: 'Peter Quint – you devil!' (121). You wonder if this peculiar 'you'-effect is not something that is being hinted at or surreptitiously played out in that celebrated comment that James makes in his Preface to the New York edition:

> Only make the reader's general vision of evil intense enough, I said to myself – and that already is a charming job – and his own experience, his own imagination, his own sympathy (with the children) and horror (of their false friends) will supply him quite sufficiently with all the particulars. Make him *think* the evil, make him think it for himself, and you are released from weak specifications.[59]

It is a curiously encrypted passage within the critical peritext, this embedded reminiscence of a soliloquy ('I said to myself . . .'), which begins with 'I' and ends with a *you*: 'you are released . . .' As for the governess's narrative itself, you stare into the spiral, you see yourself inscribed there, in fleeting spectral glimpses, just two or three times, when the governess writes: 'think what you will' (TS: 27), 'you'll see what' (61) and then 'You may imagine' (62). These are singularly strange moments, in which you can hardly *not* ask yourself: To whom does the governess address herself?

Veering belongs to no *-ism* or school of criticism or theory. It is not psychoanalysis or philosophy or literature. It is a force, altering intimacy, veering within, veering off.

You say all this. You stop. You smile. But the tears begin to roll. I have no idea who or where on earth you are.

Notes

1. Poem 1575, in *The Complete Poems of Emily Dickinson*, ed. Thomas H. Johnson (London: Faber and Faber, 1975), p. 653.
2. 'The Literary Turn' began life (in more condensed form) as a lecture at a conference entitled 'Writing in a Post-Derridean Era', at the University of Växjö in Sweden, in October 2008. I would like to record my thanks to Vasilis Papageorgiou for initially inviting me to address this topic.
3. Jacques Derrida, 'Some Statements and Truisms about Neo-Logisms, Newisms, Postisms, Parasitisms, and other Small Seismisms', trans. Anne Tomiche, in David Carroll (ed.), *The States of 'Theory': History, Art and Critical Discourse* (New York: Columbia University Press, 1990), p. 76.
4. Jacques Derrida, 'I Have a Taste for the Secret', Jacques Derrida in conversation with Maurizio Ferraris and Giorgio Vattimo, in Derrida and Ferraris, *A Taste for the Secret*, trans. Giacomo Donis (Cambridge: Polity, 2001), p. 76.
5. J. Hillis Miller, *On Literature* (London: Routledge, 2002), p. 1. Further page references to Miller's book appear parenthetically in the text.
6. Miller's idiom is familiar enough, even though the *OED* makes no reference to it and has no separate entry for 'droves' in the plural. The dictionary does, however, cite an example of the plural from Nathaniel Hawthorne, writing (in his *French and Italian Journals* in 1857): 'A ghost in every room, and droves of them in some of the rooms.' The ghostliness of 'turning in droves' is perhaps apposite.
7. Jacques Derrida, 'Envois', in *The Post Card: From Socrates to Freud and Beyond*, trans. Alan Bass (Chicago: Chicago University Press, 1987), p. 197.
8. Jacques Derrida, *Archive Fever: A Freudian Impression*, trans. Eric Prenowitz (Chicago: Chicago University Press, 1996), p. 16; *Mal d'archive: Une impression freudienne* (Paris: Galilée, 1995), p. 34.
9. See 'Everybody Needs to Get Thicker Skins', *The Guardian*, G2 (11 July 2008), p. 5.
10. Jonathan Culler, *The Literary in Theory* (Stanford: Stanford University Press, 2007). Further page references to Culler's book appear parenthetically in the text.
11. Jacques Derrida, *Béliers: Le dialogue ininterrompu: entre deux inifinis, le poème* (Paris: Galilée, 2003). This was published in English as 'Rams: Uninterrupted Dialogue – Between Two Infinities, the Poem', trans. Thomas Dutoit and Philippe Romanski, in Thomas Dutoit and Outi Pasanen (eds), *Sovereignties in Question: The Poetics of Paul Celan* (New York: Fordham University Press, 2005), pp. 135–63.
12. See Culler's 'Omniscience', in *The Literary in Theory*, pp. 183–201. On telepathy, literature and being-two-to-speak-or-think-or-feel, see Nicholas Royle, 'The "Telepathy Effect": Notes toward a Reconsideration of Narrative Fiction', in *The Uncanny* (Manchester: Manchester University Press, 2003), pp. 256–76.
13. Jonathan Culler, *On Deconstruction: Theory and Criticism after Structuralism* (London: Routledge and Kegan Paul, 1983), p. 180.
14. Culler, *On Deconstruction*, p. 182. Cf. also Culler's citation (217–18) of the passage in *Of Grammatology* in which Derrida comments: 'the writer

writes *in* a language and *in* a logic whose own system, laws and life his discourse by definition cannot dominate absolutely. He uses them only by letting himself, after a fashion and up to a certain point, be governed by the system.' See Jacques Derrida, *Of Grammatology*, trans. Gayatri Chakravorty Spivak (Baltimore: Johns Hopkins University Press, 1976), p. 158.

15. Jacques Derrida, *Mémoires: for Paul de Man*, trans. Cecile Lindsay, Jonathan Culler and Eduardo Cadava (New York: Columbia University Press, 1986), p. 96.

16. Rita Felski, *Uses of Literature* (Oxford: Blackwell, 2008). Further page references are given parenthetically in the main body of the text.

17. Jacques Derrida, 'Passions: "An Oblique Offering"', trans. David Wood, in *On the Name*, ed. Thomas Dutoit (Stanford: Stanford University Press, 1995), pp. 28ff.

18. See, in particular, Jacques Derrida, 'The University Without Condition', in *Without Alibi*, ed. and trans. Peggy Kamuf (Stanford: Stanford University Press, 2002), pp. 202–37.

19. It should perhaps be added, however, that Felski makes passing reference (though in a consistently negative vein) to deconstruction and psychoanalysis. See, for example, *Uses of Literature*, pp. 11, 59, 60, 80 and 119.

20. For two valuable recent studies in this area, see Michael Naas, *Derrida From Now On* (New York: Fordham University Press, 2008) and Martin McQuillan, *Deconstruction after 9/11* (Abingdon: Routledge, 2009).

21. Jacques Derrida, 'Deconstruction in America: An Interview with Jacques Derrida', trans. James Creech, *Critical Exchange*, 17 (1985): 9.

22. See, in particular, Jacques Derrida, 'This Strange Institution Called Literature', trans. Geoffrey Bennington and Rachel Bowlby, in Derek Attridge (ed.), *Acts of Literature* (London and New York: Routledge, 1992), pp. 33–75, and especially pp. 37–43 and 48; *Positions*, trans. Alan Bass (Chicago: Chicago University Press, 1981), especially p. 70; 'Circumfession', in Bennington and Derrida, *Jacques Derrida*, trans. Geoffrey Bennington (Chicago: Chicago University Press, 1993); *Given Time: I. Counterfeit Money*, trans. Peggy Kamuf (London: Chicago University Press, 1992), especially p. 153; 'Passions', especially pp. 27ff.

23. Jacques Derrida, *Demeure: Fiction and Testimony* (with Maurice Blanchot's *The Instant of My Death*), trans. Elizabeth Rottenberg (Stanford: Stanford University Press, 2000), p. 28.

24. See, for example, Jacques Derrida, 'Before the Law', trans. Avital Ronell and Christine Roulston, in Derek Attridge (ed.), *Acts of Literature* (London and New York: Routledge, 1992), pp. 183–220, especially here p. 199; 'Declarations of Independence', trans. Tom Keenan and Tom Pepper, in *Negotiations: Interventions and Interviews 1971–2001*, ed. Elizabeth Rottenberg (Stanford: Stanford University Press, 2002), pp. 46–54; and 'The Principle of Reason: The University in the Eyes of Its Pupils', trans. Catherine Porter and Edward P. Morris, in *Eyes of the University: Right to Philosophy 2* (Stanford: Stanford University Press, 2004), pp. 129–55.

25. Derrida, *Demeure: Fiction and Testimony*, p. 29.

26. See Derrida, *Demeure: Fiction and Testimony*, p. 27.

27. Derrida, 'This Strange Institution Called Literature', p. 52.
28. Derrida, 'This Strange Institution Called Literature', p. 69. The original French here for 'to *lead it off* elsewhere' is '*l'entraîner ailleurs*': see 'Cette étrange institution qu'on appelle la littérature', in *Derrida d'ici, Derrida de là*, ed. Thomas Dutoit and Philippe Romanski (Paris: Galilée, 2009), p. 287. The italicization is Bennington and Bowlby's.
29. Derrida, 'This Strange Institution Called Literature', p. 55.
30. See Jacques Derrida and Elisabeth Roudinesco, *For What Tomorrow . . . A Dialogue*, trans. Jeff Fort (Stanford: Stanford University Press, 2004), p. 173.
31. See Jacques Derrida, 'Afterword: Toward an Ethic of Discussion', trans. Samuel Weber, in *Limited Inc* (Evanston, IL: Northwestern University Press, 1988), p. 136. On the 'animal question' more generally, see Jacques Derrida, *The Animal That Therefore I Am*, ed. Marie-Louise Mallet, trans. David Wills (New York: Fordham University Press, 2008), and *The Beast and the Sovereign*, vol.1, trans. Geoffrey Bennington (London: Chicago University Press, 2009); and on the 'poematic' animal in particular, see 'Che cos'è la poesia?' and '*Istrice 2: Ick bünn all hier*', trans. Peggy Kamuf, in *Points . . . Interviews, 1974–1994*, ed. Elisabeth Weber (London: Routledge, 1995), pp. 288–99 and 300–26.
32. Jacques Derrida, 'Unsealing ("the old new language")', trans. Peggy Kamuf, in *Points . . . Interviews, 1974–1994*, ed. Elisabeth Weber (London: Routledge, 1995), pp. 115–31. References to the French original, where provided, are to 'Desceller ("la vieille neuve langue")', in *Points de suspension: Entretiens*, ed. Elisabeth Weber (Paris: Galilée, 1992), pp. 123–40.
33. See, in particular, *Mémoires: for Paul de Man*, and his remarks in the film *Derrida* (directed by Kirby Dick and Amy Ziering Kofman. USA: Jane Doe Films, 2002).
34. See Jacques Derrida, *Edmund Husserl's* Origin of Geometry: *An Introduction*, trans. John P. Leavey, Jr. (1962; Stony Brook, NY: Nicolas Hays, 1978), pp. 102–4.
35. See Derrida, *Edmund Husserl's* Origin of Geometry, pp. 100–1, n.108; 'Des tours de Babel', trans. Joseph F. Graham, in *Psyche: Inventions of the Other*, vol. 1, ed. Peggy Kamuf and Elizabeth Rottenberg (1985; Stanford: Stanford University Press, 2007), pp. 191–225; *Spectres of Marx: The State of the Debt, the Work of Mourning, and the New International*, trans. Peggy Kamuf (London: Routledge, 1994).
36. Derrida, 'Unsealing ("the old new language")', pp. 118–19; 'Desceller ("la vieille neuve langue")', p. 127.
37. Derrida, 'Envois', p. 160.
38. Derrida, 'Envois', p. 194.
39. Walter Pater, 'The School of Giorgione', in *The Renaissance* (New York: Modern Library, 1919), p. 111.
40. Pater, 'The School of Giorgione', p. 111.
41. 'Unsealing ("the old new language")', p. 119, tr. sl. mod.; 'Desceller ("la vieille neuve langue")', p. 128.
42. See Gilles Deleuze, 'He Stutters', in *Essays Critical and Clinical*, trans. Daniel W. Smith and Michael A. Greco (London: Verso, 1998), pp. 107–14.
43. This calls to mind some of the things he says about the relations between

music and architecture elsewhere. See, for example, Jacques Derrida and Peter Eisenman, *Chora L Works*, ed. Jeffrey Kipnis and Thomas Leeser (New York: Monacelli Press, 1997), pp. 166–8.

44. Derrida, 'Unsealing ("the old new language")', p. 118; 'Desceller ("la vieille neuve langue")', p. 127.

45. Derrida, 'Passions: "An Oblique Offering"', p. 28.

46. Derrida, *Of Grammatology*, p. 162.

47. Jacques Derrida, in Catherine Malabou and Jacques Derrida, *Counterpath: Travelling with Jacques Derrida*, trans. David Wills (Stanford: Stanford University Press, 2004), p. 147, tr. sl. mod.; *Jacques Derrida, La Contre-allée* (Paris: La Quinzaine Littéraire–Louis Vuitton, 1999), p. 147. The veering character of this co-authored work is perhaps more clearly announced in the subtitle to the original French publication: *Dérive, Arrivée, Catastrophe* (*Drift, Arrival, Catastrophe*).

48. See Derrida, 'Passions: "An Oblique Offering"', p. 30. Here again it is a question of that more radical veering towards which Derrida gestures in *Rogues* when he remarks that 'there never was in the 1980s or 1990s . . . a *political turn* or *ethical turn* in "deconstruction"'. It is not a matter of supposing that deconstruction 'veer[s] away or chang[es] tack', but rather of what such an image 'ignores or runs counter to', namely a thinking of the trace, the differential veering of the 'send-off' (*renvoi*) in relation to 'what remains to be thought'. In this more radical sense, veering would be the opening of the future itself, indissociably linked to a thinking of the trace and the 'democracy to come'. See *Rogues: Two Essays on Reason*, trans. Pascale-Anne Brault and Michael Naas (Stanford: Stanford University Press, 2005), p. 39.

49. Henry James, *The Turn of the Screw and Other Stories*, with an Introduction by S. Gorley Putt (Harmondsworth: Penguin, 1969). Further page references are to this edition and appear parenthetically in the main body of the text, abbreviated 'TS' where appropriate.

50. Nicholas Royle, *Telepathy and Literature: Essays on the Reading Mind* (Oxford: Basil Blackwell, 1990), p. 10.

51. Shoshana Felman, 'Turning the Screw of Interpretation', in *Yale French Studies*, 55/56 (1977): 94–207. Where appropriate, further page references are given parenthetically in the main body of the text.

52. See, for example, 'in turn' (120, 122), 'turning into' (133), 'turns out' (130, 131, 147, 176).

53. For further discussion of 'frame narrative' as a critical fiction, permit me to refer to my essay 'Spooking Forms', *Oxford Literary Review*, 26 (2004), 155–72.

54. Elizabeth Bowen, 'Notes on Writing a Novel', in *The Mulberry Tree: Writings of Elizabeth Bowen*, ed. Hermione Lee (London: Virago, 1986), p. 41.

55. See Derrida, *Given Time: I. Counterfeit Money*, p. 153.

56. Maurice Blanchot, 'The Pain of Dialogue', in *The Book to Come*, trans. Charlotte Mandell (Stanford: Stanford University Press, 2003), p. 153.

57. See *The Notebooks of Henry James*, ed. F. O. Matthieseen and Kenneth B. Murdock (New York: Oxford University Press, 1961), p. 161. The story to which James refers is 'The Coxon Fund'.

58. On a 'kind of magic', see Sigmund Freud, 'The Question of Lay Analysis: Conversations with an Impartial Person' (1926), in *SE* 20: 187; 'A Kind of Magic' was also the subject of a remarkable lecture by Hélène Cixous, given at the University of Leeds, 2 June 2007. For two striking recent elaborations of the interweavings of literature, psychoanalysis and magic, see Elissa Marder, 'Mourning, Magic and Telepathy', *Oxford Literary Review* 30: 2 (2008), 181–200; and Sarah Wood, 'Foreveries', *Oxford Literary Review* 31: 1 (2009), 65–77.

59. See *The Novels and Tales of Henry James*, New York edn, vol. 12 (London: Macmillan, 1908), pp. xxi–xxii.

Chapter 8

Veerer: Where Ghosts Live

How quickly the days slide away
Into where they came from. (Norman MacCaig)[1]

The self: a cemetery guard. (Jacques Derrida)[2]

Veering is about where ghosts live.[3] It entails the experience of the *where* as a kind of *atopos*, a spectralization of place that literature enables us to apprehend perhaps better than any other kind of discourse. In the following pages I want to explore the question of this *where* (still echoing from the end of *The Turn of the Screw*, in the boyish voice of Miles, relayed through the governess and through the anonymous narrator who relays the relaying of the governess, all thrown in the cryptic side-vocals of Henry James) through an engagement with the writings of Elizabeth Bowen, Raymond Williams and a few others.

*

Everything gathers inside or spreads out in order to start, right down to my bare feet, as I sit here in my study on an upper floor of this old house, 'a sea house' as Walter de la Mare might call it, in Seaford, East Sussex.[4] Why barefoot? Because it is late summer and warm enough, but it also seems right in a way I do not understand. Perhaps it has to do with death, a certain spookiness, like the cold and 'horny feet' that protrude in Wallace Stevens's 'The Emperor of Ice-Cream'.[5] But there is also a feeling of affirmation, as in that poem, also by Stevens, about a 'large red man reading' and the 'ghosts that returned to earth to hear his phrases, / As he sat there reading'. 'Large Red Man Reading' (1948) is a kind of *mise-en-abyme*, a poem falling to earth, like a meteor, evoking a scene in which we are invited to imagine ghosts, those who had not yet had enough of 'the poem of life', who die too soon and who, given the chance to return to earth (in other words, to read or listen to the large red man reading this poem) 'would have wept to step barefoot into reality', who 'would have wept and been happy'.[6] It is a version of what Mark Currie discusses in the context of narrative fiction as 'future memory', a strangely twisted effect of what he calls 'the present ... experienced in a mode of anticipation'.[7] 'Large Red Man Reading' gives us poetry itself (*'poesis*, the literal characters, the vatic lines') in the fiction of a future conditional ('would have') that alerts and alters. It is a stepping barefoot into a ghostly present.

Ghosts pass so quickly. Life, too: 'what a little short thing it is to be alive and so strange.'[8] The more quickly you try to arrive, the more quickly passed. I hear these words, 'quick' and 'passed', resonate in more than one sense – homophones without a home. A character in Elizabeth Bowen's *A World of Love* remarks: 'You're far too quick to assume people are dead.'[9] Like Montaigne, one must learn to die, to live, definitively late, piecing together one's thoughts and feelings as one goes, with the words of the dead. 'If I have only one hour's work to do before I die, I am never sure I have time enough to finish it.'[10]

*

Veerer: who or what are you?

In terms of an Authorship Question, I would be tempted to think of the Liberal Democrat MP Norman Baker, the former Shadow Environment Secretary, whom I happened to find myself walking along-side one day, early in 2008, in his constituency town, about eight miles from here. I told him I had just moved and asked did he know anything about recycling schemes in Seaford (which is part of his constituency). He immediately got out a notepad and, promising to send me details, asked for my address. When I told him, he said, without looking up: 'Oh, Vera's old house.' I must have misheard: 'Vera' was a veerer. Actually he said *Mary*, as became clear when he repeated it: Mary and Denis Crutch. When they lived here it was a secondhand bookshop. As I write this I am sitting in the late Denis Crutch's study, precisely where he sat, surrounded by books on shelves that were built for him by his son. Crutch used to be the Secretary of the Lewis Carroll Society, and published numerous things Carrollian including, in 1979, a revised edition of *The Lewis Carroll Handbook*.[11] From one shadow secretary to another: everything I am writing here passes by way of this figure, a ghostly secretary who is neither Norman Baker nor Denis Crutch but rather *veerer*.

Veerer is in the house and up out on the clifftops.

Another book might be written concerning this word 'secretary'. It would be necessary to write on its behalf, let oneself be written by it, become secretary to its secrets. One of the senses of 'secretary' is *writing-desk*. The Hatter's question veers up: 'Why is a raven like a writing-desk?'[12] It is in the context of this writing-desk that Denis Crutch may be longest remembered. It is a question of a secretarial error. Even modern editions of the *Alice* books continue to get the thing wrong. The editor of the most recent Norton Critical Edition, for example, adds an ostensibly clarifying note regarding the Hatter's question: 'In a later edition of *Alice's Adventures in Wonderland* Dodgson wrote that originally this riddle had no answer, and then he provided one: because it can produce a few notes, although they are very flat, and it is never put the wrong end front.'[13] The 'never' is a silent and erroneous emendation, Crutch argues.[14] Here, in the 1896 edition of *Alice*, is what Dodgson actually wrote: 'Because it can produce a few notes, tho they are *very* flat; and it is nevar put with the wrong end in front!' Crutch points out the literal reversal. It is the playful illustration of the impossibility of a ksedgnitirw or nevar. Which is to say, the playful illustration of the possibility. Indeed, without the rather flat note of this wordplay (the inscription of 'raven' backwards), Dodgson's reasoning would seem mere nonsense, or at least invite a further riddle: When is a raven put with the wrong end in front? In a variation of Poe, 'never' should be 'nevarmore': the desk is always a chamber door.[15]

'Veerer' is hardly a proper word. In the broadest respects, it would refer to something or someone that veers or makes veer. There is an entry for it in the *OED*, but it appears there as an early seventeenth-century translation from French and there is no 'use' of the word recorded thereafter. 'Veerer' is thus to all intents and purposes, as far as the *OED* would lead us to believe, a useless word. In his *Dictionarie of the French and English Tongues* (1611), Randle Cotgrave provides an entry for the French word *vireur*, defining this as: 'a veerer, or whirler, a round turner, or turner of things often about' (cited in *OED*, veerer, n. 1). In homage to Cotgrave (a slightly eerie name, is it not?), I hereby propose to resurrect or revivify 'veerer', as an old word to be read and understood anew.

'Veerer' is a veerer: its force and value has to do with kinetic strangeness and unpredictability. The word might be used, for example, to refer to a person, object or text, or to something veering within them; but it may also refer to something happening *between* one person and another, or one text and another, or a person and a text, and so on. In particular, 'veerer' would describe a movement in and out of writing, the effects of a kind of verbal shape-shifter, or locomotive silence, the way in which, for instance, a text at once meddles with and eludes generic and other kinds of classification or differentiation (between narrative and dramatic, for example, or between critical and creative writing). It would work, then, both in a micrological context, to designate the veering effects of a certain word, thought or image, and in a more generalized context, to designate a text that veers.

And it is also a name for what is going on in any and every experience of *environment* – from the fingers at the keyboard to what de la Mare calls 'the environment of style', from the social and political environment to the global environmental crisis.[16] There is always a *veerer* in 'environment'. Of course, it is never one: a veerer does not come alone, it is irreducibly multiple.

We might start with a veerer near at hand, immediately around us, the objects in front of our eyes and the ghosts. But veering never stays at home, it is off. It is in the street, in the air, vertigo of place.

*

On the desk in front of me, as I write, I have a stone I use as a paperweight, that comes from Bowen's Court, the house in Cork where Elizabeth Bowen lived at various periods, from her childhood onwards, until its sale and demolition at the end of the 1950s. This shard was brought back to me by a friend who visited the derelict remains a few years ago. I dream of building something out of the gravity of this stone, a reading of or with Bowen, a writer whom I never met but with whom I feel strangely intimate. I picture a sort of phantasmagoric Bowenesque discourse that might launch out from this stone my eyes invariably rest on when I pause and turn and move off who knows where.

As Jacques Derrida has remarked: 'everyone reads, acts, writes with *his or her* ghosts, even when one goes after the ghosts of the other.'[17] There is no going after ghosts without veering. And what is a ghost if not a veerer?

I imagine immersion in the extraordinary *where* of Bowen. In the space of a fleeting anachronicity I sense us writing and reading at the same time. I am reading her as she writes. She is terminally ill with cancer, working at the text whose termination will evade her, which she will die while still writing, her autobiography, published posthumously in 1975 as 'Pictures and Conversations'.[18] This is her proposed title. For she too is haunted by the magical thinkings of the *Alice* books: '. . . "and what is the use of a book," thought Alice, "without pictures or conversations?"'.[19] Moving from Carroll to Bowen and beyond, there is an eerie recalling also, perhaps, of the Latin etymology of *conversation*: turning oneself about, moving to and fro.[20] It is a question of new ghost tenses, the tenses convoked by the spectral telephony of writing and the *where* of this experience. Bowen speaks, she writes in her autobiography as if she were speaking, as a dead person, or at any rate as if she were inviting the reader to go after her, to stop her writing in the midst of life:

> Few people questioning me about my novels, or my short stories, show curiosity as to the places in them. Thesis-writers, interviewers or individuals I encounter at parties all, but all, stick to the same track, which by-passes locality. On the subject of my symbology, if any, or psychology (whether my own or my characters'), I have occasionally been run ragged, but as to the *where* of my stories, its importance in them and for me, and the reasons for that, a negative apathy persists . . . Failing to throw a collective light on my art, my places tend to be thought of as its accessories, engaging enough to read of but not 'meaningful'. Wherefore, Bowen topography has so far, so far as I know, been untouched by research. Should anyone give it a thought after I am dead, that will be too late. To it, only I hold the key. (281–2)

Everyone will have stuck to 'the same track', by-passing the question and experience of 'locality', 'the *where* of [her] stories'. Not only does Bowen write here as if she were already dead, speaking as a ghost, but she goes on to conjure doing the same to another. 'Were I to meet a writer, *living or dead*, whose work had so percolated into my own experience as to become part of it, his places would be what I should first want to discuss . . .' (282, emphasis added).

Veerer might also be a name for that experience in which you find yourself coming into another track, taking a turn with the dead. It is a fiction, of course, a fantasy perhaps of veering well: you want to veer well, reading, writing about or listening to the dead, but it is never fully or finally within your control. A veerer of this sort may involve a feeling of uncanny surprise. It might happen with a turn of phrase or image in a novel or poem, in an essay by Montaigne or a line in Shakespeare. It might also turn up – as an unexpected guest or visitor – in inadvertencies of music, photography or film. But in the case of literature the whirler is in the very words, the turning in the words that connect you with the dead, and in the silences within and between them. A veerer is not an act of identification, though a feeling of identification may be one of its effects. A veerer is what happens, if it happens, in a singular, fleeting moment of reading.

Veering in time: it would entail what she calls a 'bend back', as when time (bringing back the dead Guy for Antonia in *A World of Love*, for example) has reimposed its phantasmagoric 'clutch'.[21] I hear it, in passing, in the bow of *when* in her name. I am sitting barefoot at my desk reading her. I am holding the page down with her old house. I've just slid my copy of *Bowen's Court* out from the pile of books on one side of my desk and chanced on a passage in which she recalls going back there from Hythe, in the early summer of 1912. It is a matter of being quick, running almost feverishly, barefoot. 'This time', she writes, 'it was to be a real, triumphant return':

> 'June sun baked the steps and streamed in at the windows, the bare floors gave off their familiar smell. On my thirteenth birthday [7 June] I woke up early and ran barefoot all over the house: already the windows were standing open, and the air was fresh with mosses and woods and lawns.[22]

But now 'too late' (as she says), she is in Hythe again, writing in her modern semi-detached beside St Leonard's Church, with its weird and improbable ossuary of two thousand human skulls, in the next county along the coast from here.[23] Seaford and Hythe connect: they are on the same road, what she calls in her autobiography 'the trafficky main thoroughfare, A259' (266).[24] Seaford and Hythe both have a kind of 'illusory look of marine emptiness' (265), to recall another phrase from 'Pictures and Conversations'. Both are so-called cinque ports. She will dispute this with me. She will recall what she says in her Foreword to *The Cinque Ports* (1952) by Ronald and Frank Jessup, that some places (including Seaford) have been 'incorrectly promoted into [the] ranks' of the true and original cinque ports.[25] I am an upstart, I know, we were never going to get along in that respect. But Seaford was designated the chief subordinate port of Hastings in 1229, a limb of that 'mother' cinque port, which is a long enough pedigree for most people. And what she writes in her Foreword is as evocative of Seaford as of Hythe: 'The past of these places is of a length out of all proportion with their visible size'; this past seems 'not so much departed as contracted into . . . the ghost of a memory' (59). Along this stretch of Sussex and Kent one feels 'its layer upon layer of extinct, eroded or shrunken civilizations' (59). This 'whole belt of coastal country', she concludes, '[has] an endemic temperament: something salt and sturdy about the very set of the bricks and stones, something vital about the surrounding contours – whether stretching flats, sweeping slopes, jutting heights' (61).

Talking of 'extinct, eroded or shrunken civilizations' and the ghosts of memories, yesterday afternoon as I sat here at my desk reading her story 'Attractive Modern Homes' (1941), reflecting on the ways in which her writing perhaps constitutes a kind of newbuild tradition of the ghost story, in the sunny street below me I heard a youngish man suddenly shout out, loudly and in jubilation: 'I'm fucking back from the dead! I'm fucking back from the dead!' She is, I suspect, as pained as I am by such language. I am just saying what the man said. Nowadays, it would seem, it is not enough to come back from the dead; one must be 'fucking' back. He was evidently shouting at or to someone, and refer-ring (I surmise) to having returned from a spell in prison, but when I went over to the window I could see no sign of where the noise had come from.

Bowen topography is untouched by research – and now that I am dead, she says in effect, it will remain untouched, virgin. To it, she says, as if dead already, only I hold the key. The novelist: ghost of a prison warden. Of Hythe she recalls in these same pages: 'The edifices lining the streets or gummed at different levels above the Channel seemed engaged in just not sliding about. How much *would* this brittle fabric stand up to? My thoughts dallied with landslides, subsidences and tidal waves' (277). With the word 'fabric' the stone begins to dissolve. There is no doubt a kind of stony clarity about her writing, but the 'brittle fabric' of buildings veers off into impressions of texture, ribbons and bows, the weave and 'sheer kink' of writing, reading the threading together, 'knitting up'.[26]

Where is the ghost: in the vertigo I read in her, with her. For example, very near the beginning of *The House in Paris* (1935), there is the striking singularity of her punctuation or its absence when the narrator first refers to the unmothered young boy Leopold. Is Leopold a boy, in fact, or a monkey? The young Henrietta, on her way to visit the eponymous 'house in Paris', is not sure. She thinks that Miss Fisher, the strange woman with whom she is sitting, is perhaps referring to the toy monkey Henrietta is holding. The terrifying Madame Fisher (as yet unmet, but already back home, waiting in the house, the ghastly figure at the haunted heart of the novel) has evidently told her daughter to tell Henrietta that 'she is most anxious to see you, and also hopes to see Leopold'.[27]

> *Leopold?* thought Henrietta. The thought that Miss Fisher might have taken the liberty of re-christening her monkey, whose name was Charles, made her look round askance. She said: 'Who is Leopold?'
> 'Oh, he's a little boy,' Miss Fisher said with a strikingly reserved air.
> 'A little boy where?'
> 'Today he is at our house.' (19–20)

Thinking as Henrietta (and everything turns through this manifestation of literature as thought-reading, writing speaking feeling in the body of another), Bowen's narrator has her say: 'A little boy where?' Not 'A little boy? Where?' or 'A little boy, where?' It is a single question without punctuation – as if the 'where' were part of him, like 'little boy blue' or 'little boy lost'.[28] The pointed absence of punctuation generates a veerer. In a sense Henrietta's is a crazy question, since she and Miss Fisher are in transit, 'skidding away' (17) across Paris in a taxi, as the opening sentence of the novel makes clear. They are passing quickly, like ghosts. As if she were looking out of the taxi window and were supposed to be able to see him, Henrietta exclaims: 'A little boy where?'

This bizarre question could be said to encapsulate the novel: the 'where' of Leopold in a ghostly today, meeting his mother, or rather *not* meeting his mother, for the first time, in the house in Paris in which years earlier, unbeknownst to him, his father committed suicide. Unbeknownst – but at the same time eerily foreknown, foreseen, overlooked by the clairaudient, clairvoyant and telepathic textures of Bowen's writing. 'Oh, you oughtn't to thought-read letters to someone else!' (59), says Henrietta to Leopold, catching him 'in exalted abstraction', in the mad moment of holding 'an envelope to his forehead, his eyes shut' (58). The envelope that Leopold is trying to thought-read is a sort of headachey miniature of what it is to read *The House in Paris*. He knows it is a letter from his mother (having recognized her handwriting on the outside), but the envelope is empty, a letter purloined, in effect, ahead of time. Bowen invites us to think about telepathy and literature, telepathy in literature, the telepathy of literature. Novelistic narration is an eerie weave of thought-reading and feeling-sharing, shifting about within and through one body or point of view and another, never at home, never properly 'in place'. *The House in Paris* is also a zigzagging encounter with the question of telepathy as an experience of suffering, the suffering of distance and distant suffering (tele-*pathos*). To read this novel is to find oneself sharing Henrietta's sense of being 'like a kaleidoscope often and quickly shaken' (54). The reader is drawn into a relationship that is, in A. S. Byatt's apt phrase, 'odd, continuous and shifting'.[29]

While its title suggests an envelopment of the novel as itself a house, with Paris the determined location, Bowen's novel never settles down *anywhere*. It is, to recall her own phrasing from 'Pictures and Conversations' (284–5), a 'non-stop narrative' of 'fluidity', composed in an 'anti-static', 'liquefying' language. It veers about from present to past to present, by letter and by telephone, by taxi, ship and train, between Paris and Ireland, London and Boulogne and Hythe.

'Today he is at our house': Leopold, like Henrietta, like a ghost, is just visiting. The novel is just visiting.[30]

'Just visiting': strange phrase. If you pay a visit to the passages in the *OED* in which 'visit' is defined, you might be slightly surprised at how pervasively this word is linked to suffering, punishment and affliction. Its sense is also, of course, to do with the religious and supernatural: originally 'visit' is used 'Of the Deity: To come to (persons) in order to comfort or benefit' (*OED*, visit, v., I, 1. a). Its ghostly, less markedly Christian inflection goes back only a couple of hundred years. For the word 'visitation' explicitly in conjunction with the figure of the ghost, the *OED* cites Dickens's *A Christmas Carol* in 1844 (*OED*, 'visitation', n., II, 6. d). The visiting of ghosts and ghosts of visiting: the space of literature would be, more than philosophy or any other kind of writing, where this happens, if it does. Thinking about literature as 'just visiting' would engage with its lightness, transience and play (it is 'just' a story, 'just' a poem), but also with its capacity to unnerve, confront or afflict, to descend or impose on us. To read a powerful work of literature is not so much to visit as to feel oneself visited. And likewise to write: when Bowen, for example, reflects in her autobiography on *where* the characters in her stories come from, she describes them precisely as 'visitations' (296).

'Just visiting' can always be ironic, a discombobulating litotes. Correspondingly, its resources or reserves are not confinable simply to appearances of the word 'visit' and its cognates, however rich that vein itself might prove – from the 'visitation' of the Ghost in *Hamlet* to Lockwood in the opening words of Emily Brontë's *Wuthering Heights* ('I have just returned from a visit to my landlord . . .'), from Thomas Hardy's 'His Visitor' to Bowen's 'The Visitor'.[31] The first visitor would perhaps be the author. Roland Barthes's celebrated formulation might be recalled: 'It is not that the Author cannot "come back" into the Text, into his text; however, he can only do so as a "guest", so to speak' – in other words, just visiting.[32] It would be a matter of orienting oneself to an analysis and understanding of literature as a discourse essentially preoccupied with visits and visitors, visitants and visitations, figures of quest or wandering, the stranger or outsider, inspiration or influence, the coming into oneself of suffering and affliction, the uncanniness of colonization and the foreign body, the uncertainly abiding, transitory residence that is every home.

In the case of the novel or short story, 'just visiting' would also be a way of getting at that flickering affectivity, the phantomatic ventriloquism, the shifting character of magical thinking and telepathic narration. The narrator is a fiction, a kind of ghost just visiting, without determinable location, now transcribing the thoughts of Henrietta, now describing how for instance the little girl 'look[ed] round askance'. 'A little boy where?' asks Henrietta, asks the narrator, asks Bowen: asking askance, being two or more to think, to ask. Constitutionally unstable, literary narrative is this shifting layering of multiple voices and perspectives, in ghostly veerings of location.

'The locale of the happening always colours the happening, and often, to a degree, shapes it', as she says in 'Notes on Writing a Novel' (1945) and says again, quoting herself, locating and relocating her own words, nearly thirty years later in 'Pictures and Conversations'.[33] But alongside

Bowen's petulantly posthumous insistence on the primacy of place in her work, and readers' apparent indifference to it in her lifetime, goes the soaring, vertiginous affirmation of the dislocated and unlocatable. One might, a shade outlandishly, imagine her writings being made into a TV property programme: *Dislocation, dislocation, dislocation.*[34] Bowen's fiction is driven and riven by a sense of the ghostly, captivating potencies of place. For any lover, in life or literature, it is necessary to beware the where. As the narrator observes of the star-crossed Karen and Max, who are just visiting Boulogne (with its 'oppressed' and 'stricken' atmosphere), in *The House in Paris*: 'People in love, in whom every sense is open, cannot beat off the influence of a place' (144). Animistic language secures the suspicion of a sort of lurking wherewolf: as the couple sit high up on an 'unsafe parapet', with a sheer drop below them, the leaves of the trees 'kept sifting in the uncertain air', 'an incoming tide of apartness began to creep between Max and Karen', 'the apse of the cathedral, the sad windows of houses . . . looked at them through the boughs' (144–5).

Bowen's fiction combines what, in another context, Theodor Adorno calls 'the utopia of what is close at hand with that of the utmost distance'.[35] The utopian veers into the *atopos*. She understands – and lets it show in virtually every page of her writing – that 'anywhere, at any time, with anyone, one may be seized by the suspicion of being alien'.[36] An intense specificity of place, accuracy of locale, even a quite classic affirmation of *genius loci*, is haunted by a pervasive and more radical disorientation. In this latter respect, Bowen's *where* is never far from the vocable that concludes Poe's crazy and magnificent 'The Imp of the Perverse'. The murderer-narrator is due to be 'consigned . . . to the hangman and to hell' the following day. In prison (which is thus again the apparent location of the narration, another fiction that effectively imprisons itself), he sounds his final words: 'To-day I wear these chains, and am *here*. To-morrow I shall be fetterless! – *but where?*'[37] You can wear all the chains in the world but you cannot, so to speak, wear where.[38] Bowen's *where* is funny, as well as menacing or menaced. It is veering between the spectralized, intimate but ambiguous 'Where?' that is the final agonized word of the little boy Miles at the end of Henry James's *The Turn of the Screw*, just before 'the cry of a creature hurled over an abyss', and the 'where' that pervades Lewis Carroll's *Alice* books, above all perhaps the 'where' that comes through in the dialogue of the two little boys, Tweedledum and Tweedledee, when the former tells Alice that the Red King is dreaming about her and the latter claps his hands triumphantly, exclaiming: 'And if he left off dreaming about you, *where* do you suppose you'd be?'[39]

The House in Paris is a work of cryptaesthetic force that, perhaps more compactly than any other of Bowen's novels, brings to mind the spooky ending of her autobiography, the moment at which she signs, in effect, its living death sentence, by offering a few notes about how the unwritten 'Pictures and Conversations' would or could have been continued. Just after noting the moment of a book's publication (in particular that of 'a novel or long short story') as a time of veering – when 'the cable having been cut between it and the author, it enters upon an unforeseeable life of its own' – she adds a note about the last section she will never write:

> WITCHCRAFT: A QUERY. Is anything uncanny involved in the process of writing? General conclusions drawn by the author, with regard in part to her own work, but also no less, if anything more, to that of the hierarchy of other writers. (298)

There is something about her writing, from time to time, makes me want to laugh aloud like a madman. It has to do with that 'almost telepathic' sense of rapport that she talks about in 'The Bend Back'.[40] It comes upon me here, this uncanny veerer –

Sheer drop. Stepping over a cliff.

*

A newbuild tradition of the ghost story, I was saying. 'A story, to be a story, *must* have a turning-point', she declares.[41] The more haunting the story, I would suggest, the more the turning-point is a veerer. Bowen's 'Attractive Modern Homes' is about the Watsons, a couple who move about eighty miles across country to a 'box-like' 'semi-detached house' that has just been built, on the edge of a new estate that has not yet been completed.[42] It is the very unhauntedness of the place that becomes disturbing. Everyone is a newcomer: 'everybody feels strange and has no time for curiosity' (522). Until moving house Mrs Watson 'has been happy without knowing, like a sheep or cow always in the same field' (524).

Step over a cliff –

The narrator comments: '[Mrs Watson] never needed to ask what was happening really. No wonder the move had been like stepping over a cliff. Now no one cared any more whether she existed; she came to ask, without words, if she did exist . . .' (524). Mr Watson also becomes prone to 'dread' (524–5). They become less alive than ghosts, as if in a surreal yet absolutely mundane confrontation with the meaning of the family name: *what's on?* (And even perhaps, in more teasingly phallogocentric tenor: what son? what future?) It is a story that peculiarly pivots on a walk up the half-funnily named Nut Lane, into the woods. Mr Watson does not know that his wife has already wandered off in the same direction. As he makes his way, 'recoiling from branches in the thickety darkness', he thinks that seeing a ghost would be a comfort compared with the 'entombed', 'unliving' nature of the new estate he is walking away from: 'The idea of a ghost's persistent aliveness comforted some under part of his mind' (525). Suddenly, he comes upon 'a woman's body face down on the ground'. Is she masturbating? Miming a crucifixion? Making love to the earth? Simulating burial? We read:

> Her arms were stretched out and she wore a mackintosh. With a jump of vulgar excitement he wondered if she were dead. Then the fair hair unnaturally fallen forward and red belt of the mackintosh showed him this was his wife, who could not be dead. (525)

The language, as so often in Bowen, is quietly but ineluctably erotic. Mr Watson 'could not have been more stricken in his idea of her if he had found her here with another man. He did not like to see her embrace the earth' (525–6). This is not where ghosts live, Bowen suggests, it is not animated enough for that. It is not 'decent', the man tells his wife: 'Get up.' As she finds her feet she 'keep[s] her face away' from him, then:

> 'Decent?' she said. 'This place isn't anywhere.'
> 'It's round where we live.'
> 'Live?' she said, 'What do you mean, live?'
> 'Well, we – '
> 'What do you mean, we?'
> 'You and I,' he said, looking sideways at her shoulder.
> 'Yes.' She said. 'It's fine for me having you. Sometimes anyone would almost think you could speak.'
> 'Well, what is there to say?'
> 'Don't ask me.' (526)

Harold Pinter's dialogues are closer to Bowen's than has perhaps been appreciated.[43] These lines recall Bowen's nice dictum that dialogue is 'what the characters *do to each other*'.[44] These characters are neither living nor ghosts. 'Attractive Modern Homes' could indeed be regarded as part of a newbuild tradition, uncertainly humorous and disquieting, that challenges us to think anew about where ghosts live. Rather than think of them as merely fearful, Bowen's work suggests that not to live with ghosts, not to be able to acknowledge that you *are* where ghosts live, is not to be alive at all.

The Watsons also have two children, a boy called Freddie and a girl called, as chance would have it, Vera. Bowen herself seems unable to resist some play on the girl's name, when she writes: 'Vera was a child with naturally nice ways who would throw anything off' (523). It is Vera's capacity to throw anything off that, perhaps above all, intimates the unsteady but quirky hopefulness of Bowen's story. As the couple return from their strange encounter in the wood, they are intercepted by a neighbour who introduces herself as Mrs Dawkins (a further play perhaps, with 'door' and 'kin') and asks if Vera could come to tea that afternoon and play with her daughter Dorothy (another 'dor'). Mr Watson now having 'edged past them', the two women concur that, when it comes to 'settl[ing] into a place', men 'don't feel it in the same way' (528). There is 'a crimpled dead leaf' (527–8) in Mrs Watson's hair, come from her escapade in the wood: at the very end of the story, standing by the gate in conversation with her new acquaintance, she 'pluck[s] the leaf from her hair' and remarks: '"Still, I've no doubt a place grows on one . . ."' (528).

*

What's in a name? In the raven's book and testing of a Vera ever verging on a veerer, or *vice versa*, one door after another, to adore a veerer, neither proper name nor common noun, beyond names, it keeps shifting. On my desk I also have a letter from Jacques Derrida, written on his birthday (15 July 1999), in which he tells me of the birth of his granddaughter: 'Elle s'appelle Vera . . .' *Chambers* dictionary tells me the name *Vera* is from Russian, meaning 'faith', but is 'understood as Latin "true"'. 'Vera' means one thing but is understood as something else: faith is truth, truth is faith. 'Vera' veers from one into the other. It opens onto the very vertigo of belief. It recalls what Derrida says, playing the ghost in the film bearing his name, when asked what philosopher he would like to have been his mother: 'a philosopher is a Father, not a Mother. So the philosopher that would be my mother would be a post-deconstructive philosopher, that is, myself or my son. My mother as a philosopher would be my granddaughter, for example. An inheritor. A woman philosopher who would reaffirm the deconstruction'.[45]

Writing about Vera's birth on his own birthday, Derrida's letter is about birthdays and ghosts. He is writing also in response to an essay in which I suggest that it is 'difficult to imagine a theory of the ghost or double without a theory of *déjà vu* . . . The double is always ghostly and cannot be dissociated from a sense of *déjà vu*'.[46] The context for this is Freud's argument (in 'On Narcissism', 'The Uncanny' and elsewhere) that there is something called 'primary narcissism' and that this is something that we abandon.[47] If, for Freud, we get over this as we do other sorts of 'primitive thinking' (such as believing in the return of the dead), the presence of primary narcissism itself remains somewhat ghostly, something to be confirmed, as he puts it, 'by inference from elsewhere'.[48] In his letter, immediately after announcing the birth of Vera, Derrida adds three dots, then writes, in English: '. . . "Primary narcissism . . . revival and reproduction of [my] own narcissism, why [I] have not abandoned yet..", as you would say with our grand, grand father Freud..' [*sic*]. It is an extraordinary threading together of phrases – bizarre, elliptical, poematic, in short what I would like to call a veerer. In this sentence (if it is one), in micrological fashion, Derrida is doing something very similar to what happens in the text entitled 'Telepathy', where he projects himself into Freud, and becomes Freud's ghost, or invites Sigmund Freud's ghost to become Jacques Derrida. It is a spectralization of quotation and voice, a 'just visiting' in which Derrida stitches together a couple of phrases from Freud, then adds another ('why [I] have not abandoned yet') that is not in Freud's text at all. In the same precipitous movement he has added in square brackets the words 'I' and 'my' to refer to himself, but then (in the twist given by the concluding phrase, 'as you would say') apparently also to refer to me, spoken as if by our grand, grand father, and yet flatly opposed to what Freud (in the essay 'On Narcissism') actually says. Or rather, perhaps, it is what the ghost of Freud says, or what comes from the ghost that Derrida is after.

There is at least one other Vera on my desk. It is a book about the art of Maria Chevska entitled *Vera's Room*.[49] A sort of phantomatic architectural development flips to mind, a ghostly procession that moves from Bowen's 'attractive modern homes' via Pinter's interiors to Vera's. It evokes the dream of that other sense of 'environment', a fictive or fantastical sense pertaining to art (and dating, according to the *OED*, to 1962): 'A large structure designed to be experienced as a work . . . for all (or most) of one's senses while surrounded by it, rather than from outside' ('environment', n. 1, d). There are many remarkable photographs in this book, including a section (67–72) called 'Vera's Room, 2000 (Ongoing)', showing an installation that was originally exhibited in 2003, in Berlin, Paris and elsewhere in France, then again in London in 2005. Vera's room is mostly white and beige. There is a small white box, a light brown wooden chair and dresser, and a black bicycle. Otherwise the principal objects in the room are pieces of white or beige-coloured cloth or paper, some draped or half-draped (is it an apron, a shawl, a curtain?), some lying on the floor, some worked up into strange cones (evidently solidified using kaolin) and placed on the floor or on the wall.[50] In his introduction to *Vera's Room*, Tony Godfrey notes: '[Maria Chevska's] work seems static, still, near-monochromatic. But, as one moves closer, every surface is to some extent agitated. Everything is moving.' Vera's room has 'the air of the dream', he goes on, 'as though we looked at memories or ghosts of things rather than things themselves'. It invites us to think of painting-installations as 'philosophical gymnasiums' (13), Godfrey remarks. These cloths and fabrics strangely suggest nakedness, it is true, the gymnast of truth, and the peculiar, sometimes comical correlation of ghosts with sheets, with white or pale cloth of different sorts, as well as the white sheet of a page or blankness of a so-called 'Word-document' screen, the strange textures of writing, spinning and weaving.

Vera's Room also contains a piece called 'K – A Notebook (Vera's Room)', written by that 'thief of little cotton cloths' as she calls herself, Hélène Cixous.[51] In what could be described as a kind of textual installation *in* the book, writing about *Vera's Room*, the installation *and* the book, Cixous asks:

> Is Maria's book a strolling of ghosts [*une promenade de spectres*]? Or the ghost of a stroll of ghosts? On the fractured stage of the book, human beings are distant, vague, traces. The human world is in the past. The sheets and towels are in the present . . . I leaf through the book of hours of a traveller who remembers times when she wasn't born . . .

In *Vera's Room* Cixous reads a luxuriation of metamorphoses: 'all the inertia and all the movement meet in this piece of fabric . . . From this rag can come men, women, children, birds, drapes, hairstyles, parasols, handkerchiefs, marriage veils, clouds, dolphins.' It composes a 'clothpoetic'. But this is not a space of aesthetic comfort. 'We will understand nothing from this trembling, troubled archive,' writes Cixous, 'without recollecting the history of war in the century scarcely past.' *Vera's Room* speaks to her of 'some recent catastrophe, like Chernobyl', of war, eviction and exile. It is 'A still room, with no one inside. No one's room.' And there is no door: 'We see the walls clearly, the windows, the floors, but no door. You, who wander, are you inside? are you outside? who were you, invisible subject of the enigma?' Cixous's notebook records as it spins, inside-out and *vice versa*. And the movements of this stillness do not stop. She writes: 'I search, I look, I follow, I receive. The towel changes and spins another cotton. Suddenly the slide alters speed and trajectory.'[52] *La serviette vire*. It turns. It veers.

*

Like Hythe in Bowen's descriptions, Seaford is a town strangely out of time. It seems to be suspended but you cannot say whether in memory or mere oblivion. It is only ten miles or so east of Brighton, yet its impressively long shingle beach is, by comparison, quite deserted. The promenade leads past the most westerly of all the Martello towers in Kent and Sussex, up to that most impressive of 'jutting heights' (to recall Bowen's phrase), the great grassy, chalk-faced promontory known as Seaford Head. The promenade is lined with commemorative benches bearing examples of prosopopeia, voices-to-or-from-beyond-the-grave: 'In Loving Memory of David Milne, 7.2.1937 – 9.9.1993. "Finished With Engines"'; 'In Memory of Walter Clapham, 7.10.1916 – 24.2.2005. Writer and Bomber Command Veteran'; 'Mausi's Special Grandstand Seaside Seat. Rest Awhile to View Her Much Loved Sunset and Moonrise'; and so on. It brings to mind Paul de Man's contention, in 'The Rhetoric of Temporality', that 'Wordsworth is one of the few poets who can write proleptically about their own death and speak, as it were, from beyond their own graves.'[53] This has always struck me as one of de Man's more maverick remarks, as if there were a Top Twenty prosopopeia chart, with Wordsworth up there, near the top, week after week, year after year. The epitaphic voice or ghost of prosopopeia may be, as de Man suggests, the governing trope of autobiography, but it also haunts all so-called living speech.[54]

The desire for this fiction is never going to end, but its most incisive articulations, analyses and trajectories in recent decades have been part of the literary turn, in other words the opening up of new possibilities, a new vocabulary and new ways of construing survival, future memory or what Mark Currie calls the 'performative prolepsis [that] produces the future in the act of envisaging it', the effects of living backwards (in Lewis Carroll's phrase) and living on (in Derrida's) – above all, perhaps, in the light of a new appreciation of the ghostliness of fiction, the spectral virtualities of literature in which our culture and society, law and institutions are inscribed.[55] The literary turn is about a new sensitivity to the ghostliness of literature, both in the experience of reading a novel or a poem, say, and in the fabric of apparently non-literary experience: law, technology, witnessing, the street, the environment. This formidable generalization of what might be called the ghost powers of literature is at the same time also singular. For the general is haunted by the singular, and *vice versa*; and another name for a singularity would be a veerer.

How readily a *vice versa* is reckoned as a symmetry, a neat and tidy turnaround. To think the veering in *vice versa*, its versatilities: that way lies the jouissance of deconstructive desire.[56] As Hélène Cixous puts it: 'I adore miswanderings. Versatility is life and vice-versa-tility.'[57] Seaford appears not to have any well-known former inhabitants: there are none of those blue plaques that are the customary if absurd signposts of 'where ghosts live'. While other English towns go out of their way to commemorate (including Eastbourne, with its tribute to Lewis Carroll who spent many summer holidays there, and Hythe, with its charming, slightly incongruous-looking plaque on the wall of Bowen's semi), Seaford seems intent on concealing all its literary historical richness as thoroughly as possible. 'F. Anstey' is the nom de plume of Thomas Anstey Guthrie (1856–1934), a man who lived and is buried in East Blatchington, once a separate village but now part of Seaford. Yesterday afternoon, wandering around the churchyard, the place so overgrown and neglected, I could not even locate his gravestone. Yet *Vice Versa*, first published in 1882, is an elegant comic novel that has inspired numerous films, from Peter Ustinov's 1948 version to more recent Hollywood remakes.[58] Among the many more specifically literary charms of *Vice Versa*, we might note its introduction into the English language of the word 'telegrafts', a playful Cockney version grafting 'telegraphs' and 'telegrams', appearing in the same year (1882) as the word 'telepathy' was invented.[59] The family cook attempts to console Dick, 'remark[ing] cheerily' as he prepares to leave home for another term at boarding school: 'Lor bless his heart, what with all these telegrafts and things, time flew so fast nowadays that they'd be having him back again before they all knew where they were!' (14).

Vice Versa is, by chance, all about the magical qualities of a stone, the Garudâ stone 'as ready as ever to awake into action at the first words which had the power to evoke it' (21). This stone enables Dick to have his father experience life from the son's perspective. Dick tells his father to look in the mirror and see what has happened to him. 'He had expected to see his own familiar portly bow-windowed presence there – but somehow, look as he would, the mirror insisted upon reflecting the figure of his son Dick' (27). The 'unspeakably delightful' (14) fantasy of being one's own father is sent whirling in reverse. Anstey's novel provokes the thought of a completely other 'telegraft' of Freudian psychoanalysis, a fiction of future memory in which everything would veer about the figure of the son in the father.[60]

*

Another scarcely visible Seaford ghost: George Meredith. His house is, literally, less than a stone's throw from where I am sitting. Who even reads him now? How to begin to respond to his extraordinary *Modern Love* (1862), the sequence of fifty sonnets that he wrote in the wake of the collapse of his marriage?[61] The poems have usually been read as a candid, searing account (without naming names) of how his wife, Mary Ellen Nicolls (the daughter of Thomas Love Peacock) fell in love with a young artist called Henry Wallis, leaving Meredith (and their young son

Arthur) in Seaford and eventually eloping with Wallis to Capri in the summer of 1857. (Mary Ellen herself would be dead by the time *Modern Love* was published.) Robert M. Cooper evokes the scene:

> In the summer of 1856 [Seaford] was a nondescript fishing village when George Meredith came there to reach a pivotal point in a personal domestic tragedy that was to find expression in *Modern Love*, that series of monodramatic poems that so shocked the Victorians.
>
> Meredith found Seaford an 'ill-conditioned sort of place with a struggling row of villas facing a muddy beach' ... At first it offered [him] compensations: the towering South Downs, grand for walking, and cheap lodgings with good food at the home of the local carpenter. But by December his despair is clear: 'I remain here as I can work better than elsewhere, though, engaged as I am, the DULNESS is something frightful, and hangs on my shoulders like Sinbad's Old Man of the Sea.'[62]

Being shipwrecked (like Sinbad, before and after he has to veer about under the weight of the Old Man of the Sea) is a recurrent motif of *Modern Love*, along with numerous other nautical images. It is about 'our old shipwrecked days' (XVI), in which the poet-speaker attempts ambiguously, despite being 'wrecked', to affirm his sense of control: 'The wind that fills my sails, / Propels; but I am helmsman' (XX). In a later sonnet we read: 'Helplessly afloat, / I know not what I do, whereto I strive ...' (XL).

Modern Love is a kind of poetic ghost novel, haunted by the shining of 'Love's corpse-light' (XVII), apparently possessed by 'the promptings of Satanic power' (XXVIII), as if written by the light of the 'dancing spectre [of] the moon' (XXXIX). It details a sense of suffering that begins with the couple (not yet separated) 'looking back through their dead black years' (I), where the world itself comes to be 'forgot' and 'Looked wicked as some old dull murder spot' (II). The first-person speaker in these poems comes to 'claim a phantom-woman in the Past' (III), in a time that no longer exists since these lovers have already 'suffered shipwreck with the ship' (IV). These fifty sonnets constitute an intricately veering work about 'Love's ghost' (VI), railing at Cupid with 'his magic whisks and twirls' (VII), the speaker picturing his lost beloved as a '[p]oor twisting worm' (VIII). He finds himself jerked about like 'the puppet of a dream' (X), haunted by 'Love's great bliss, / When the renewed for ever of a kiss / Whirls life within the shower of loosened hair!' (XIII).[63]

Love is the great veerer in Meredith's work. Is the 'tragedy' of this love 'alive or dead?' (XXXVII), asks the speaker. 'What's my drift?' (XXXI), he wonders, of all this '[s]trange love talk' (XXXIII). The lyric present of Meredith's writing is constantly dislocated by the traumatic sense of not knowing when this dead love is truly dead, by '[t]he dread that my old love may be alive' and will already have 'seized [any] nursling new love by the throat' (XL). Take sonnet XIV:

> What soul would bargain for a cure that brings
> Contempt the nobler agony to kill?
> Rather let me bear on the bitter ill,
> And strike this rusty bosom with new stings!
> It seems there is another veering fit,
> Since on a gold-haired lady's eyeballs pure,
> I looked with little prospect of a cure,
> The while her mouth's red bow loosed shafts of wit.
> Just heaven! can it be true that jealousy
> Has decked the woman thus? and does her head
> Swim somewhat for possessions forfeited?
> Madam, you teach me many things that be.
> I open an old book, and there I find,
> That 'Women still may love whom they deceive.'
> Such love I prize not, madam: by your leave,
> The game you play at is not to my mind.

Here, as elsewhere, Meredith probes the ironic and crazy ways in which jealousy can be aroused by appearances, especially when couples 'act [the] wedded lie' (XXXV). 'Hiding the skeleton' (as Sonnet XVII calls it) is 'in truth a most contagious game', in which a married couple feigning love can (in a twisted version of the song of Keats's nightingale) 'waken envy of [their] happy lot'.[64] *Modern Love* is superbly eloquent about the necessity but perhaps also the impossibility of separating love and deception. Is the veerer called love an experience of faith or truth? Who or what are you, Veerer? Sonnet XIV pivots around the marvellously compressed phrase, 'another veering fit'. The 'another' gives us to sense a prior veering (and even to suppose that veering is a sort of organizing trope for the poem as a whole), while the inversion of syntax accentuates the ambiguity in 'fit' – both an (ironically) apt or suitable veering and an attack or convulsion of veering.

Later on in the sonnet-sequence the speaker records that he is in a 'dullard fit' (XXIII) and still later, in sonnet XLIII, we encounter 'a fitting spot to dig Love's grave':

> Mark where the pressing wind shoots javelin-like,
> Its skeleton shadow on the broad-backed wave!
> Here is a fitting spot to dig Love's grave;
> Here where the ponderous breakers plunge and strike,
> And dart their hissing tongues high up the sand:
> In hearing of the ocean, and in sight
> Of those ribbed wind-streaks running into white.

Such would be 'the fitting spot', a skeletal and ghastly convulsion of locus, the very repetition of 'here' and 'where' unsettling its specificity, *here-where* ghosts live. It is perhaps difficult not to pick up the eerie assimilation, the 'crave' only half-buried in 'Love's grave'. These lines make up a ghostly apostrophe, a plea ('Mark') that recalls the Ghost of Hamlet, a vision or sounding of the sea and wind that is a singular commingling of the real and phantasmagoric. 'Mark' marks the ghostliness of the poem itself, as its waves of densely figurative and animistic language cast up the fleeting apparitions of other poems, such as Coleridge's 'Ancient Mariner' (the shooting movement of the spectre ship, 'the ribbed sea-sand', 'the water-snakes' rearing in 'the shadow of the ship'), and the monstrous 'hissing' of tongues in Milton's *Paradise Lost*.[65]

*

Death in the sea at Seaford: that was evidently also one of Virginia Woolf's fantasies, like a weird prefiguring of her suicide in the river that meets the sea just nearby, at Newhaven. On 26 October 1937 she writes to Ethel Smyth:

> We were on the front at Seaford during the gale ... The waves broke over the car. Vast spouts of white water all along the coast. Why does a smash of water satisfy all one's religious aspirations? And its [*sic*] all I can do not to throw myself in – a queer animal rhapsody, restrained by L[eonard].[66]

*

'In hearing of the ocean': ghostly in its ambiguity (while hearing the ocean, within hearing distance of the sea, but also within the ocean's range of hearing), that is one of the things that makes where I write a sea house. Last night, for example, *the last night* (I told myself) before I finish writing this essay, it is driving me mad, I lay awake, sleeping only fitfully, in hearing of the sea. I had tried to end the day by reading, as I have been doing last thing every night for a few days now, a story by Walter de la Mare. Lying awake, I found myself pondering his remarkable explorations of voice and sound, his fascination with the idea of being possessed or driven by 'the ghost of a voice', his dreamy but persistent preoccupation with the ghostliness of English words – with the notion, for example, of 'an English slurred, broken, and unintelligible ... yet clear as bell, haunting, penetrating, pining as voice of nix or siren'.[67] His stories evince, with a disquieting regularity and insistence, an explicit and passionate concern with veerings in hearing, with what 'faintly swirl[s] in the labyrinth of [the] ear', with the way that a few 'hollow, challenging, half-stifled words [can ring] out oddly in the silence', with the sense that 'Nothing is more treacherous . . . than the ear. It magnifies, distorts, and may even invent.'[68]

*

Step off a cliff –

What is this thing I am writing anyway? Is it a piece of autobiography, literary criticism, spectral topography, eco-writing, cultural theory?

*

The picturesque terrace where the author of *Modern Love* lived at least preserves a visible vestige of this detail of its history: it is called Meredith House. But there is nothing, neither plaque nor any sort of legible sign to let you know that Raymond Williams (1921–88) lived in Seaford for several years, starting in 1946. In the basement of Seaford town library, which is due shortly to be demolished, he had a kind of epiphany. He describes it as a sort of *déjà vu*, 'a shock of recognition'. It is when he looks up the word *culture* in the OED. This was the inspiration for his classic work of 1958, *Culture and Society*. He reports this powerfully shaping moment in his Introduction to *Keywords: A Vocabulary of Culture and Society* (1976): 'Then one day in the basement of the Public Library at Seaford, where we had gone to live, I looked up *culture*, almost casually . . .'.[69] In a sense, it might be said, cultural studies and cultural materialism begin in Seaford: that is a topocriticopoeticospectrographical inheritance to reckon with. And yesterday afternoon, *en route* to East Blatchington churchyard, when I stopped off to visit this shabby but still endearing little library basement, to find the thirteen-volume edition of the OED in which Williams had his revelation long since gone, I had a strange creeping realization of my own. In the absence of the dictionary I found myself flicking through a worn old paperback called *Bygone Seaford* and coming upon a photograph of our sea house, as it was perhaps fifty or so years ago, when Williams was living in the town, and suddenly, in an absolutely unforeseen fashion, I glimpsed a *semblable*.

Thoroughly improbable, the feeling nonetheless stole over me that Williams's project has haunted my own, without my noticing it, for at least thirty years. I never possessed a copy of *Keywords* before coming to live in Seaford. I recall reading a library copy, in rather desultory fashion, when I was a student in Oxford around 1977. I remember thinking it inventive and informative, admirable yet peculiarly dry. I now perceive with a certain dismay, a kind of revulsion at my own ignorance, that in the intervening years I have been slowly and blindly working on another version of the same project, another 'keywords', doubtless a scattered and haphazard version, not bound within the covers of a single book, but a sort of ghostly vocabulary of keywords gathering itself over the years. How many times, without the slightest conscious thought of Raymond Williams's work, have I found myself writing essays or even books organized around a single word or phrase, and around the capacity it has for locking and unlocking? So here, just one more keyword: 'veering'. (See also: 'veerer'.)

It is perhaps fitting to recall what Williams writes in *Keywords* apropos the focus of his Seaford revelation. The entry for 'Culture' is characteristically direct, meticulous and discriminating.[70] He starts with a sentence that makes me smile: '*Culture* is one of the two or three most complicated words in the English language' (87). The assertion has affinities with Paul de Man's prosopopeia chart. Up at the top with 'culture', it turns out, is 'nature'. '*Nature*', Williams remarks, is 'perhaps the most complex word in the language' (219). It is a question, of course, not of any old words: *Keywords* is not a dictionary, as he stresses in his Introduction, it is Williams's 'vocabulary', *his* strategic but also subjective selection of particular 'words . . . which involve ideas and values' (17). A bit oddly perhaps, the priority accorded to 'nature' and 'culture' (the 'most complex' or 'most complicated' words in the English language) is not an occasion for critical reflection as such. ('Culture' is cross-referenced at the end of the entry on 'Nature', though not *vice versa*.) More specifically, there is no reflection on the fact that this couple is *a couple*.

In the entry for 'Culture', Williams sketches the role and significance of the work of Johann Gottfried von Herder, especially his unfinished *Ideas on the Philosophy of the History of Mankind* (1784–91): 'nothing is more indeterminate than this word [*Cultur*]', Herder remarks, 'and nothing more deceptive than its application to all nations and periods' (quoted in Williams: 89). It is to Herder, Williams suggests, that we owe the 'decisive innovation' of 'speak[ing] of "cultures" in the plural: the specific and variable cultures of different nations and periods, but also the specific and variable cultures of social and economic groups within a nation' (89). Thus Williams comes to stress the development of an opposition, especially in the Romantic period and through the nineteenth century, between 'culture' and the more 'orthodox and dominant "*civilization*"' (89). He goes on:

> It was first used to emphasize national and traditional cultures, including the new concept of *folk-culture* . . . It was later used to attack what was seen as the '*mechanical*' character of the new civilization then emerging: both for its abstract rationalism and for the 'inhumanity' of current industrial development. It was used to distinguish between 'human' and 'material' development.

Politically, as so often in this period, it veered between radicalism and reaction and very often, in the confusion of major social change, fused elements of both. (It should also be noted, though it adds to the real complication, that the same kind of distinction, especially between 'material' and 'spiritual' development, was made by von Humboldt and others, until as late as 1900, with a reversal of the terms, *culture* being material and *civilization* spiritual. In general, however, the opposite distinction was dominant.) (89–90)

How ever tacitly, this passage sharply brings out Williams's commitment to dialectical thinking, in particular vis-à-vis what he calls (under the entry for 'Dialectic') 'the interactions of contradictory or opposite forces' (108). Everything is apparently susceptible to the organizational logic of oppositions and hierarchies (culture vs civilization, human vs material, radical vs reactionary, material vs spiritual, and so on). And yet, at the same time, sense veers. No *culture* without veering: Williams himself seems to say as much. But what is hereby broached, perhaps, is a notion of veering that cannot be held within any kind of dialectical figuration.

The account of 'culture' is anthropocentric through and through. The various 'contradictory or opposite forces' Williams evokes inevitably bring to mind the other major opposition noted a few moments ago, between 'culture' and 'nature' (the latter succinctly described elsewhere in *Keywords* as 'what man has not made' (223)). It might be helpful, in this context, to draw on Timothy Clark's recent work on literature and the environment. Clark argues that it no longer makes sense, if indeed it ever did, 'to take the opposition of "culture" on one side and "nature" on the other and to argue about the point or line of their differentiation': rather, it is necessary 'to question the coherence of making any such distinction in the first place, and the anthropocentric fantasy that sustains it.'[71] Recent ecocritical writing has made clear the need for a deconstructive understanding of 'culture'. As Clark summarizes it:

culture itself has a context – the biosphere, air, water, plant and animal life – and more radical ecocritical work tends to be, so to speak, *meta-contextual*, opening on issues that may involve perspectives or questions for which given cultural conceptions seem limited.[72]

But it is not as if Raymond Williams did not have a sense of what was coming. This is evident in *Keywords* itself, in particular in the light of the inclusion – in the 1983 revised edition – of an entry for 'Ecology'. Regarding ecopolitics, ecology groups and parties, and so on, he writes with pithy prescience: 'Economics, politics and social theory are reinterpreted by this important and still growing tendency' (111).

Who is Raymond Williams? Who will he have been? More of a veerer, I would venture to conclude, than may at present generally be supposed.

*

Picture walking up Seaford Head. Despite its spectacular beauty and comparative isolation, there is no point pretending it is simply 'nature' up there, or that even the culturally packaged section called Seaford Head Nature Reserve is not gravely imperilled by the most local as well as world-wide environmental crisis. Picture it: a man makes his way to the end of the promenade, then wanders up above the cliff with its remarkable kittiwake colony, with the manicured sward of Seaford Head Golf Club on the left, clambering ever higher, accompanied by veering gulls and crows and the ceaseless sounding expanses of the sea. Looking back westward from up there on the jutting heights, he notes in the distance the hazy industry of Shoreham and Portslade, and the higher buildings of Brighton (the first and only Green Party-controlled constituency in the UK). Closer to hand, just three miles or so along the coast, he observes the port of Newhaven with its brand-new temple of destruction, the huge incinerator commissioned by the Conservative-controlled East Sussex County Council, built to deal with 210,000 tonnes of waste per annum (with an estimated 125 lorryloads arriving every day), filling the atmosphere with dioxins, carcinogens and other toxins. Located in the heart of Newhaven, one of the most socially and economically deprived little towns in England, and immediately adjacent to an area of Outstanding Natural Beauty (the South Downs), the Hades Project (as this man likes to call it) will be in operation from August 2011 onwards. He walks a further hundred feet east along the grassy cliff path and this entire swathe of coastline disappears, out of sight if not of mind or body. The astonishing beauty of the Seven Sisters rears into view. Sheep graze in the fields nearest to the cliff edge. Inland the rolling South Downs stretch to the horizon. There are rabbits everywhere, and many different species of butterfly and moth. The air is ringing with the song of skylarks. He walks, carefully, to the very edge and there he sits, feet over the edge, dangling modifiers.

Williams would often come up here. Southdown Road, where he lived in the spacious ground-floor flat of a house called Betton, leads directly up onto the lower part of the Head.[73]

He changes the name 'Seaford' to 'Brenton'. As yet unpublished, Williams's novel *Adamson* begins with a section called simply 'Event', which describes a man walking up here.

For he stepped abruptly from his regular walk, and jumped, feet together, to test with his heels the hardness of the frozen verge. And the turf yielded slightly, so that he saw, turning away, the faint impression of his strike. And he stepped again to the road, recovering his pace.

The white gradient rose firmly towards the Head. The land which it traversed was suddenly free of detail, as if it were wholly contour. It rose before him as a sudden statement of shape, a finely drawn articulation of down and ridge and combe, edged by the tiny nesses of the cliff. The mild light of the coronal January sun, falling eastward along olive slopes of grassland and under dark lively bushes and into brown turned earth, modulated each pitch and re-entrant, touching the land and briefly scoring its structure. The hachured lines of the ridges leaped into sharp relief, black against the warm bronze light which moved over scarp and hollow. Within each fold the grass seemed alive with light, and the earth itself seemed warm and living, a single presence that moved against and dominated the pale sky and the mild gray-blue sea.[74]

Williams's attention to details of landscape and light comports with the sort of 'intense observation of people and objects' he writes about in what is perhaps his finest critical book, *The Country and the City* (1973).[75] The novel, then, begins with a veering – the peculiarity of the 'For' that starts it off, the 'stepping abruptly' away – and the simulacrum of a cliff jump, on the 'frozen verge'. Adamson (as his name transpires to be) seems compulsively drawn to the cliff edge: he 'strained forward to the very edge of the cliff, looking down at the rocks and the breaking waves three hundred feet below' (2).

He walks on and discovers there is someone else up there, 'sitting at the edge' (8), evidently poised to throw himself off. Cautiously he approaches and finally calls out 'One moment! Wait!' (9). This seems, however, to achieve only the opposite effect:

> But at the first words, the man had started violently, and in the same movement, with a single loud cry, was gone over the edge of the cliff. The line of the edge sprang out suddenly, and Adamson shouted and ran forward. At the edge from which the man had fallen, he threw himself prone, looking down through the darkness towards the sea. (9)

Shortly after this traumatic witnessing, he finds the man's car and other former belongings. Then, in what is no doubt the strangest shift, he assumes the dead man's identity.

Raymond Williams is dead, but the pictured man cannot help experiencing this 'just visiting'. With Williams he shares a fascination for what is vertiginous in writing and where ghosts live, for literature as suicidal substitutability. All these words and silences, tingling in his ears. It has his head spinning.

Notes

1. Norman MacCaig, 'By the Three Lochans', in *The Many Days: Selected Poems of Norman MacCaig*, ed. Roderick Watson (Edinburgh: Polygon, 2010), p. 12.
2. Jacques Derrida, '*Fors*: The Anglish Words of Nicolas Abraham and Maria Torok', trans. Barbara Johnson, in Nicolas Abraham and Maria Torok, *The Wolf Man's Magic Word: A Cryptonymy*, trans. Nicholas Rand (Minneapolis: University of Minnesota Press, 1986), p. xxxv.
3. I would like to record my thanks here to Graham Allen and David Coughlan for inviting me to speak on the subject of 'where ghosts live', at a conference at the University of Cork, in September 2009. This essay is a revised and expanded version of a lecture initially presented on that occasion.
4. See 'Music', in Walter de la Mare, *Short Stories 1927–1956*, ed. Giles de la Mare (London: Giles de la Mare Publishers, 2001), p. 371.
5. See *The Collected Poems of Wallace Stevens* (New York: Alfred A. Knopf, 1954), p. 64.
6. See 'Large Red Man Reading' in *The Collected Poems of Wallace Stevens*, pp. 423–4. Further citations of the poem are from this edition.
7. See Mark Currie, *About Time: Narrative, Fiction and the Philosophy of Time* (Edinburgh: Edinburgh University Press, 2007), p. 5.
8. So says someone called Clancy Yeats, in Russell Hoban's *Angelica Lost and Found* (London: Bloomsbury, 2010), p. 83.
9. Elizabeth Bowen, *A World of Love* (Harmondsworth: Penguin, 1983), p. 37.
10. Michel de Montaigne, 'To philosophize is to learn how to die', in *The Complete Essays*, trans. M. A. Screech (London: Penguin, 2003), p. 98.
11. *The Lewis Carroll Handbook*, Being a New Version of *A Handbook of the Literature of the Rev. C. L. Dodgson* by Sidney Herbert Williams and Falconer Madan, rev. and augmented Roger Lancelyn Green, further rev. Denis Crutch (Folkestone: Dawson – Archon Books, 1979).
12. Lewis Carroll, *Alice in Wonderland*, 2nd edn, ed. Donald J. Gray (New York: Norton, 1992), p. 55.
13. See Carroll, *Alice in Wonderland*, p. 55, n.4.
14. See Denis Crutch, 'The Hunting of the Snark: A Study in Fits and Starts', *Jabberwocky*, Journal of the Lewis Carroll Society, 5 (Winter 1976): 103–9.
15. See 'The Raven', in *Complete Stories and Poems of Edgar Allan Poe* (New York: Doubleday, 1966), pp. 754–6. What transpires to be a raven 'croaking "Nevermore"' is initially envisaged in vaguer or more general terms as someone just visiting, turning up, tapping, in a nodding scene of hypnopoetic reading:

> Once upon a midnight dreary, while I pondered, weak and weary,
> Over many a quaint and curious volume of forgotten lore –
> While I nodded, nearly napping, suddenly there came a tapping,
> As of some one gently rapping, rapping at my chamber door.
> ''T is some visitor,' I muttered, 'tapping at my chamber door –
> Only this and nothing more.'

16. See Walter de la Mare, 'The Lost Track', in *Short Stories 1895–1926*, ed. Giles de la Mare (London: Giles de la Mare Publishers, 1996), where the narrator speaks, apropos Henry James, of 'the environment of his style' (384).

17. Jacques Derrida, *Spectres of Marx: The State of the Debt, the Work of Mourning, and the New International*, trans. Peggy Kamuf (London: Routledge, 1994), p. 139.

18. See 'Pictures and Conversations' (first published in 1975), in *The Mulberry Tree: Writings of Elizabeth Bowen*, ed. Hermione Lee (London: Virago, 1986), pp. 265–98. Further page references appear parenthetically in the main body of the text.

19. Carroll, *Alice in Wonderland*, p. 7.

20. On the etymology of 'converse', as a verb, the *OED* includes the Latin '*conversārī* lit. to turn oneself about, to move to and fro, pass one's life, dwell, abide, live somewhere, keep company with.'

21. On 'The Bend Back' (1950), see Bowen, *The Mulberry Tree*, pp. 54–60. The 'clutch' is in *A World of Love*, p. 77.

22. Elizabeth Bowen, *Bowen's Court* (New York: Alfred A. Knopf, 1942), pp. 423–4.

23. On the peculiarity of 'ghosthood' as 'being in two places at the same time' in Bowen, see Neil Corcoran's perceptive reading of 'The Back Drawing-Room', in *Elizabeth Bowen: The Enforced Return* (Oxford: Oxford University Press, 2004), pp. 33–4.

24. It is this same tricky, slow and twisting road that passes (between Seaford and Hythe) through Rye, where Henry James lived from 1897. Rye too, of course, is a cinque port.

25. See Foreword to *The Cinque Ports* (1952), by Ronald and Frank Jessup, in *People, Places, Things: Essays by Elizabeth Bowen*, ed. Allan Hepburn (Edinburgh: Edinburgh University Press, 2008), pp. 59–61: here, p. 59. Further page references to this foreword appear parenthetically in the main body of the text.

26. On 'sheer kink', see Andrew Bennett and Nicholas Royle, *Elizabeth Bowen and the Dissolution of the Novel* (Basingstoke: Macmillan, 1995), pp. 82–103. On 'stony clarity' and 'knitting', in particular, see pp. 84 and 86–8.

27. Elizabeth Bowen, *The House in Paris* (1935) (Harmondsworth: Penguin, 1976), p. 19. Further page references to Bowen's novel are given parenthetically in the main body of the text.

28. For another instance of Bowen's sensitivity to the veering effects of an absent or present comma, see *Eva Trout* (1968) (Harmondsworth: Penguin, 1982): '"Charles the First walked and talked half an hour after his head was cut off." You put in a comma somewhere, then that made sense but was not so interesting' (193). Cf. also 'Happy Autumn Fields' (1944), in *The Collected Stories of Elizabeth Bowen* (Harmondsworth: Penguin, 1983), p. 681.

29. See A. S. Byatt, 'Introduction', in Elizabeth Bowen, *The House in Paris* (Harmondsworth: Penguin, 1976), p. 7.

30. I borrow this formulation from Jacques Derrida who says in an essay about deconstruction in the United States, entitled 'The Time is Out of Joint',

'*deconstruction is just visiting*'. See 'The Time is Out of Joint', trans. Peggy Kamuf, in *Deconstruction is/in America: A New Sense of the Political*, ed. Anselm Haverkamp (New York: New York University Press, 1995), p. 29.

31. See William Shakespeare, *Hamlet*, ed. Philip Edwards, updated edn (Cambridge: Cambridge University Press, 2003), III, iv, 109; Emily Brontë, *Wuthering Heights*, ed. William M. Sale and Richard J. Dunn (New York: Norton, 1990), p. 3; Thomas Hardy, *The Complete Poems*, ed. James Gibson (London: Macmillan, 1976), p. 347; Elizabeth Bowen, 'The Visitor' in *The Collected Stories*, pp. 124–35.

32. Roland Barthes, 'From Work to Text', in *Textual Strategies: Perspectives in Post-Structuralist Criticism*, ed. Josue V. Harari (London: Methuen, 1979), p. 78.

33. See Bowen, *The Mulberry Tree*, pp. 39 and 283.

34. For 'dislocations' in 'Pictures and Conversations', see p. 283, and on 'dislocation' as 'the modern uneasiness', see 'English Fiction at Mid-Century' (1953), in *People, Places, Things*, p. 322. With such 'dislocation' comes a new thinking of topology, home and environment. By a nice coincidence Timothy Morton proposes 'dislocation, dislocation, dislocation' as the 'slogan' of what he calls 'the ecological thought'. See Morton, *The Ecological Thought* (Cambridge, MA: Harvard University Press, 2010), p. 28.

35. Theodor W. Adorno, 'On Lyric Poetry and Society', in *Notes to Literature*, vol. 1, trans. Shierry Weber Nicholsen (New York: Columbia University Press, 1991), p. 48. Adorno here is writing about Eduard Mörike's poem, 'On a Walking Tour'.

36. She actually 'locates' this statement in her travel memoir of Rome: see Elizabeth Bowen, *A Time in Rome* (1959) (Harmondsworth: Penguin, 1989), p. 19.

37. See Edgar Allan Poe, 'The Imp of the Perverse', in *Tales and Sketches, Volume 2: 1843–1849*, ed. Thomas Ollive Mabbott (Chicago: University of Illinois Press, 2000), pp. 1219–26: here, p. 1226.

38. For a link between 'wear' and 'veer', see *OED*, 'wear', v. 2, sense 1, intransitive: 'Of a ship: To come round on the other tack by turning the head away from the wind. Often with *round*. Opposed to *tack*.' The dictionary notes that it is 'of obscure origin' even if (or even though) 'in sense it coincides with *veer* [i.e. 'veer', v. 2, sense 2]'. We shall return to the question of such *whereabouts* later in this book, in the context of 'wheer' in D. H. Lawrence (in Chapter 10 'Veering with Lawrence').

39. See Henry James, *The Turn of the Screw and Other Stories*, with an Introduction by S. Gorley Putt (Harmondsworth: Penguin, 1969), p. 121, and Lewis Carroll, *Alice in Wonderland*, p. 145 (emphasis added).

40. See Bowen, 'The Bend Back', p. 56.

41. This is in 1949, in her Preface to the second edition of her first collection of short stories, *Encounters* (1923). See Bowen, *The Mulberry Tree*, p. 122.

42. Elizabeth Bowen, 'Attractive Modern Homes', in *The Collected Stories*, pp. 521–8. Further page references are given parenthetically in the main body of the text.

43. Pinter's interest in Bowen's writing is of course manifest from his screen-play, *The Heat of the Day*, adapted from the novel by Elizabeth Bowen (London: Faber, 1989). Cf. also Neil Corcoran, who sees 'Pinter discovering Beckett in Bowen', in *Elizabeth Bowen: The Enforced Return*, p. 200.
44. See Bowen, 'Notes on Writing a Novel', in *The Mulberry Tree*, p. 41.
45. See Kirby Dick and Amy Ziering Kofman (Directors), *Derrida: Screenplay and Essays on the Film* (Manchester: Manchester University Press, 2005), p. 97. Derrida had described himself as a filmic 'ghost' already in the earlier film *Ghost Dance* (directed by Ken McMullen. UK: Cornerstone Media, 1983).
46. Nicholas Royle, 'Déjà Vu', in Martin McQuillan, Graeme Macdonald, Robin Purves and Stephen Thomson (eds), *Post-Theory: New Directions in Criticism* (Edinburgh: Edinburgh University Press, 1999), pp. 3–20: here, p. 15. This essay later appeared, in slightly modified form, in *The Uncanny* (Manchester: Manchester University Press, 2003), pp. 172–86.
47. See Sigmund Freud, 'On Narcissism: An Introduction' (1914), in *SE* 14: 90–1, and 'The Uncanny' (1919), in *SE* 17: 235, where Freud remarks that 'primary narcissism' (the 'unbounded self-love [which] dominates the mind of the child and of primitive man') is a 'stage' that is in due course 'surmounted'. Cf. 'An Outline of Psychoanalysis' (1938) in which he comments that primary narcissism 'lasts till the ego begins to cathect the ideas of objects with libido, to transform narcissistic libido into object-libido' (*SE* 23: 150).
48. Freud writes: 'The primary narcissism of children *which we have assumed* and which forms one of the postulates of our theories of the libido, is less easy to grasp by direct observation than to confirm *by inference from elsewhere*. If we look at the attitude of affectionate parents towards their children, we have to recognize that it is *a revival and reproduction* of their own narcissism, which they have long since abandoned.' See 'On Narcissism', *SE* 14: 90–1 (emphases added).
49. *Vera's Room: The Art of Maria Chevska* (London: Black Dog Publishing, 2005). Further page references appear parenthetically in the main body of the text.
50. The Slought Foundation project website for the exhibition in London in October 2005 informs us: 'The installation is of varying sizes and components and has been installed according to a series of prescriptive procedures determined by the artist and enacted by the curators. It has both "real" objects in it—functional furniture, for example—and a number of "imaginary" sculptures made up of both found and made objects. The objects, simple forms made from cloth or paper rendered solid in kaolin, look familiar and functional; however, they are not quite the same as the articles they resemble. This uncanny and abstract quality is given further tension in the installation due to the intimate setting and a sense of transient domesticity. This in turn suggests the fragile and nomadic existence of a stranger who achieves visibility on account of his or her sheer resourcefulness.' See http://slought.org/press/11300/.
51. There is no pagination for the section of the book given over to Cixous's notebook, which appears in facsimile handwriting (in French), as well as in an English translation by Susan Sellers.

52. Translation slightly modified. The original French reads: '*Je cherche, je regarde, je suis, je reçois. La serviette vire et file un autre coton. Soudain l'affalement se retourne en vitesse et trajectoire*' (79).

53. Paul de Man, *Blindness and Insight: Essays in the Rhetoric of Contemporary Criticism*, 2nd edn (London: Methuen, 1983), p. 225.

54. On prosopopeia as the 'dominant figure of . . . epitaphic or autobiographical discourse', see de Man, 'Autobiography as De-Facement', in *The Rhetoric of Romanticism* (New York: Columbia University Press, 1984), p. 77. For an elaboration of the argument that prosopopeia entails 'a fictive voice' that nonetheless 'already haunts any said real or present voice', see Jacques Derrida, *Mémoires: for Paul de Man*, trans. Cecile Lindsay, Jonathan Culler and Eduardo Cadava (New York: Columbia University Press, 1986), p. 26.

55. On performative prolepsis, see Currie, *About Time*, p. 44.

56. For a rich exploration of the figure of *vice versa*, especially apropos the eroticism of 'crossing over', see Marjorie Garber, *Vice Versa: Bisexuality and the Eroticism of Everyday Life* (New York: Simon Schuster, 2000). Garber's book offers a provoking range of turns on the sort of position adumbrated in its first epigraph, drawn from Freud's 'Analysis Terminable and Interminable' (1937): 'A man's heterosexuality will not put up with any homosexuality, and *vice versa*' (*SE* 23: 244).

57. Hélène Cixous, 'The Book as One of Its Own Characters', trans. Catherine Porter, in *Volleys of Humanity: Essays 1972–2009*, ed. Eric Prenowitz (Edinburgh: Edinburgh University Press, 2011), p. 134.

58. F. Anstey, *Vice Versa* (London: Puffin Books, 1981). Further page references are given parenthetically in the main body of the text.

59. On the invention of 'telepathy' and its significance for thinking about literature and literary theory, permit me to refer to *Telepathy and Literature: Essays on the Reading Mind* (Oxford: Blackwell, 1990); see also Roger Luckhurst's cultural history, *The Invention of Telepathy, 1870–1901* (Oxford: Oxford University Press, 2002).

60. We might, to begin with, go back to the sheer oddity of that passage in *The Interpretation of Dreams* in which Freud discusses Shakespeare's *Hamlet* in terms of its having 'its roots in the same soil as *Oedipus Rex*' (*SE* 4: 264). The shiftings, subtractions and accretions of later footnotes (including the 'mad' note of 1930 in which he dismisses the very idea that Shakespeare wrote the play in question), together with the implications of his deferred realization of the role of his own father's death in the writing of the book (acknowledged only in the 1908 Preface to the 2nd edn: see *SE* 4: xxvi) make this one of the most haunted passages in all Freud's writings. At the heart of this, perhaps, is the still unthought potential of that moment in which Freud notes (but does not elaborate on) the idea that *Hamlet* might be not only or not so much about 'the death of Shakespeare's father', as about the death of a son: 'It is known, too, that Shakespeare's own son who died at an early age bore the name of "Hamnet", which is identical with "Hamlet"' (265–6). Glimpsed here, perhaps, is the trembling strangeness of a *vice versa* of *Hamlet*, of all the thinking of an 'Oedipus complex', of the logic of cause and effect, mourning, temporality and anachronicity of the spectre: a play about the father's relation to the son.

61. George Meredith, *Modern Love* (n.p.: Kessinger Publishing, n.d.). All quotations are from this edition.

62. Robert M. Cooper, *The Literary Guide and Companion to Southern England*, rev. edn (Athens, OH: Ohio University Press, 1998), p. 126.

63. Elsewhere in *Modern Love*, the kiss is specifically figured as a whirler no more: 'A kiss is but a kiss now! and no wave / Of a great flood that whirls me to the sea' (XXIX).

64. The seeming ease of Meredith's lovers, who are 'enamoured of an acting nought can tire' (XVII), stands in stark ironic contrast to Keats's nightingale: ''Tis not through envy of thy happy lot, / But being too happy in thine happiness, – / That thou . . . / . . . / . . . / Singest of summer in full-throated ease.' See 'Ode to a Nightingale' in *The Poems of John Keats*, ed. Jack Stillinger (London: Heinemann, 1978), p. 369.

65. See 'The Rime of the Ancient Mariner', in Samuel Taylor Coleridge, *Poems*, ed. John Beer (London: Dent, 1974), ll. 202, 227 and 272ff; and the 'dismal universal hiss' of serpentine metamorphosis in *Paradise Lost*, ed. Gordon Teskey (New York: Norton, 2005), Book X, ll. 508ff.

66. *The Letters of Virginia Woolf*, vol. 6 (1936–41), ed. Nigel Nicolson and Joanna Trautmann (New York: Harcourt Brace Jovanovich, 1980), p. 185.

67. See Walter de la Mare, 'Pretty Poll' and 'The Creatures', in *Short Stories 1895–1926*, pp. 334 and 155 respectively.

68. See Walter de la Mare 'Strangers and Pilgrims' and 'All Hallows', in *Short Stories 1895–1926*, pp. 198 and 355.

69. See Raymond Williams, *Keywords: A Vocabulary of Culture and Society*, rev. and expanded edn (1983; London: Fontana, 1988), p. 13.

70. See Williams, 'Culture' in *Keywords*, pp. 87–93. Further page references appear parenthetically in the main body of the text.

71. See Timothy Clark, 'Climate and Catastrophe – A Missed Opening?', in Sean Gaston and Ian Maclachlan (eds), *Reading Derrida's* Of Grammatology (London: Continuum, 2011), p. 165.

72. Timothy Clark, *The Cambridge Introduction to Literature and the Environment* (Cambridge: Cambridge University Press, 2011), p. 4.

73. For a fuller account of Williams's life in Seaford, see Dai Smith's *Raymond Williams: A Warrior's Tale* (Cardigan: Parthian, 2008). Smith describes Betton, Southdown Road, as 'overlooking the gorse-covered Downs running down to the sea with, in the distance, the white-chalked Seven Sisters cliffs' (222). In fact the Seven Sisters are not visible from here: it is necessary to climb up Seaford Head before coming into sight of them.

74. Raymond Williams, *Adamson*, at Swansea University Library, ts, p. 1. Further page references are to this typescript. I am grateful to colleagues at Swansea, especially Rob Penhallurick and Daniel Williams, as well as Katrina Legg and Elaine Gale in the Library, for their kindness and assistance in enabling me to consult this fascinating text. Dai Smith also provides some valuable commentary on the novel in his *Raymond Williams: A Warrior's Tale*, pp. 318–22.

75. See Raymond Williams, *The Country and the City* (New York: Oxford University Press, 1975). Of Georgian poets and writers he acutely notes: 'Intense observation of people and objects dissolves, without transition,

into forms of fancy which in the end, indeed, are more historically significant' (255). As Williams makes clear at the outset, *The Country and the City* is a work of 'social, literary and intellectual history' that is also autobiographical – the product of a 'personal pressure and commitment' (3).

Chapter 9

Veerer: Reading Melville's 'Bartleby'

'Nobody should ever forget the debt of eternal gratitude they owe to whoever it was first got them to read Herman Melville properly.' (John Burnside)[1]

The aircraft veered into position, halting. (Don DeLillo)[2]

Veering is my subject. My subject is veering. I would like to leave these sentences side by side here, in all their undisambiguated simplicity, as a kind of Tweedledum and Tweedledee entrance-way to a reading of Melville's 'Bartleby'. I propose to begin with a recapitulation of what I have been trying to explore in this book. There is something a bit odd, even perverse about the gesture of recapitulating. As Rachel Bowlby has noted, recapitulation has 'the peculiar quality of being an ending that includes a beginning. To recapitulate is to go over the main points of an argument, at the end, but from the start.'[3] In short, there is something veerable about a recap. To veer – just to recap – is to change direction, to turn aside or away, to alter course; veerable is 'tending to veer; changeable' (*OED*, 'veerable', adj.). It is perfectly possible for a person to veer, but just as likely there is a vehicle of some sort involved: a ship veers round, a car veers off the road. Non-human animals veer. Veering is not necessarily human. It points, we might say, in significantly non-anthropocentric directions. Often the word is connected with the wind: you have perhaps had the pleasure of listening to the UK shipping forecast, learning that the wind is north 5 or 6 veering northeast 7 to 8 increasing, the sea state moderate to rough, the weather squally, the visibility poor to very poor, and of feeling comforted by the sense that you are not out there, or, conversely, and perhaps perversely, by imagining that you *are* out there, braving the elements, in Coleridge's words, 'Alone, alone, all, all alone, / Alone on a wide wide sea!'[4] When we speak of a person veering, there is a kind of ambiguity: veering can be something that happens in a controlled way, or something that involves a loss, often a sudden and unexpected loss of control. This ambiguity may amount to something akin to the 'Is this pint-glass of beer half full or half empty?' Some people may be inclined to think about veering in an orderly and controlled manner, others in a riskier, less agent-centred way. My aim is to reckon with both of these inclinations, but also to try to respond to the ambiguity itself, in other words to consider the possibilities of 'veering' as a sort of primal word, in Freud's sense, a word of antithetical meaning, that can mean its own opposite.[5] It is neither one thing nor the other, or it might be both. Put differently, 'veering' is susceptible to perverse inclinations: there is a sort of veering within 'veering' that demands critical reflection. And, at the same time, this thing called 'veering' is decidedly slippery and rather ghostly.

As I have been attempting to make clear, thinking about *veering* has a certain revolutionary potential. It might indeed help generate new inflections of the revolutionary. *Veering* is a little word, but an investigation of its strange nature brings into consideration a rich freight of other words, including the many English words that entail turning, and perhaps especially those that relate to the Latin *vertere*, such as 'version', 'verse', *'vice versa'*, 'vertigo', 'versatility', 'converse', 'conversion', 'perverse', 'averse', 'reverse', 'inversion', 'diversion' and 'subversion'. Some of these words, like 'conversely' and 'perversely', you may have noticed, have already shown up in the preceding paragraph. Others, such as 'inclination' and indeed 'ambiguous', are also drifting about here in a not entirely innocent or insignificant way. How should one sense the *leaning* in 'inclination' (the Latin verb *inclinare* means to lean inwards or outwards) or the uneasiness of ambiguity with its literal sense of 'driving both ways'? What happens if we try to take on board the supposition that all of these words and concepts, all these forms of feeling and thinking, are susceptible to effects of veering, that veering is a necessary inflection, that any and every inflection entails veering? What kinds of turn does 'veering' give?

My concern, then, is with exploring the possibilities of veering at the most general level conceivable, as a sort of unbounded term for thinking about thinking, for relating to the world around us, for notions of community, ethics and politics. Some of the most challenging and vital aspects of this may be most concisely illustrated in terms of the concept of the environment. However small or hard to notice, the word 'environment' has 'veering' inscribed within it. The 'vir' of 'environment' is from the French *virer*, 'to turn' or 'to veer' (see *OED*, 'environ', adj. and prep.). Ultimately at issue, then, is a new thinking of 'environment'. Affirming the uncertainties and ambiguities, the elusiveness and otherness of 'veering' is part of an attempt to take a stand (a perhaps imaginative or eccentric, but also an ethico-political stand) against all the centrisms that have dominated the concept of 'environment' and that have played such major roles in producing the dire current 'world situation'. The environment environs and, according to the most powerful and seemingly entrenched logic (the logic, indeed, of *logos*), at the centre of this environing is, first of all, the I, the ego, the so-called individual and, by the same movement, the human. Logocentrism, anthropocentrism, egocentrism ('That's me in the middle!'): the future of environmentalism is inseparable from a questioning and dislocation of all these centrisms. An attention to the strangeness of 'veering' is bound up with a deconstructive thinking of the environment and environments. I should perhaps stress that 'environment' here means not only what people used to call the 'natural world' but also being in the world in the sense of being in the world of Wall Street, say, or Heathrow. 'World' makes one's head whirl. No world without a whirled head: in its most general or exorbitant form, veering is a way of thinking about relativity, quantum theory, string theory. It is about how we conceive the universe and our place in it. It has to do with the swirl of stars and space, with shifting galaxies and spinning pulsars, but also with what is singular about each of us (and what is not – or not only – human about this singularity). Everyone has singular ways of veering, even or especially if they do not realize it. Analysis of veering is, among other things, an attempt to think in new ways about manner of being, conduct, style and idiom.

Our place in the universe: literature is the primary focus here for an appreciation and understanding of the 'our' and the 'place'. The figure and concept of veering opens up new perspectives on literary works, but also, conversely, literary works are a key to thinking about the experience and value of veering. Veering in these respects is closely related to those aspects of literature we perhaps consider most unnerving but also potentially thrilling: danger, extreme pleasure, losing a sense of oneself, losing control, sensing something secret, the unforeseeable, absolute surprise and radical transformation. Veering is thus linked to new ways of reading and responding to literature, in the light of what I have called the literary turn. Literature comes to be construed in terms of unexpected, undecidable movements and effects that do not stay within oppositional theory/practice, creative/critical and even fictional/juridical divides. It is a matter of reading all these words anew. As Michael Naas has recently observed, apropos what has been widely referred to as 'the end of Theory':

> If the golden age of Theory is indeed long past, then perhaps we can begin to read again, and to read without having to buy into the opposition between

theory and practice, to begin to read again – and, yes, perhaps even a novel – as a way of posing and analysing the most pressing philosophical *and* political questions of our time.[6]

The focus for exploration in the following pages is sometimes described as a novel, though more usually as a short story, Melville's 'Bartleby'.[7]

*

Before proceeding to Melville, however, I would like to make a few brief summary remarks regarding the word 'veerer'. Rather than pretend to confine it to a single definition or even series of definitions, here are fifteen aphorisms:

1. A veerer is someone or something that veers or makes veer. You cannot pin down a veerer any more than you can categorize the place of a supplement or finalize the relationship between literature and the secret.
2. A veerer does not have a proper place. It is always already on the move, elsewhere.
3. Here is what Lorrie Moore says about the writings of Clarice Lispector: 'Lispector reads as a lively intelligence sometimes veering toward hysteria, then falling back, as if in a faint, and flattening to aphorism and pronouncement.'[8] Like so many other cases where 'veering' appears, it is just as much a disappearing. No veerer without contretemps, anachronism, temporal slide. This is enacted in the form of Moore's sentence, which itself comprises a sort of interrupted or off-course pseudo-iterative: 'sometimes' it is 'veering', we are told, as if to imply that at other times it is not, but then the way Moore goes on suggests it is just a one-off 'sometimes', without 'other times', a veering in her own prose or intelligence. Is this a description of Lispector reading, or of reading Lispector? The lively intelligence of Moore's own writing suggests, in the midst of all that 'f'-alliteration, a play on 'faint' (a ruse or 'feint'), as well as a hysterical faint that would in turn veer off from the ostensive claim she appears to be making.
4. No aphorism without a veerer.
5. A veerer always involves a question of tone. In a discussion of the 'deep, dividing forces' that are at work in Mark Twain's *Pudd'nhead Wilson* (1894), the critic and novelist Malcolm Bradbury writes:

> The result is in many ways ambiguity – but ambiguity that comes not only from identifiable weakness in the writing (themes not fully assimilated, stories not fully worked out, sudden veerings of tone) but also from the most exacting kind of literary control, from the exercise of an

irony so persistent, sharp, and farsighted that it can scarcely leave its objects alone until every possible turn of the screw has been tried.[9]

This is another difficult sentence to parse. There seems to be an ambiguity about ambiguity: there is ambiguity that is connected with veerings (a pleasing, if rare plural in critical writing), and another with 'the most exacting kind of literary control'. 'Literary control', I confess, makes me smile. As we have already noted, veering can be controlled.[10] But it can also be otherwise: a lack or loss of control, absolute diremption. No irony without veering or without, in Bradbury's phrase, 'veerings of tone'. Tone is never single.

6. The veerer is a figure of irony par excellence. That is in part what ties veering to democracy. Without irony, without the right to irony in the public space, there can be no democracy.[11]

7. A veerer is ghostly. Its very place is to veer, to vanish, gone no sooner than you think you have spotted it. It moves at strange speed, at once unnaturally fast and slow. It is a matter of a kind of quickness *on slow*. It happens in the space of what Hélène Cixous refers to as 'the slowness inside the speed'.[12] It is off.

8. A veerer is versatility itself.

9. The veerer is in truth a literary will-o'-the-wisp in the scene of writing. It offers another way of thinking about narrative and point of view. It veers off from that fundamentally Christian critical terminology of 'omniscient narration' and offers new directions for exploring the structure of telepathy or magical thinking in literature. Consider, first of all, the figure of the narrator as a veerer.

10. There is no doubt a temptation to suppose that there is something of the magical or miraculous about it – yes, why not? There is a kind of magic in literature. But 'veerer' would be a figure for a new, demystified, non-mystical thinking of the magical, and of the sovereign, the univocal, the subject.

11. The veerer entails a new model, ghostly by nature, for thinking about digression in literature. It dislocates, it frees up in advance the teleological structure that digression installs. Digression is always, in effect, digression *en route to*. The digression ends, at which point the reader returns to, or is reacquainted with, where things had reached prior to that. To speak of a veerer, of what is going on when a literary narrative veers, enables a more dynamic, riskier, less certain model for what is happening, in the moment, in the strange grain of the writing in which the end of the digression is not foreseen, in which the very nature of a digression is in question, various forms of 'critical control' (and no doubt the fantasy of 'literary

control' that goes with it) are relinquished, and the language of the text is allowed to do its thing, in other words veer.

12. 'Veerer' is at once micrological and macrological. It might refer, for example, to a movement to be picked up in a single word or piece of a word, or indeed a single item of punctuation or spacing, as well as to an entire text.

13. Once upon a time people talked about literary sources and allusions. Then along came the great battleship 'Intertextuality', to blow them all out of the water. Nowadays the sea seems calm and empty again, without a wrinkle, as Conrad might say. People still talk about sources and allusions. Sometimes they do so by calling them intertextual. 'Veerer' would be a ghost ship from another time, coming in peace, in pieces. It offers new ways of illuminating the relations between texts, new ways of thinking about 'influence', 'allusion', the 'intertextual' and so on.

14. A not much remarked upon aspect of Freud's essay on the antithetical meaning of primal words: his stress on the *sounds* of words, the way words sound backwards, the way they can turn about in our mouths, in our dreams.[13] Freudian slips: micrological veerers. The rêve, ever, reverie, revere, reave, bereave.

15. The greatest literary works, the most haunting and compelling but also the most resistant to reading, are the most veering. A masterpiece is always a veerer.

*

Let us, then, turn to 'Bartleby'. I say that with at least a flicker of irony, for it may be evident that I turned in that direction some time ago. 'Bartleby' or, as it is more fully titled, 'Bartleby, The Scrivener', or indeed, 'Bartleby, The Scrivener: A Story of Wall-street', written and first published in 1853, is famous, above all, for the phrase that Bartleby repeatedly comes out with: 'I would prefer not to.' It recounts how this young man called Bartleby comes to be employed as a scrivener or copyist in a lawyer's office in Wall Street, in New York, but soon proves resistant to his employer's requests. Asked to 'examine a small paper' with the lawyer, Bartleby says mildly, 'I would prefer not to' (10). The lawyer (who is also the narrator) relates his mounting sense of frustration at Bartleby's apparent unwillingness or inability to carry out any of his tasks as an employee. The lawyer makes various attempts to get rid of him, but the young scrivener would prefer not to move. So rather than evict Bartleby, the lawyer himself moves chambers. This rather peculiar course of action, however, fails to resolve matters. In continuing to station himself in the lawyer's former offices, Bartleby proves an unacceptable imposition on the new tenant, another lawyer, who seeks out the narrator and demands his assistance in removing Bartleby, rather as if the latter were an item of furniture or pile of papers the narrator had left behind. The complications in all of this devolve principally from the fact that the narrator, for all his cool reasoning and apparent aloofness, actually has a good deal of sympathy and indeed affection for the young man. Eventually, however, Bartleby is arrested as a vagrant and imprisoned. He dies shortly afterwards in the notorious New York prison known as the Tombs. The lawyer concludes his 'little narrative' (34) by recounting a rumour he heard a few months after Bartleby's death, namely that the young man had formerly been employed as 'a subordinate clerk in the Dead Letter Office at Washington, from which he had been suddenly removed by a change in the administration' (34).

'Bartleby, The Scrivener' has been the subject of a great deal of critical and philosophical reflection and discussion, including work in recent years by Giorgio Agamben, Branka Arsić, Gilles Deleuze, Jacques Derrida, Peggy Kamuf and J. Hillis Miller.[14] The philosophical richness of Melville's masterpiece has been acknowledged and elaborated in notable detail by the thinkers and critics just named. Together these analyses bear witness to what Hillis Miller (in an essay entitled 'Who Is He? Melville's "Bartleby the Scrivener"') calls the story's 'inexhaustible power to generate commentary'.[15] I must confess, however, that my own experience of reading 'Bartleby' and trying to write on it has not confirmed the apparent ease of proliferating commentary implied here. I cannot think of any other text, in fact, that seems to have had such a disarming effect on my ability to write about it. I begin to write, it is very hard-going, but I get a paragraph completed, then I realize it is no good, it has missed the point: I have to delete it. I feel rather like Jack in *The Shining*, or at least I am overly aware of what Stephen King calls the 'basement guy'.[16] Except that the man in this case might just as much be a woman, or then again not human at all, and not in a basement but in that queerly invaginated space or crypt that is the singular experience of reading 'Bartleby, The Scrivener'.[17]

When Michael Naas makes his claim about our 'post-theory' moment, in which it becomes possible to see how a novel can pose 'some of the most pressing philosophical and political questions of our time', his example is from contemporary literature, and specifically Don DeLillo's *Cosmopolis* (2003). 'Bartleby, The Scrivener' is discombobulating in part because it is *not* contemporary, and yet seems to resonate in such powerfully topical ways. It is not 'a story of Wall Street' in the way that DeLillo's novel is. Melville's story predates the Wall Street that we today recognize as a name for the heart of global capital. The New York Stock

Exchange was not established until 1865. Already Wall Street was well established, however, as a location for the machinations and processes of the law, which are of course a constant point of reference in Melville's story. Law and money are very old bedfellows, and Wall Street did not become 'the inferno of injustice' (in Jacques Derrida's memorable phrase) overnight.[18] Melville's text is an indispensable document for any rigorous reflection on the cultural and political history of 'Wall Street' and on what it has become.

Melville's subtitle, 'A Story of Wall-street', has a kind of parabolic generality that invites an irreducible plurality of readings, especially given its emphasis on the ways in which property, law and finance are inextricably linked. And at the same time the text is explicitly a story about writing, about the essential relation between writing and law, and between law and literature. It is also, more specifically perhaps, a story about justice, homelessness and vagrancy: Bartleby is eventually taken 'as a vagrant' to 'the Tombs, or to speak more properly,' as the narrator puts it, 'the Halls of Justice' (31). Vagrancy is the reason given for his incarceration, despite the lawyer-narrator's classification of this classification as 'absurd'. Bartleby is, he suggests, the very opposite of a vagrant: 'What! he a vagrant, a wanderer, who refuses to budge? It is because he will *not* be a vagrant, then, that you seek to count him *as* a vagrant. That is too absurd' (27–8).

What is a vagrant? What kind of vagrant is Bartleby, if he is one? What is *just*, when it comes to dealing with vagrancy? How might the 'just' here reverberate in the notion of literary works as 'just visiting'? What is the relation between vagrancy and literature? At the same time, Bartleby is and remains, literally and figuratively, perhaps the most *stationary* character in American or any other so-called national literature: the text relentlessly foregrounds his strangely 'still', 'motionless' nature. How can 'refus[ing] to budge' (in the narrator's words) be compatible with vagrancy? What is the law, the lawyer or the law-maker to do with this 'unaccountable' (26) and 'unaccountably eccentric' (31) young man? In what ways is Bartleby the scrivener a portrait of the artist as a young man, or indeed of anyone who writes or is expected to write, including literary critics or philosophers? How does the scrivener's 'passive resistance' (13), as the narrator calls it, relate to notions of civil disobedience and thus render Bartleby perhaps a singularly subversive figure for our time? How are we to deal with the fact that this text is so tonally divided, at once heart-rendingly sad and side-splittingly funny? These are some of the questions with which Melville's little story compels us to reckon.

And how does it do all this? Because it is a veerer. As I suggested earlier, every great work of literature is a veerer, and indeed every such work will also, by a dynamically corresponding turn, have significant things to say *about* veering. But 'Bartleby, The Scrivener' is exemplary in its reflexive intensity, above all in provoking singular kinds of quandary about the social, ethical, judgemental nature of a reading, and about the relations between reading and justice. I quoted Hillis Miller a moment ago but did so in a somewhat fragmentary manner. 'Although "Bartleby, The Scrivener" has an inexhaustible power to generate commentary', Miller remarks, 'none of it seems to get quite to the point, as if it too were fugitive and vagrant' (177). With what might be called a lawyer-like clarity, orderliness and attentiveness to detail, Miller gives an admirable account of how the figures of vagrancy and the vagrant (literally, one who 'wanders about') pervade Melville's text. Vagrancy is at issue not only apropos Bartleby's own status and the eventual bogus reason for his imprisonment, but also with regard to the narrator's specific business as 'a conveyancer and title hunter' (9) – in the strange legal world in which properties and titles wander about between one owner and another – and with regard to his various responses to the scrivener. Miller cites a passage in which the lawyer-narrator recounts how he deals with being held responsible for the fact that Bartleby will not leave the lawyer's former chambers:

> I now strove to be entirely care-free and quiescent; and my conscience justified me in the attempt; though indeed it was not so successful as I could have wished. So fearful was I of being again hunted out by the incensed landlord and his exasperated tenants, that, surrendering my business to Nippers [one of the narrator's other employees], for a few days I drove about the upper part of the town and through the suburbs, in my rockaway; crossed over to Jersey City and Hoboken, and paid fugitive visits to Manhattanville and Astoria. In fact I almost lived in my rockaway for the time. (31)

Miller nicely sums up: 'the narrator himself is made into a vagrant by Bartleby. He wanders pointlessly from one place to another in a kind of fugitive movement in place that is wonderfully expressed by the name of his conveyance [that is, the rockaway]' (161).[19]

In his concern to foreground the 'unaccountable' (146, 174), Miller finely alerts us to the ways in which the 'fugitive and vagrant' seem not only to pervade the work itself, but to characterize any and every critical or philosophical reading of it. Miller knows as well as anybody that, in Jacques Derrida's celebrated formulation, '*blindness to the supplement* is the law': there is always something vagrant, fugitive or errant in a reading, and the identification of that vagrancy can in turn enable another reading which will in turn transpire to have been dependent on missing 'the point'.[20] My elaboration of the 'veerer' is merely an attempt to sharpen and refine a critical and (I dare to hope) creative appreciation of this vagrancy. The power of Derrida's account of the supplement has to do, after all, with what is in effect already gone or not yet there, a ghostly logic of what is 'neither a presence nor an absence'.[21] Miller sees himself as a critical police officer but also implicitly situates all future readers in these terms: 'All readings of the story, including my own, are more ways to call in the police' (174). Must every reading be in the name of the law or in the form of a policing? What happens then, for example, to the question of reading and civil disobedience, to a sense of justice at odds with the law?

At the same time, Miller affirms his own strangeness as a haunted man. As he puts it: 'we remain haunted by Bartleby, but haunted also by "Bartleby the Scrivener: A Story of Wall-Street"' (174). This remark is in accord with his focus on Bartleby himself ('Who Is He?' is, we may recall, the title of Miller's essay), rather than, for example, the anonymous narrator or on so-called narrative perspective. If 'Bartleby, The Scrivener' haunts, it is a ghost story of an especially complex kind. There is a correlation here with what Shoshana Felman says about Henry James's *The Turn of the Screw*, namely that it has 'uncanny trapping power' as a 'reading-effect'.[22] Indeed, I would suggest that 'Bartleby, The Scrivener' is in a sense the first modern ghost story, specifically in its showing (decades earlier than *The Turn of the Screw*, for example, or 'The Jolly Corner') how the ghost is not only or not primarily a character or apparitional 'presence' in the text, but is also the 'I' of the narrator or reader, the one who hunts after the ghost only to veer round to see that the ghost is, in truth, the 'I' itself, along with language as such. The lawyer, in Melville's story, repeatedly refers to Bartleby as '[l]ike a very ghost' (15), as an 'apparition' (16), as not so much 'man' but 'rather ghost' (27). But the power of the story consists just as much in its spectralization of the lawyer himself – and then the opening up, the veering in the direction of the reader in turn.

'Bartleby, The Scrivener' veers in itself, out of itself. Melville's writing is, in a word, zigzag.[23] Reading becomes at once an experience and an analysis of veering. This is in part a matter of signature, style and tone. Hillis Miller gives relatively little attention to this, despite his eloquent foregrounding of the thematic oscillation between mobility and stillness that seems to organise the narrative. The lawyer may himself prove vagrant, rocking away in his rockaway, but, as Miller notes, Bartleby's primary effect on him is one of stilling or immobilizing. As the narrator recalls his response to Bartleby's first saying, 'in a singularly mild, firm voice . . . "I would prefer not to"' (10): 'I sat awhile in perfect silence,

rallying my stunned faculties' (11). Miller proposes that we see the narrator in terms of what he calls 'a neutral state in which immobility and
mobility come to the same thing, since motion is no longer directed to
a goal' (160). But veering is not neutral. Neither is it confined to movement in the outside world: it is at work in language, in signature, style
and tone, and in the mind. Veering is always at least a bit mental, even
(or especially) if it is a question of the unconscious or of dreaming.

Gilles Deleuze's 'Bartleby; or, The Formula' brilliantly brings out
this dimension of Melville's writing, in particular with respect to what
he calls the 'alternations ... between stationary, fixed processes and
mad-paced procedures: *style*, with its succession of catatonias and
accelerations'.[24] Deleuze captures, perhaps better than any other commentator on 'Bartleby', this sense of veering between stillness and rapid
movement, between one perspective and another, the sense that, in the
context of Melville's work, 'Truth always has "jagged edges"' (86). As
is often the case with Deleuze, this leads him in the direction of cinema,
toward a cinematographics of literature: thus he proposes that Melville's
work calls for 'a new perspective, an archipelago-perspectivism that
conjugates the panoramic shot and the tracking shot' (87). While
opening up fascinating slants on cinema, literature and 'becoming', this
emphasis tends to take us away from the zigzag strangeness of signature
and style as such, the shifting tones and encrypting voices, the swirling
energies and allergies of words. For the veering in and of 'Bartleby, The
Scrivener' is first and foremost an event generated out of words, and
out of their subatomic activities or passivities. (We may recall Maurice
Blanchot's discussion of passivity in *The Writing of the Disaster*, and in
particular his remark that Melville's text – and above all its most cited
line, 'I would prefer not to' – entails an 'infinity of patience'.[25])

*

Infinite patience is probably not what you are feeling by this point. I
fear you will think it a digression but, before proceeding further with
'Bartleby', some clarification is called for vis-à-vis the question of these
activities or passivities of words and indeed of particular sounds or
parts of words. There is a temptation to talk about it in terms of 'word-
consciousness'. This is a neat critical convenience, alluding to a given
writer's feeling for words. It may be noted that 'word-consciousness'
is also ambiguous, in fact, since it carries the mildly bizarre suggestion of the word's consciousness of itself, of its place in the text and
its relation to other texts, as well as of its place in the world. A strange
scenario, it may seem, especially if we push things a little further and try
to think of these verbal effects as only uncertainly aware of themselves

– less consciousness, perhaps, than demonic possession or catatonic dreaming.

Every description of word-consciousness would tend towards the singularity of a signature, and perforce a kind of madness. This is how Hélène Cixous puts it, in the remarkable text entitled 'Writing Blind':

> Words . . . are our dwarfs, our gnomes, our minuscule workers in the mines of language. They perforate our deafness. They forethink . . . Naturally they know what goes on in the more or less well-tended corners of the back of our mind. As everyone wants not to know, we all have the words we deserve. These little so ancient agents never stop joking and bringing us gifts in secret. Too bad for those who consider words to be worn down pebbles. An etymological presentiment guides me. Call it a good nose. I smell the odour of origins on the most familiar words . . . And what words do between themselves – couplings, matings, hybridizations – is genius. An erotic and fertile genius. A law of life presides over their crossings [*croisements*]. Only words in love sow. [*Seuls les mots qui s'aiment sèment.*][26]

I would like to suggest that this is the kind of 'genius' that we find in Shakespeare but also in Melville. This is not the 'genius' of a writer or individual: 'Bartleby, The Scrivener', as we will see in a moment, is quite ironic and satirical in this regard. At issue is not so much a writer's consciousness of words, even if we were to include in that Cixous's notion of 'etymological presentiments', with its own intimations of eerie provenance and alterity. Rather it is the things words do with themselves and with one another, the things words do with a writer, the jokes they make, the gifts they bring in secret.

While 'word-consciousness' has a certain appeal, especially in the double-meaning just noted, the phrase is nonetheless perhaps too easily recuperated into a language of mastery and control. It might be more helpful to think about *wordlife*.

I want to try to illustrate this, then, by turning to a passage from Melville's story. It comes just after the lawyer-narrator has given Bartleby what he believes are his marching orders. He has told the young man he is to leave the premises and not come back: 'slip your key underneath the mat, so that I may have it in the morning. I shall not see you again; so goodbye to you' (23). The lawyer considers this strategy to have been 'masterly'. As he puts it: '[w]ithout loudly bidding Bartleby depart – as an inferior genius might have done – I *assumed* the ground that depart he must; and upon the assumption built all I had to say' (23). But when he wakes up next morning he has his doubts:

> My procedure seemed as sagacious as ever, – but only in theory. How it would prove in practice – there was the rub. It was truly a beautiful thought

to have assumed Bartleby's departure; but, after all, that assumption was simply my own, and none of Bartleby's. The great point was, not whether I had assumed that he would quit me, but whether he would prefer so to do. He was more a man of preferences than assumptions.

After breakfast, I walked down town, arguing the probabilities *pro* and *con*. One moment I thought it would prove a miserable failure, and Bartleby would be found all alive at my office as usual; the next moment it seemed certain that I should see his chair empty. And so I kept veering about. At the corner of Broadway and Canal-street, I saw quite an excited group of people standing in earnest conversation.

'I'll take odds he doesn't,' said a voice as I passed.

'Doesn't go? – done!' said I, 'put up your money.'

I was instinctively putting my hand in my pocket to produce my own, when I remembered that this was an election day. The words I had overheard bore no reference to Bartleby, but to the success or non-success of some candidate for the mayoralty. In my intent frame of mind, I had, as it were, imagined that all Broadway shared in my excitement, and were debating the same question with me. I passed on, very thankful that the uproar of the street screened my momentary absent-mindedness. (23)

'Theory' and 'practice' here dissolve in a strange dramatization of magical thinking. We encounter in elliptic and condensed form a sort of 'inside narrative' of the workings of Melville's text.[27] The lawyer is walking down Broadway 'arguing the probabilities *pro* and *con*': is this 'arguing' happening only *in his head*, as one says, or is he talking out loud? The way the account develops (leading up to the corresponding case of 'debating') serves retrolexically to exacerbate the uncertainty. Here, more sharply perhaps than anywhere else in Melville's text, any sense of the lawyer as a rationalizing and calculating character, a figure of reason and order, goes awry. Will Bartleby be 'all alive at [his] office as usual' or will he have vanished, like the 'very ghost' (15) that the narrator has earlier called him? At the moment of reiterating the difference between himself and Bartleby ('he was more a man of preferences than assumptions'), the lawyer slips into the very conditional forms ('it would', 'I should') of Bartleby's 'I would prefer not to'. Bartleby hath the lawyer in thrall. 'And so I kept veering about': he is walking, we suppose, in an orderly enough fashion; the veering is all in his head. He keeps it. He keeps veering about.

And in this suspended time of veering, we encounter the most explicit moment of magical thinking in Melville's text, the moment at which the wall between inside and outside falls, the fall of this 'Story of Wall-street'. In this continual, continuous-discontinuous time of 'veering about', the lawyer is engulfed by an experience in which he fails to register the distinction between what is inside and what is outside his head. 'Veering about' in his head becomes a veering about in the world, a veering in and of the world. And here the very distinction between assumption and preference collapses: the lawyer has the conviction, so to speak, that his thoughts are not his own, that others are sharing his thoughts. He had, 'as it were, imagined that all Broadway shared in my excitement, and were debating the same question with me'.[28] Now this moment, indissociably entangled with the figure of 'veering about', is of course a moment of madness, but it is also in effect the most literary moment in the text, a moment of exscription (to adopt Jean-Luc Nancy's term)[29] in which the very workings of literary narration are laid bare. For literary fiction consists in a mode of telepathic or magical thinking, speaking or writing, in which there is always at least one 'I' (whether narrator or author-figure) who can access or indeed invade and take over the thoughts and feelings of another (whether that be a character or the narrator). In this moment of telepathic 'uproar', in which the lawyer's 'absent-mindedness' is allegedly 'screened', we are presented with a singular exposition of the internal logic of the text. In truth, the lawyer is not screened either from Bartleby or from Melville as author-figure. On the contrary, the space of literature is where thoughts and feelings are indeed *shared*, and its mode of operation is what we might call (after Melville) *veering about*.

'Bartleby, The Scrivener', we are invited to suppose, is written by an anonymous lawyer. He is writing about a young scrivener, but he is not a scrivener himself. Melville is evidently nowhere to be seen or heard. But of course we all know that this is not the case. Not to be caught up in the very kind of delusion that the lawyer experiences on Broadway, it is necessary to keep in mind that this is a work of fiction, that the lawyer is, to follow the strange letter of the literary law, at once a fictional narrator and himself a scrivener. For every fictional narrator is a scrivener of the author. There is no first-person literary fiction without the logic and operation of a scrivener, a narrator whose words (whether initially spoken or written) are a precise and faithful copy of the author's. They do not need to be 'examined': to go there would be to enter into the circularity and repetitiousness of Borges's 'Pierre Menard, Author of the Quixote', or to conform to what Hillis Miller calls the lawyer's apparent compulsion for the 'orbicular' (150). Bartleby, in this sense, would be the very embodiment of a kind of resistance literature. And while we love a story, we also know that it is all a set-up, that the credit we give to linearity and the rectilinear unfolding of a plot, including the critical reliance on terms such as prolepsis, analepsis and digression, point of view, focalizer and focalization, is itself a fiction, and that what is really going on are forms and instances of veering about.

Correspondingly, the lawyer is not Bartleby, nor is he Melville, but one cannot begin to construe tone and voice in 'Bartleby, The Scrivener' without reckoning with this logic of veerings of tone and *more than one voice*. When, for example, Bartleby says on one occasion, 'I prefer not to', and we are told that this is 'in a flute-like tone' (12), with how many ears or in how many voices should this be heard? Or when, on another occasion, the narrator describes Bartleby's 'I would prefer not to' as a 'mulish vagary' (14), from whose point of view, in whose tongue is that verbal vagrancy to be read? The disturbing, pervasive nature of 'tongue turning' that Melville's text explores (the ways in which other characters become 'turned' (21), ventriloquized or possessed by Bartleby's language, and especially by his use of the word 'prefer') is another haunting enactment of this strange veering about in language.[30]

Wordlife is not simply, or not necessarily at all, a matter of Melville's 'creative genius', his inspired 'word-consciousness' or linguistic inventiveness. It seems more closely bound up with notions of gifts and hospitality, radical passivity and states of trance or possession – all of which can be associated in significant ways with the figure of Bartleby. Wordlife entails an attention to what is going on in 'the mines of language', as Cixous says, the 'jokes' and 'gifts' that words bring us 'in secret', the 'couplings, matings, hybridizations'. It is turning about, for example, in the very word 'veer'. Once you start immersing yourself in the mines of 'Bartleby, The Scrivener' it becomes difficult not to be struck by the subterranean shiftings and substitutions, the insistence and the laughter of a 'veer' in the word 'scrivener' itself (a word that occurs more than twenty-five times in the text), in the word 'remove' or 'removed' (which appears some eight times), in the repeated references to Bartleby's 'revery' or 'reveries' (15, 18, 21, 26) and his emphatic 'reserve' (18, cf. 19), as well as in the lawyer's apparent penchant for the word 'severe' or 'severer' (15, 20, 24, 27). The vagrancy of these verbal reverberations reaches out in every direction, turning up in such apparently distinct and unrelated words as 'ever', 'never', 'moreover', 'every', 'several', 'conveyancer', 'perverse', 'irreversible', 'inadvertently', 'revolved', 'recovered', 'discovered', 'hovered', 'delivered', 'endeavor', 'interview', 'overpowering', 'services', 'privileges', 'receiving', 'reserving', 'vegetarian', 'resolved', 'revealed', 'retrospectively', 'inveteracy'. To work in such a subatomic bomb factory it would be necessary to verse oneself in the thinking of a completely other scrivener, a veritable scrivener of the irreceivable.

Nevertheless, with more time and with sufficient patience, the micrology of Melville's veerers, including perhaps the *veer* in the name 'Herman Melville', might be traced and analysed all the way up to his last work, 'Billy Budd, Sailor', and the maddening reserve of the inscrutable Captain Vere.[31] What makes 'Billy Budd, Sailor' among the most breathtaking, excruciating, paralysing works of short fiction ever written ('the most beautiful story in the world', in the view of Thomas Mann) might be said to turn on the appalling silent play in the name 'Vere'.[32] For everything in a sense is twisted up in the tacit homophonic madness of this word which signifies 'truth' and 'faith' but also (as 'Bartleby, The Scrivener' encourages us to suppose) a *veering about*. It is all about how this astonishing 'inside narrative' at once reveals and resists, gives and withholds an account of Captain Vere's 'unhinged' (147) state of mind, his becoming (or not becoming) 'the sudden victim ... of aberration' (147–8), his 'absent fits' and his 'inly deliberating' (152). Vere is a veerer.[33] So the 'inexhaustible' winds of Melville blow, as Albert Camus puts it, 'for thousands of miles across empty oceans'.[34]

Permit me to add one further remark on wordlife and intertextuality in the context of 'Bartleby, The Scrivener'. At issue here would be the queer veering or veer-queering of Melville's story. In the course of some succinct and fascinating observations about irony, sacrifice, humour and the uncanny in this text, Jacques Derrida comments: '"Bartleby, The Scrivener" doesn't make a single allusion to anything feminine whatsoever, and that is all the more the case for anything that could be construed as a figure of woman.'[35] At a certain level this is doubtless true: the apparent absence of female characters is obvious. But in other respects things are perhaps less certain. Thus we might consider the moment at which the lawyer remarks that 'it was [Bartleby's] wonderful mildness chiefly, which not only disarmed me, but unmanned me, as it were' (16). This *unmanning* is a small but crucial indicator of the cryptic queerness of Melville's text.[36] More subtle and elliptical, perhaps, is the intertextual encounter that Melville's work appears to stage in rela- tion to John Keats's poem, 'La Belle Dame sans Merci'.[37] Both works are concerned with a pervasive sense of anguish, of being haunted and possessed.[38] So far as I am aware, no critic has remarked on this but, from its opening words onwards ('O what can ail thee, knight at arms, / Alone and palely loitering?'), there is an insistent resonance of Keats's poem in 'Bartleby'.[39] The word 'pale' (or 'palely') provides an almost hypnotic refrain in both texts, along with 'alone'.[40] Bartleby also is said to 'loiter' (33), in the yard of the Tombs at the end; he too has, literally, 'starv'd lips', since he has been 'liv[ing] without dining' (33). And in this deathly yard that is 'entirely quiet' ('no birds sing'), just as the haunted man in Keats's poem 'shut her wild wild eyes / With kisses four', so the narrator of Melville's story, touching Bartleby (now dead) for the first time, 'closed the eyes' (33). Keats's poem is a veerer in Melville's work. The queer veering of wordlife in 'Bartleby, The Scrivener' is suggestively identified with an uncanny woman or uncanny feminization. The sense of ghostly possession affects both lawyer and scrivener. Sexual difference is veering. If Bartleby speaks, like *la belle dame* herself, 'in language strange', her 'I love thee true' is his 'I would prefer not to'.[41]

*

I would like to conclude by reverting finally to these words for which 'Bartleby, The Scrivener' is most celebrated, if not revered. Above all, it is a matter of responding to the kind of crazy imbalance of Melville's text. As Elizabeth Hardwick has noted: 'Out of some sixteen thousand words, Bartleby, the cadaverous and yet blazing centre of all our attention, speaks only thirty-seven short lines, more than a third of which are a repetition of a single line ["I would prefer not to"].'[42] 'I would prefer not to': everything seems to culminate in this line which is, of course, hardly a line. As Deleuze points out, it is 'agrammatical'.[43] Initially we understand it as the young man's referring to the lawyer's request that he 'examine a small paper with [him]' (10), but it soon becomes a kind of general statement or (in Deleuze's phrase) a 'formula': 'I would prefer not to [*anything*]'.

What Deleuze sees as 'the formula', Giorgio Agamben characterizes in terms of anaphora, a matter of the successive repetition of a phrase. Indeed he suggests that 'I would prefer not to' is exemplary, a kind of enactment of the etymological sense of anaphora as 'carrying back'. Agamben writes:

> The final 'to' that ends Bartleby's phrase has an anaphoric character, for it does not refer directly to a segment of reality but, rather, to a preceding term from which it draws its only meaning. But here it is as if this anaphora were absolutized to the point of losing all reference, now turning, so to speak, back toward the phrase itself – an absolute anaphora, spinning on itself, no longer referring either to a real object or to an anaphorized term: *I would prefer not to prefer not to prefer not to* . . .[44]

This image of the phrase 'spinning on itself' suggests a kind of vertigo – and where there is vertigo there is veering – but Agamben seems to want to freeze things there, in a circular self-referencing that is, I would argue, quite heterogeneous to the revolutionary openness of Melville's text. '*I would prefer not to prefer not to prefer not to*' is Agamben, not Melville. And in any case, it is not simply Melville either, it is a character in a literary narrative. 'I would prefer not to' is spinning, yes, but not merely on itself, indeed never purely on itself. 'I would prefer not to' is an aposiopesis, in other words an example of the rhetorical figure for an unfinished . . . 'I would prefer not to': this is the veerer at the heart of the work. Every time it is different, and differently disruptive, interruptive, incomplete.[45] With Cixous's notion of etymological presentiment in mind, we may note that 'to prefer' is from the classical Latin *praeferre*, to place before or in front, to put forward, to advance. Bartleby's phrase, then, is a going or putting forward *not*: it goes in front, only to be immediately withdrawn, taken away. It is an advancing-off-course. It seems to me that, if there is a single phrase in the lawyer's own discourse that corresponds with this, it would be 'veering about': like Bartleby's 'I would prefer not to', it is between one thing and another, a strange bending and suspending in space and time, unfinished.

I have focused here on *wordlife* in part because I believe people are too hasty in consigning Bartleby to death, to do as the lawyer does and envisage him, in the midst of his story, already as a corpse, 'laid out, among uncaring strangers, in its shivering winding sheet' (18). What makes 'Bartleby, The Scrivener' arguably the first modern ghost story has to do with what might be called its spectral turn – the way it compels us to reckon with a ghostliness that is a condition of perception and experience, not merely the ghostliness of some projected afterlife. A crucial dimension of Melville's text, in this respect, is its peculiar realism: the 'story' maintains a sufficiently strong air of credibility, a consistent enough grounding in actuality for it to be possible to believe that the lawyer's is a true and faithful account that might, at least in principle, stand up in a court of law. (The everyday details of the lawyer's office and its New York environment, as well as the numerous historical figures evoked, function in the service of this realism.) At the same time, as I have tried to suggest, 'Bartleby, The Scrivener' is one of the most delirious, cryptic and playfully reflexive fictions in modern literature. With 'Bartleby, The Scrivener', verisimilitude veers. It is not a matter, then, of an opposition between literature and the real, the environment of 'Bartleby' the literary fiction as distinct from the environment of Wall Street, law and justice, any more than it is a question of what Slavoj Žižek (entirely eliding the literary dimensions of Melville's writing) calls 'the parallax gap between the "Bartleby" attitude of withdrawal from social engagement and collective social action'.[46] Shifting in a singular and uncertain fashion between registers, Melville's text embodies at once a force of literary or cryptaesthetic resistance and an openness that, today perhaps more than ever, it is difficult not to read in the direction of a justice beyond the law, an instantiation of a logic of civil disobedience, an 'I would prefer not to' or, in Derrida's words, 'don't count me in'.[47]

Notes

1. John Burnside, *Glister* (London: Vintage, 2009), p. 86.
2. Don DeLillo, *The Names* (London: Picador, 1987), p. 137.
3. Rachel Bowlby, *Freudian Mythologies: Greek Tragedy and Modern Identities* (Oxford: Oxford University Press, 2007), p. 226.
4. See 'The Rime of the Ancient Mariner', in Samuel Taylor Coleridge, *Poems*, ed. John Beer (London: Dent, 1974), ll. 232–3.
5. See Sigmund Freud, 'The Antithetical Meaning of Primal Words', in *SE* XI: 153–61.
6. Michael Naas, *Derrida From Now On* (New York: Fordham University Press, 2008), p. 149.
7. It is, ironically, designated as a 'short novel' in the edition to which I am referring in this chapter, viz. 'Bartleby, The Scrivener', in *Melville's Short Novels*, ed. Dan McCall (New York: Norton, 2002), pp. 3–34. Further page references are to this edition and are given parenthetically in the main body of the text. While it seems faintly comical to refer to a thirty-page story as a novel, this designation does perhaps have the value of intimating its extraordinary complexity. 'Bartleby, The Scrivener' is, in a sense, far more considerable as a text than innumerable other novels that are hundreds of pages in length.
8. Lorrie Moore, 'The Brazilian Sphinx', in *The New York Review of Books* (26 September 2009). Moore is reviewing Benjamin Moser's *Why This World: A Biography of Clarice Lispector* (Oxford: Oxford University Press, 2009). For some fine reflections on veering in Lispector, especially apropos 'obliqueness', 'sliding away', 'slanting', 'sloping', 'cutting', 'sidestepping', 'jumping' and 'leaping', see Hélène Cixous's *Reading with Clarice Lispector*, trans. Verena Conley (Minneapolis: University of Minnesota Press, 1990), pp. 30–2, 68–77 and 158–9.
9. See his Introduction to Mark Twain, *Pudd'nhead Wilson and Those Extraordinary Twins*, ed. Malcolm Bradbury (London: Penguin, 1986), p. 9.
10. Thus, for example, in Lorrie Moore's story 'Which is More Than I Can Say about Some People', there is a fractious moment when the mother is driving and the daughter announces that she needs to go to the bathroom:

    > Mrs. Mallon veered the car over to the left and slammed on the brakes. There were some black-faced sheep haunch-marked in bright blue and munching grass near the road.
    > 'Here?' asked Abby.
    > 'I don't want to waste time stopping somewhere else and having to buy something. You can go behind that wall.'

    Here the 'veered' is used, unusually, in a transitive mode and suggests deliberateness and control. But, even so, there is uncertainty, a kind of ambiguity (accentuated by the suddenness of 'slammed . . . brakes') that would not exist had Moore written, say, 'directed' or 'steered'. See Lorrie Moore, *The Collected Stories* (London: Faber and Faber, 2008), p. 91.
11. Cf. Jacques Derrida, *Rogues: Two Essays on Reason*, trans. Pascale-Anne

Brault and Michael Naas (Stanford: Stanford University Press, 2005), pp. 91–2, where he also explores what links democracy to the secret and to literature.

12. Hélène Cixous, 'Writing Blind: Conversation with the Donkey', trans. Eric Prenowitz, in *Stigmata: Escaping Texts* (London: Routledge, 1998), p. 144.

13. See Freud, *SE* XI: 160–1.

14. See, in particular, Giorgio Agamben, 'Bartleby, or On Contingency', in *Potentialities: Collected Essays in Philosophy*, ed. and trans. Daniel Heller-Roazen (Stanford: Stanford University Press, 1999), pp. 243–71; Branka Arsić, *Passive Constitutions, or, 7½ Times Bartleby* (Stanford: Stanford University Press, 2007); Gilles Deleuze, 'Bartleby; or, The Formula', in *Essays Critical and Clinical*, trans. Daniel W. Smith and Michael A. Greco (London: Verso, 1998), pp. 68–90; Jacques Derrida, *The Gift of Death*, 2nd edn, and *Literature in Secret*, trans. David Wills (London: Chicago University Press, 2008), pp. 75–7; Peggy Kamuf, '"Bartleby", or Decision: A Note on Allegory', in *To Follow: The Wake of Jacques Derrida* (Edinburgh: Edinburgh University Press, 2010), 34–42; and J. Hillis Miller, 'Who Is He? Melville's "Bartleby the Scrivener"', in *Versions of Pygmalion* (Cambridge, MA: Harvard University Press, 1990), pp. 141–78.

15. Hillis Miller, *Versions of Pygmalion*, p. 177. Further page references to Miller's essay are given parenthetically in the main body of the text.

16. See Stephen King, *On Writing: A Memoir of the Craft* (London: Hodder and Stoughton, 2000), p. 112.

17. For more on the weird senses of space and architecture of Melville's story, see Branka Arsić's remarkable book, *Passive Constitutions*; on 'invagination' in particular, see Peggy Kamuf's fine discussion in '"J" Is for Just a Minute: It's Miller Time When It Shimmers', in Barbara Cohen and Dragan Kujundžić (eds), *Provocations to Reading: J. Hillis Miller and the Democracy to Come* (New York: Fordham University Press, 2005), pp. 205ff.

18. See Jacques Derrida, 'Force of Law: The "Mystical Foundation of Authority"', trans. Mary Quaintance, *Cardozo Law Review*, 11: 5/6 (1990), 997.

19. Miller likewise comments on the 'uncannily appropriate' name of 'Wall Street': it is, he suggests, 'an embodied oxymoron' (149–50). Elsewhere he notes the playfulness of other names while singling out 'Bartleby': 'Just as the name Bartleby has, unlike the names Turkey, Nippers, and Ginger Nut, no metaphorical or allegorical resonance whatsoever, at least none that I can identify, but is a pure proper name if there ever was one, so he has a gift for making absolutely literal remarks that seem just slightly off the point' (159–60). Bartleby's remarks, in a word, veer. We might, however, query Miller's claim about the 'pure proper name': does the young man's name not suggest, for example, a world of capital and commerce, in which to 'barter' and 'buy'?

20. See Jacques Derrida, *Of Grammatology*, trans. Gayatri Chakravorty Spivak (Baltimore: Johns Hopkins University Press, 1976), p. 149.

21. Derrida, *Of Grammatology*, p. 314.

22. See Shoshana Felman, 'Turning the Screw of Interpretation', in *Yale French Studies*, 55/56 (1977), 102. Dan McCall makes a provoking comparison between *The Turn of the Screw* and 'Bartleby, The Scrivener': while the

latter 'is not exactly a ghost story', he says, it shares a Jamesian devious-ness apropos the idea that the writer can increase the ghostliness of a text through silence, elision and unnecessary specification (see *Melville's Short Novels*, p. 276). As McCall goes on to put it: 'what we bring to Bartleby might be more eerie and convincing than the Dead Letter Office and deeper than anything Melville could say' (276). It is perhaps a further illustration of the topicality of Melville's text that its status as ghost story has some-what shifted in the years since the publication of McCall's book *The Silence of Bartleby* (1989). These days, I suspect, most critics would be less likely to quibble over the idea that 'Bartleby' is a ghost story. We have witnessed something like a new turn of the ghostly.

23. The word 'zigzag' appears in Melville's texts on numerous occasions: see, for example, 'The Piazza', pp. 100 and 102, and 'The Lightning-Rod Man', p. 227, in *Billy Budd and Other Tales* (New York: Signet Classic, 1998).

24. Deleuze, 'Bartleby; or, The Formula', p. 80. Further page references appear parenthetically in the main body of the text.

25. Maurice Blanchot, *The Writing of the Disaster*, trans. Ann Smock (Lincoln, NE: University of Nebraska Press, 1986), p. 17, tr. sl. mod.

26. Cixous, 'Writing Blind', pp. 147–8. I have translated 'croisements' here as 'crossings', in an attempt to evoke the veering of intersections and transver-sal movements, but there is also a sense here (as Eric Prenowitz's transla-tion has it) of 'crossbreedings'.

27. 'An Inside Narrative' is the subtitle of 'Billy Budd, Sailor': see *Melville's Short Novels*, p. 103. Melville's notion of 'inside narrative' is at the same time, I believe, a key to understanding the apparently inverse logic accord-ing to which Bartleby is, in Branka Arsić's reading, 'someone who comes from "without"'. (See Arsić, *Passive Constitutions*, pp. 9–10.) For a detailed discussion of the phrase 'inside narrative', see Jinan Joudeh, who first taught me to read Melville's writings, if not properly, at least (which is perhaps more) as singular improprieties: 'The text's uncanny captivat-ing power is perhaps already intimated in the queerness of its subtitle, *An Inside Narrative*. With the strange snapping together of these otherwise seemingly familiar words, "inside" and "narrative", Melville's text locates itself in a new space of historical fiction. As "an inside narrative", it com-bines the art of ostensibly disinterested and detached historical report with some of the most bizarrely manipulative and unsettling strategies of storytelling ever deployed in the history of American Literature. The decep-tive simplicity of the phrase "an inside narrative" in truth wreaks havoc on all presuppositions concerning what is "inside" and what is not.' Jinan Joudeh, *Hoax Literature: Reading Edgar Allan Poe, Herman Melville, and Mark Twain* (Yale PhD dissertation, 2009), p. 218.

28. This is not the only moment in which the lawyer shows what we might call tendencies toward 'magical thinking'. There are at least three earlier instances: he refers to Bartleby's appearing, 'agreeably to the laws of magical invocation, at the third summons' (15); he recalls how 'presenti-ments of strange discoveries hovered round me' as he pictured the scrivener as a corpse, 'laid out, among uncaring strangers, in its shivering winding sheet' (18); and on another occasion he reports that he 'strangely felt something superstitious knocking at my heart' (20), discouraging him from

simply dismissing Bartleby from his employment. But what happens at this moment on Broadway is the only explicit instance in which magical or telepathic thinking supervenes on the external world.

29. See Jean-Luc Nancy, 'Exscription', in *The Birth to Presence*, trans. Brian Holmes and others (Stanford: Stanford University Press, 1993), pp. 319–40. Nancy observes: 'Writing, reading, I exscribe the "thing itself" – "existence", the "real" – which *is* only when it is exscribed, and whose *being* alone is what is at stake in inscription' (338–9). As Patrick ffrench nicely glosses it: 'The term *exscription* thus comes to mark the relation between literature and the real, between language and the world, which can displace and interrupt the logic of mimesis.' See Patrick ffrench, 'Sacrifice, Technique: Exscription', in Ian James and Patrick ffrench (eds), 'Exposures: Critical Essays on Jean-Luc Nancy', *Oxford Literary Review*, 27 (2005), 103–18: here, 111.

30. Bartleby says 'I would prefer not to' and others have their tongues turned and start speaking the language of the scrivener: 'I thought to myself, surely I must get rid of a demented man, who already has in some degree turned the tongues, if not the heads of myself and clerks' (21). But this tongue-turning is the very condition of the narration: the word 'prefer' haunts the language of the narrator from the start. It is already at work in the seemingly anodyne opening words of the text: 'I am a rather elderly man' (3). Melville's text plays on this little word, 'rather', throughout: it is rather a rhetorical tic in the lawyer's discourse, one that seems already to show up an association with the word 'prefer'. 'Prefer' itself is declared a 'queer word' (21) – this is the only instance of the word 'queer' in Melville's text (I will return in a few moments to the question of queering and veering: suffice to suggest that they are a passionate couple that go together, in the context of reading Melville) – but it is part of the queerness of 'prefer' that it can always entails a 'rather', and *vice versa*. You might say that one seems to preserve and bury the other within. Veering from first to second person, the lawyer wonders: 'What shall I do? what ought I to do? what does conscience say I *should* do with this man, or rather ghost. Rid myself of him I must; go, he shall. But how? You will not thrust him, the poor, pale, passive mortal, – you will not thrust such a helpless creature out of your door? you will not dishonor yourself by such cruelty? No, I will not, I cannot do that. Rather would I let him live and die here, and then mason up his remains in the wall' (27). The second 'rather' here ('*Rather* would I . . .') – given additional stress by the inverted syntax – is the only occasion on which the lawyer appears to use this word as a straightforward synonym for 'prefer' and is also perhaps the closest he comes to ventriloquizing or allowing himself to be ventriloquized by Bartleby's 'I would prefer not to'. But the sense of a twisting or turning of the lawyer's apparent preference for 'rather' *remains*, as it were, from the start.

31. 'Billy Budd, Sailor', in *Melville's Short Novels*, pp. 103–70. Further page references appear parenthetically in the main body of the text.

32. In Anthony Heilbut's *Exiled in Paradise: German Refugee Artists and Intellectuals in America from the 1930s to the Present* (Berkeley: University of California Press, 1997), we read: 'The last thing [Thomas Mann] wrote was a tribute to "the most beautiful story in the world", Melville's *Billy*

Budd: "O could I have written that!"' (496). Cited in *Melville's Short Novels*, p. 369.

33. An anagrammatic reading of 'vere' and 'veer' also corresponds with the play Melville's text makes over the anagram of 'Angles' ('meaning *English*, the modern derivative') and 'angels' (see 'Billy Budd, Sailor', p. 161).
34. See *Melville's Short Novels*, p. 370.
35. Derrida, *The Gift of Death*, p. 76.
36. A related further example of the 'figure of woman' is when the lawyer records that, in reaction to one of the earliest instances of Bartleby's 'I would prefer not to', '[f]or a few moments I was turned into a pillar of salt', that is, figuring himself as Lot's wife (Genesis 19: 26).
37. 'La Belle Dame sans Merci: A Ballad', in *The Poems of John Keats*, ed. Jack Stillinger (London: Heinemann, 1978), pp. 357–9. Little seems to have been written about Melville and Keats. One notable essay in recent years, however, is Debbie Lopez's 'Ungraspable Phantoms: Keats's *Lamia* and Melville's Yillah', in Larry H. Peer and Diane Long Hoeveler (eds), *Comparative Romanticisms: Power, Gender, Subjectivity* (Columbia: Camden House, 1998), pp. 159–70. Lopez explores the idea that '[i]n *Mardi* and *Pierre*, Melville employs Lamian figures both in responding to Keats in particular and in inquiring what it means to be, simultaneously, a Romantic and an American artist' (162).
38. 'Anguish' is a prominent word in Keats's poem: 'I see a lily on thy brow / With anguish moist and fever dew . . .'. Intriguingly, this is the key word for Dan McCall in his account of 'Bartleby, The Scrivener': 'The anguish in the story is real, of course, and I know of no other word than "anguish" to use.' See McCall's *The Silence of Bartleby*, quoted in *Melville's Short Novels*, p. 279.
39. Stillinger's text gives 'O what can ail thee, knight at arms, / Alone and palely loitering?' but also notes the original form of first publication: 'Ah what can ail thee, wretched wight / Alone and palely loitering . . .' (pub. in Leigh Hunt's *Indicator*, in 1820). Melville evidently encountered the poem in this earlier version: he may first have come across it in the New York *Arcturus* in 1842 (see *The Poems of John Keats*, p. 644), but we know for certain that he read a slightly later book containing this earlier version of Keats's poem, *The Indicator: A Miscellany for the Fields and Fireside*, published by Leigh Hunt in 1845. (See Geoffrey Sanborn, 'Lounging on the Sofa with Leigh Hunt: A New Source for the Notes in Melville's Shakespeare Volume', *Nineteenth-Century Literature*, 63 (June 2008): 104–15.) It is thus worth noting that 'Bartleby, The Scrivener' contains an instance of the archaic 'wight' (the lawyer at one point describes Bartleby as 'this lean, penniless wight': 15), and there is also a haunting suggestion of homology between 'Ah . . . wretched wight' and the lawyer's final words: 'Ah Bartleby! Ah humanity!' (34). My thanks to Andrew Bennett and Stephen Matterson for their help with clarifying the question of Melville's reading here.
40. For 'pale' in 'Bartleby, The Scrivener', see pp. 11, 15, 18 (on four occasions), 27, 31, 33 and 34; for 'palely', see p. 10; for 'alone', see pp. 21, 22 (twice), 25 (twice), 29 and 31. The emphasis on 'pale' and 'alone' in Keats's poem may be recalled especially in the closing stanzas:

I saw pale kings, and princes too,
   Pale warriors, death pale were they all;
They cried – 'La belle dame sans merci
   Hath thee in thrall!'

I saw their starv'd lips in the gloam
   With horrid warning gaped wide,
And I awoke and found me here
   On the cold hill's side.

And this is why I sojourn here,
   Alone and palely loitering,
Though the sedge is wither'd from the lake,
   And no birds sing.

One should not seek to close things down here, however: to propose veering as a way of thinking about intertextuality is to affirm a kind of radical openness. The notion of veerers in this respect is concerned with a thinking of intertextuality that is, as Graham Allen has argued, irreducible to 'stability and order' and resistant to all 'authority'. (See Graham Allen, *Intertextuality* (London: Routledge, 2000), p. 209.) We might consider this description of Bartleby, for example: 'But he seemed alone, absolutely alone in the universe. A bit of wreck in the mid Atlantic' (22). Bartleby's veering about in the mid Atlantic cannot be anchored to Keats's poetry any more than to Coleridge's 'Alone, alone, all, all alone, / Alone on a wide wide sea!' (see n.4, above). Intertexts are veerers: ghostly, fleeting, cryptic.

41. This sense of strangeness is linked to mystery in and of the name. The question of *mercy* haunts both texts: Keats's 'lady' is known only as 'la belle dame sans merci'. Correspondingly, in Melville's story, a stranger asks the lawyer about the 'ghost' (27) we know as Bartleby: 'In mercy's name, who is he?' (29) To which he replies, rather disingenuously: 'I certainly cannot inform you. I know nothing about him' (29).

42. Elizabeth Hardwick, 'Bartleby in Manhattan', qtd in *Melville's Short Novels*, p. 257.

43. Deleuze, 'Bartleby; or, The Formula', p. 68.

44. Agamben, 'Bartleby, or On Contingency', p. 255.

45. Cf. Hillis Miller's suggestion that 'Bartleby's "I would prefer not to" is a syncope, like a missed heartbeat, in the ongoing march of business, history, reasoning, and narrativity' (164).

46. Slavoj Žižek, *The Parallax View* (Cambridge, MA: MIT Press, 2006), p. 10.

47. See Jacques Derrida, 'I Have A Taste for the Secret', in Jacques Derrida and Maurizio Ferraris, *A Taste for the Secret*, trans. Giacomo Donis (Cambridge: Polity, 2001), p. 27. Cf. also his remark in the essay 'Resistances': 'deconstruction is also a logic of the spectral and of haunting, of surviving, neither present nor absent, alive nor dead: "I would prefer not to," and so forth.' See Jacques Derrida, *Resistances of Psychoanalysis*, trans. Peggy Kamuf, Pascale-Anne Brault and Michael Naas (Stanford: Stanford University Press, 1998), p. 30.

A Small Case of Civil Disobedience

I'm giving you this on the spur, live, as they say, recording it over the phone as I advance up the line, ostensibly speaking to my room-mate, three minutes and my name becomes a household word, if you suspect it, report it, Rob Bevington, Rob on the mob, you'll think I'm follow-ing in the shoes of Richard Reid, who isn't, I mean who else has had a greater individual impact on life in the twenty-first century, 24/7, for all the millions going through airport security it's time to take your shoes off, pay obeisance, fetishize that nutter, if you read me, my room-mate's quietly fooling around with a mobile as well, took a surreptitious photo of me in the queue already, another with luck at the big moment, something for all the networks, my name and face flashed on TVs and websites, in papers and magazines across the world, because I'm an intellectual terrorist, always have been, and now it's time to act, wishing you were here at Heathrow, talking low because I don't want to attract attention, furtive smile at room-mate, this is so glamorous I can't tell you, over the first hurdle of psychopathic security, ordered to remove all liquids and pastes from hand baggage and put them in a plastic bag and, if you don't have the correct small transparent zip-up kind, woe betide you and your nitroglycerine toothpaste and other toiletry items, and we're in line for the security point and body search, snaking about like snails, if you'll pardon the creepy metaphors because it is excruciat-ing after all, squashed into these concentration camp lines heading up to the X-ray machines and the conveyor belts where everyone takes off their jackets, coats and belts and all coins, keys, personal stereos and mobile phones out of pockets, and any laptop in a separate tray and finally, in recognition of His Holiness Richard Reid, remove shoes, Mr Reid read this, you thought YOU were big, well here's Rob Bevington, I'm going to have to switch this off, we're just a minute from security, this, folks, is the Bevington Effect, following a double-strategy offensive, I'm white as a kite, my room-mate's part Arab but they don't usually pick up on that, sky high like I said, the guy who's going to be fleecing me looks like a Pakistani gentleman, stories he's going to have, do nicely out of the whole business himself I imagine, I'm sweating a lot by now, picturing the havoc while I'm telling it, pitched clearly in my best actorly voice so others can bear witness, as I bring Heathrow to a standstill, the bloke's done with feeling me up and I announce as loud as the grave, Oh sir, but you haven't looked carefully enough, not at all, no no, this is when my room-mate takes the world-famous-for-a-nanosecond snapshot, Oh no sir, I cry, check out these deconstructive glasses, sir, and I take them off, because they're placebo glasses, I'm wearing my contacts underneath, and as you can see there are steel skewers specially fitted into the spectacle-frames and with them I blind my way into the cockpit, overcome the pilots and bring down the aircraft, better than a poke in the eye with a sharp stick I exclaim, by now I'm surrounded, but it doesn't stop me delivering my lines at the top of my lungs, the most thespian voice I can manage, I'm Rob Bevington, no one in future will be able to go onto an aircraft wearing glasses, and if you'd care to examine my laptop there at the end of the conveyor belt you'll find it contains a device, of course you won't have failed to spot it, and now the sirens start, evacuate the building, there is no need to panic, proceed calmly to the designated exits, no more laptops on planes, no more business first terrorism second, it's the Bevington Effect, the laptop also contains a file, my very own version of bomb making for dummies, called a small case of civil disobedience.

Chapter 10

Veering with Lawrence

For hours, in fall days, I watched the ducks cunningly tack and veer and hold the middle of the pond, far from the sportsman. (Henry Thoreau)[1]

Literature is perhaps essentially . . . a power of contestation. (Maurice Blanchot)[2]

Nothing in the 'western literary canon' is solid and unshifting, starting with the 'western' and the 'literary' themselves. Even the most apparently settled and established figures (Shakespeare, Dickinson, Dostoevsky or Proust, for example) slide and twist about, depending on a kaleidoscopic mix of factors – from singularly influential readings of the writer's oeuvre, life or historical context to the vaguer but no less imposing influence of cultural and intellectual trends. The flows that constitute 'influence' are never smooth or uni-directional.

What has happened to D. H. Lawrence? And how should we read him today?

Over the decades his reputation has veered. Anne Fernihough's phrase is 'see-sawed', but that suggests a sort of regulated up and down or backwards and forwards.[3] Lawrence's reputation has veered – from the days of F. R. Leavis's *The Great Tradition* (in which Lawrence's name seems written in the stars) to the great put-down initiated by Kate Millett's *Sexual Politics* (1969), and thereafter into the politically correct pastures of a sort of hazy and complacent disregard. The reputation of Lawrence's work can never return to what it was, when the canon of 'literature in English' was primarily a gathering of dead white men and there was little or no critical reflection on questions of misogyny or the dominance of 'phallic consciousness'. There is no reason for regret on that front, even if his current critical reputation seems skewed and bizarre in different ways. From a certain perspective we may suppose that Lawrence's canonization has, in recent years, been quietly completed with the impressive (if, for the average punter, unobtainable) Cambridge edition of his writings. One wonders how he might have reacted to this magnificent yet exclusive scholarly publication, whereby copies of his novels and other writings are prohibitively expensive and, in a good number of cases, only 'manufactured on demand'.[4]

If literary traditions and reputations veer, we can also think about veering as a way of exploring what makes a work canonical. In the most original and influential contemporary account of its subject, *The Western Canon: The Books and School of the Ages* (1994), Harold Bloom argues that canonicity is a matter of 'uncanny startlement': 'the authentically daemonic or uncanny always achieves canonical status'.[5] Thus in the case of Emily Dickinson, for example, 'her canonicity results from her achieved strangeness, her uncanny relation to the tradition' (308). This canon-achieving quality, Bloom writes, comprises 'a strangeness that we either never altogether assimilate, or that becomes such a given that we are blinded to its idiosyncrasies' (4). Elsewhere he proposes that the 'unrealized truth about the Western Canon' is that 'works are appropriated by it for their singularity, not because they fit smoothly into an existing order' (147). Picking up on the jaggedness that this last quotation implies, I would argue that works become canonical on account not only of their uncanniness but also of their veering character. Great works of literature do not conform, they veer, they take off in a new direction or new directions.

The theory of veering offers a fuller and more variegated conception of the swerve or clinamen that Bloom regards as a tropological feature of the rhetorical composition of strong poems. Veering is integral to a would-be canonical work's conduct, a prerequisite quality for breaking with and altering – while perhaps inevitably also becoming a part of – the tradition. Moreover, veering is always figured *in* the work in question: the great novel, poem or play is not just a veerer as regards what it makes of its readers or (in Bloomian terms) what it makes of its literary precursors, but also as regards what it does with figures of veering in itself. Veering is not only a figure of swerve or clinamen at a formal level (this story veers away from traditional conceptions of the human, this poem veers off from a Whitmanian aesthetic, and so on), but also figures in more explicit and reflexive ways in the text itself. Analysis of the ways in which veering is at work in literary texts can provide a new illumination and understanding of the canonical as such. This might in turn enable a new and sharper sense of a writer's persisting strangeness. Thus we may come to a fresh assessment of why Lawrence's novels, stories and poems matter, and see the politically correct pastures in which he is currently confined, like other fashions or trends, as a faintly comic mirage.

*

Reflecting on the figure of veering in Lawrence, loitering with the word 'veer' in its various forms, you might begin to feel something like a signature at work, that singularity that marks the work out from anyone and everyone else. It is right in front of you. No, over there, you have to

daVid hErbERt
Lawrence

One of the ironies of what is called modernism, and of the sort of academic critical industry that situates Lawrence as a modernist writer, is that people come to disregard, overlook or disavow precisely what is modern, in other words current, urgent and of the moment about it. Veering with Lawrence is a matter of reading him as a contemporary, a strange contemporary certainly, a contemporary in whose work the time is out of joint, but also a contemporary whose work seeks to explore right now, in the very moment of our reading, new forms and experiences of being, new conceptions of the self and human relationships, as well as a new apprehension of correspondences and distinctions between the human and non-human animal. You have to read Lawrence *veering*.

*

Consider what he says in *Studies in Classic American Literature* (1923): 'we must make a great swerve in our onward-going life-course'.[6] He says this, in effect, in virtually every poem, letter, essay, story or novel he writes.

Reading Lawrence opens up uncanny vistas of thought and feeling, vistas of space but also time (as in his haunting evocation of the 'vista of years' in the 1913 poem 'Piano'[7]), vistas perhaps initially solicited by a realization of how poetry or fiction is not a separate and enclosed space (neatly printed on a page or screen) but an experience, an exposure to quickness, in which one's entire sense of the world, life and being is susceptible to being transformed. We might here remark Lawrence's vehement resistance to the notion that there is anything theatrical about his fiction:

> I can't bear art that you can walk round and admire. A book should either be a bandit or a rebel or a man in the crowd . . . I hate the actor and audience business. An author should be in among the crowd . . . After all, the world is *not* a stage – not to me: nor a theatre: nor a show-house of any sort. And

art, especially novels, are not little theatres where the reader sits aloft and watches . . . and sighs, commiserates, condones and smiles . . . [T]hat's what my books are not and never will be.[8]

Lawrence's stories and novels (but also, no doubt, his poems) attest rather to a sort of bandit country, in which thinking and experience veer away, whether rebelliously open or hidden, across and beyond any conventional borders between literature and real life.

It is in this context that we should acknowledge the disruptive lessons and treacherous fidelities of the work of Gilles Deleuze and Félix Guattari, in particular *Anti-Oedipus* and *A Thousand Plateaus*, as well as Deleuze's writing on Lawrence elsewhere: in, for example, 'On the Superiority of Anglo-American Literature' and 'Nietzsche and Saint Paul, Lawrence and John of Patmos'.[9] Deleuze and Guattari take up Lawrence's 'great swerves' with extraordinary energy and conviction. Hence their concern with lines of flight, flows, multiplicity, deterritorialization, the anomalous and becoming-animal. Deleuze and Guattari give us Lawrence as a Nietzschean, counter-Freudian ('anti-Oedipal') philosopher, a radical theorist of society and life: no pastures of benevolent neglect for *their* Lawrence. Their work also responds *in kind* (as oddly little recent critical writing on Lawrence does) to the fluxes and energies of Lawrence's own writing. Their work is in many ways more Lawrentian than that of anyone writing in English on Lawrence in recent years. And on this very account it also makes swerves of its own. Deleuze and Guattari veer in their own fashion. Their lines of flight are neither Lawrence's nor anyone else's. As Deleuze remarks, everyone has his or her 'line of slope or flight'.[10] Or to put it in terms of what I have been arguing in this book, in a reworking of Freud's celebrated contention that each human organism 'wishes to die only in its own fashion': *each organism veers in its own fashion.*[11] And the *organism* here is not only or not necessarily the human organism. Moreover, veering is as much about living as dying, about the desire for life as much as about any 'death wish'. This is also where the notion of treachery comes in. Not least as part of the effort to avoid falling into the 'twiddle-twaddle' category to which Lawrence assigned much if not all literary critical writing, it is necessary to veer in a singular way, not to toe the line but to jump or fly off somewhere else, differently.[12]

This is clear from Deleuze's remarkable essay 'On the Superiority of Anglo-American Literature' (1977). No other text conveys more sharply how important a figure Lawrence cuts for Deleuze (or Deleuze and Guattari). Deleuze casts himself as 'a novelist in philosophy', for whom Lawrence is a constant inspiration and point of reference.[13] For him,

Lawrence is one of those writers 'who create their line of flight, who create through a line of flight': with Lawrence, 'everything is departure, becoming, passage, leap, daemon, relationship with the outside' (27). 'There is always betrayal in a line of flight' (30), Deleuze remarks, a betrayal of 'the fixed powers which try to hold us back, the established powers of the earth' (30). It is a force of 'becoming', a creative treachery in which 'one has to disappear, to become unknown' (33). To read Lawrence is to encounter lines of flight, written through love, always a bit 'demoniacal' and 'delirious' (30). As Deleuze puts it: 'One only writes through love, all writing is a love-letter: the literature-Real' (38). Lawrence's work is concerned with what Deleuze calls (in a Blanchotic turn of phrase) 'a love of life which can say yes to death' (49). His writing breaks away from the festering narcissism of 'resentment' and the whimpering logic of the 'taste for castration' (37). It is a nomadic writing in which one has 'neither past nor future' (28). Lawrence, perhaps better than any other Anglo-American writer, shows us that

> [i]n reality, writing does not have its end in itself, precisely because life is not something personal . . . [T]he aim of writing is to carry life to the state of a non-personal power . . . to be a flux which combines with other fluxes. (37)

Deleuze's 'On the Superiority of Anglo-American Literature' is a crucial essay for orienting or provoking new readings of Lawrence. Indeed Deleuze's writing (with or without Guattari) on Lawrence, more generally, prompts a rephrasing of their own formulation concerning the importance of D. H. Lawrence for thinking about psychoanalysis: 'let us keep Deleuze and Guattari's reaction to Lawrence in mind and never forget it!'[14] At the same time, however, it has to be said that Deleuze and Guattari actually provide very little in terms of readings of specific literary works. (One exception is the attention they give to Lawrence's tortoise poems, to which we shall return.) Veering with Lawrence, in short, is not and never will be a matter of simply veering with Deleuze and Guattari.

'Lines of flight' are about veering. As Deleuze comments in the Preface to the English Language Edition of *Dialogues* (in 1986): 'A line does not go from one point to another, but passes between the points, ceaselessly bifurcating and diverging, like one of Pollock's lines'.[15] The reference to Jackson Pollock is suggestive: Deleuze relates the line to image, to the visual and painterly. Without wishing to understate the role of the visual in Lawrence, however, I would like to suggest that veering (or what Deleuze evokes here as the 'ceaselessly bifurcating and diverging') is crucially intertwined with the question and experience of language: in short, formations, transformations and deformations of English, sounds and silence, rhythms and repetition, rhetoric and syntax, vocabulary and wordplay, the poetic and poematic, narrative drive and desire, and so on.

Veering with Lawrence, that is to say, has first and foremost to do with the texture and detail of his language. It is a matter of veering between the kind of macrological mode of Deleuze and Guattari, then, and a new micrology. To veer with Lawrence is to read him as a thinker and inventor in the context of philosophy, psychoanalysis and society, but also to encounter him as a storyteller and poet, in other words to reckon with the force and strangeness of his writing as it moves across the fictional and poetic and beyond. In attempting to trace a sort of alternative tradition here, a veering lineage from Melville to Lawrence and beyond, everything turns on the importance of attending to the question of language – of what Lawrence does with and to English.

*

In a sense there is nothing very surprising about Deleuze and Guattari's general lack of engagement with the singular character of Lawrence's language, the vocabulary, syntax and spacing, rhetoric and narrative strategies of his novels, stories and poems. It might seem, in fact, a decidedly Lawrentian gesture. For Lawrence himself repeatedly proclaims the secondariness of language, its peripheral or impertinent nature in relation to those fluxes and becomings, the *jouissance* and self-shattering with which his work is most deeply concerned.[16] Language has a very strange role in Lawrence. This has been the focus of the work of perhaps the most thought-provoking Lawrence critic of our time, Gerald Doherty. Doherty illuminates the radical paradox of Lawrence as a writer for whom language is at once superfluous and indispensable, nothing and everything.[17] On the one hand, Lawrence's work is concerned with what Doherty calls 'true desire', with what 'is presymbolic, presocial' and 'eludes the logocentrism that grounds being in language, and the self in rational thought'.[18] Hence Lawrence's concern with what Doherty terms 'the depersonalizing excess of the orgasm', with 'that uncanny manifestation of maximum being before social discourse and habit usurp it' (7). Thus, for Lawrence, 'the subject in language is a mere thought-construction, which deep meditation or the access to *jouissance* dissolves' (150, n.23). On the other hand, language is of course essential to Lawrence's project. As Doherty puts it, 'language at once precedes constructions of the conventional self, and works toward their final undoing' (5). In addition, as I have sought to suggest at various moments in this book, *jouissance* and veering go together. Lawrence's fictions and poems are love stories or love letters that invite us to reckon with the force of Jacques Lacan's remark that 'speaking of love is in itself a *jouissance*'.[19]

*

With these sorts of paradox and shifting uncertainty in mind, then, I want to argue for a new reading and new evaluation of Lawrence through the figure and force of *veering*. Let us try, then, to reckon with this little word, image and vocable, this figure or feeling, this movement and force, as it appears in Lawrence's work. Let us try to see how it fits with the incessant, unarrestable character of his work, its engagement with the uncanny and the non-human, its radical quickness. Quickness: life and speed, but also wordplay. For veering also embroils us in an experience of Lawrence's language – its tensions and pleasures, turns and rhythms, its notorious contradictoriness, its playfulness and, finally (how ever odd or un-Lawrentian this may sound), its reflexivity, its critical or analytical involvement with itself and its sheering off from itself. If Lawrence's is, in Docherty's phrase, 'an aphrodisiac art' that is ultimately concerned with 'a hovering, high-tensional *frisson*', the trembling solicitation or *jouissance* of 'an ecstatic no-self',[20] if Lawrence's work is a space of flight, multiplicity and the anomalous (to recall the terms of Deleuze and Guattari), we might experience this most forcefully as a veering – a veering in reading, in feeling, beyond language. No *jouissance* without veering – in and out of language.

Veering can be physical, mental or linguistic, apparently foreseen or unforeseen, uncertainly internal or external. It shifts between one and the other, and *within* one and the other. Veering can be seen to operate in Lawrence's work as a sort of node or nodal point. It has to do with suddenness and surprise, unexpected change of direction, tone or sense, loss of control, a turn or turning bound up with otherness.

*

Allotropic. That is the adjective in the well-known letter to Edward Garnett (5 June 1914), in which Lawrence declares of *The Wedding Ring*: 'You mustn't look in my novel for the old stable ego of the character.'[21] Rather, one has to be attentive to what he calls 'allotropic states' (183), states of mind or being that are perhaps not so much *states* as veerings. A classic dictionary definition of 'allotropic' would suggest that it means 'having different physical properties, though unchanged in substance' (*OED*), and in his letter to Garnett it is evident that Lawrence is primarily concerned with this sense, specifically apropos carbon (the difference as well as continuity, that is to say, between coal and diamond). But there is also a more literal and more mobile sense at work in reading Lawrence, closer to that of the original ancient Greek, namely the allotropic as loss of state, as *turning other*, another turning, turning *as* other, turning of or to otherness. *Veering* would be allotropic. A good deal less familiar than the reference to dispensing with 'the old stable ego of the character' is the way the letter to Garnett goes on to evoke a corresponding or alternative movement:

> Again, I say, don't look for the development of the novel to follow the lines of certain characters: the characters fall into the form of some other rhythmic form [*sic*], like when one draws a fiddle-bow across a fine tray delicately sanded, the sand takes lines unknown. (184)[22]

Allotropology of rhythm, fiddling unknown lines of music in sand. Lawrence's *again* ('Again, I say, don't look . . .') is as much difference as repetition; and it becomes clear that the shifting line or lines are not only about 'character' but about a vibratile and more diffuse experimentation: allotropic writing.[23]

*

At the beginning of chapter 2 of *Fantasia of the Unconscious* (1923), Lawrence writes:

> We are all very pleased with Mr Einstein for knocking that eternal axis out of the universe. The universe isn't a spinning wheel. It is a cloud of bees flying and veering round. Thank goodness for that, for we were getting drunk on the spinning wheel.
>
> So that now the universe has escaped from the pin which was pushed through it, like an impaled fly vainly buzzing; now that the multiple universe flies its own complicated course quite free, and hasn't got any hub, we can hope also to escape.
>
> We won't be pinned down, either. We have no one law that governs us. For me there is only one law: *I am I*. And that isn't a law, it's just a remark. One is one, but one is not all alone. There are other stars buzzing in the centre of their own isolation. And there is no straight path between them. There is no straight path between you and me, dear reader, so don't blame me if my words fly like dust into your eyes and grit between your teeth, instead of like music into your ears. I am I, but also you are you, and we are in sad need of a theory of human relativity.[24]

The universe is 'a cloud of bees flying and veering round'. After Einstein, Lawrence suggests, we must conceive space and time anew. Everything is buzzing: we might note again the emphasis on sound and vibration here, as well as the metamorphosis of music into dust and grit, Lawrence's singularly jarring music of the spheres. There are no straight paths in between the stars or between 'you and me'. Everything in the universe is veering. And Lawrence's language, also, is veering: it is 'we' one moment, 'you' and 'I' in isolation the next; law one moment, lawless the next; a spinning wheel becomes bees become fly, flying's veering, fly flies, words fly, words dust, in your eyes, in all these you and I's.

Lawrence is perhaps not the first writer who springs to mind in terms of linguistic play but, in truth, the quickness of his language calls for a quite new and different understanding of what 'wordplay' might be. As Gerald Doherty has made clear, it might seem easy to construe Lawrence's work in terms of logocentrism – the foundational author-ity of presence, the self-identity of the 'I', an unproblematic relation between language, on one side, and the world or universe, on the other, and so on.[25] This is implicit, for example, in Lawrence's declaration, in the passage just cited, that 'One is one' or 'I am I'. But any straightfor-ward reading here is sent off course. I believe that we have not yet really begun to get a measure of the perversity of language in Lawrence, of its singularly perverse relation to the world or universe 'around us' (to use an anthropo-logo-geocentrism his work also sends spinning). For all the avowed commitment to oneness there is just as sharp a sense of erotic treachery, division and diremption, the anomalous or odd, delirious flux. Sometimes this seems deliberate, at other times inadvertent. Are the puns of 'flies' and 'eyes' in the passage from *Fantasia of the Unconscious* deliberate or not? It is perhaps not finally a question of intention, but rather of what, earlier in this book, I called *inadvertention*, the blind designs of language as it veers. This is closely related, in turn, to the swarming *wordlife* of Melville.

Lawrence's affirmation – not simply of the world off its hinges, but of the universe off its hub – corresponds to what he says in his essay 'Art and Morality' (1925): 'Each thing, living or unliving, streams in its own odd, intertwining flux, and nothing, not even man nor the God of man, nor anything that man has thought or felt or known, is fixed or abiding.'[26] The universe, the very '-verse' of the universe is veering. In its singular, demonic and allotropic way, Lawrence's writing seeks to affirm and counter-sign this veering. This flux, this veering of the universe is perhaps best evoked in poetry, in the spiralling aspirations of the poetic. Thus in his Preface to the US edition of *New Poems* (1920) Lawrence writes about 'another kind of poetry', a poetry of 'the immedi-ate present', in which 'the strands are all flying, quivering, intermingling into the web', a poetry of 'wind-like transit', 'the spinning of sky winds', 'the quick of the ever-swirling flood', of 'all the universe', in which nothing is 'at rest, static, finished'.[27] Veering in Lawrence, then, is in the homonym and homophone, it swirls about at the atomic and subatomic level of letters. It is there, it is happening in the bees veering, in the flying becoming fly becoming flies becoming words in your eyes, in the anthropomorphic oxymoronic 'multiple universe' escaping, in the crazy relation evoked between 'relativity' (Einstein) and 'relativity' (Lawrence). What is relativity in Lawrence? It is a kind of poetry. Indeed there is a poem by that name ('Relativity'), in which the speaker proclaims: 'I like relativity and quantum theories / because I don't understand them / and they make me feel ... / ... as if the atom were an impulsive thing / always changing its mind' (*CP*: 524).

Veering *with* Lawrence is a necessarily perverse matter, for it also means veering 'without', 'against', 'away from'. As noted earlier, veering is always a betrayal. You have to veer in your own fashion. As Lawrence stresses, you are you, you are veering in what he calls (just a paragraph or so further on from this passage in *Fantasia of the Unconscious*) 'the long curve of your own individual circumambient atmosphere' (26). But the environment of this circumambience is not simply yours, any more than your words ever can be. For you are also caught up, a-whirl in the mind-changing movements of language, in what might be called allotropes of *beeing*. This pun is terrible, perhaps, but not so different from what is going on in the passage. It may also help to show up another seemingly crazy relation, a certain affinity between Lawrence and Lewis Carroll. Wordplay here bespeaks a veering within and out of words, wordsplying and wordsplay, wildlife of wordlife, a kind of unarrestable banditry.[28] It would be a matter of what Deleuze calls, apropos Carroll, '"indefinite" plays on words which would be like a becoming instead of a completion'.[29]

Veering in Lawrence is inseparable from opening to the inhuman (the 'multiple universe', without its 'hub') and to non-human animal life (here, primarily perhaps, the 'cloud of bees'), but it is also – already and in spite of any particular agent, any author or self – at work in language itself, in the capacity that words themselves have to veer in direction, sense and meaning, to veer in themselves and in relation to every other word, a veering in and around every buzzing sound. It recalls the poem called 'Sinners', where 'the bee that blunders / Against me goes off with a laugh': the 'bee' that veers, rhyming, into 'me' as it buzzes out of 'blunders'.[30] In this context we might recall another suggestion made by Lacan, in one of his last seminars, that the 'chain of signifiers' identified by Ferdinand de Saussure is, in fact, less a chain and really more like a swarm of bees.[31] Here it might be noted how, over many decades now, Lawrence's own repeated and consistent evocations of what is 'wordless', 'unspeakable', 'beyond language' have, at once aptly and paradoxically, helped to encourage a lack of critical attention to his language

and especially, perhaps, its crazy relations. We need to be newly attentive to the quickness of his writing – to Lawrentian veering *in* language
as well as beyond it, spinning out of language, out of control.

*

'Samson and Delilah', first published in 1917, is not perhaps one of
Lawrence's greatest short works.[32] He himself calls it a 'story . . . which
I don't much care for'.[33] It may look in many ways like 'unremarkable Lawrence', to echo a formulation from Geoffrey Hartman on
Wordsworth. But 'Samson and Delilah' has the distinction of being the
only story that Lawrence set in Cornwall (despite his living there for
almost two years, between 1915 and 1917), as well as being a story spun
out of a story's pun, out of a double and duplicitous *veering*.

It is about a man, apparently a stranger, arriving by bus near
Penzance, who makes his way on foot through mining country to an inn
called The Tinners Rest. There he sits alone, eats and drinks, observes
the landlady and her daughter, and is an object of scrutiny for the landlady in turn. At the end of the evening he refuses to leave. He claims that
the landlady is his wife and her daughter his. She claims not to recognize
him and eventually calls upon some soldiers, who happen to be in the
pub, to help get rid of him. They get some rope and manage to bring him
down. The woman, we are told, 'pinned down his arms like a cuttle-fish
wreathed heavily upon him' (117). After which they tie him up so that
he is 'like a bound animal' (119). (These are just a couple of examples
of the ways in which Lawrence's story insists on a thinking of the non-
human animal.) They take him outside, then 'loosen the knot' so that he
can work himself free on the understanding that he 'go without creating
any more disturbance' (119). Freeing himself, in due course, the stranger
walks away, stops to rest, leaning against a wall for a long time, then
'turn[s] again in the silent night, back towards the inn' (119).

To spoil the denouement for you as completely as possible, I have to
say that the man is surprised to find the door open, goes quietly inside
and, by the fire in the kitchen, confronts the woman again, now alone.
Until this point the reader does not know what the nature of the couple's
relationship is, or even whether there is any relation beyond the fact
of his having spent the evening in the inn. Now, however, we discover
that he is indeed returning to her after an absence of 'over fifteen year'
(120) spent in the United States. The story ends with an ellipsis, a sort
of aposiopesis of speech and action – suspended on the brink, the reader
is left to imagine, of 'something sexier' (to recall a teasing phrase from
Gerald Doherty).[34] Here is the ending, then, which pauses on a question
of meaning and denial, reneging and silence, aposiopesis and *jouissance*:

'Wonderful fine woman you be, truth to say, at this minute.'

She only sat glowering into the fire.

'As grand a pluck as a man could wish to find in a woman, true as I'm here,' he said, reaching forward his hand and tentatively touching her between her full, warm breasts, quietly.

She started, and seemed to shudder. But his hand insinuated itself between her breasts, as she continued to gaze in the fire.

'And don't think I've come back here a-begging,' he said. 'I've more than *one* thousand pounds to my name, I have. And a bit of a fight for a how-de-do pleases me, that it do. But that doesn't mean as you're going to deny as you're my Missis . . .' (122)

We could analyse at length what is characteristic about Lawrence's language here, as it shifts between (figural) positing and (physical) positioning, veering between proposition and the unspoken, subtle and brazen, in the ironic twists of appearance, in the allotropic 'But' ('She . . . seemed to shudder. *But* his hand . . .'; or '. . . a bit of a fight for a how-de-do pleases me, that it do. *But* that doesn't mean . . .' (emphases added)), in the play of 'pluck' (with its associations of fighting, courage and innards which are uncertainly those of a human and non-human animal, as well as the tacit rhyme beginning with 'f'), in the peculiar echo of Hamlet and 'tak[ing] the ghost's word [*this* revenant's word] for a thousand pound' (III, ii, 260–1), and in the turns of the little word 'as' as its sheers off in several directions at once ('*as* grand a pluck *as*', '*as* I'm here', '*as* she continued to gaze', 'that doesn't mean *as* you're going to deny *as* you're my Missis . . .' (emphases added)).

But I want to turn back to the opening of the story and simply comment on what is 'veering' from the start or, perhaps, from before the start. Here, then, is a short paragraph that occurs on the first page, describing the man's journey in 'the lonely homeliness of the Celtic night' towards The Tinners Rest:

> Now and again short, stumpy, thick-legged figures of Cornish miners passed him, and he invariably gave them goodnight, as if to insist that he was on his own ground. He spoke with the west-Cornish intonation. And as he went along the dreary road, looking now at the lights of the dwellings on land, now at the lights away to sea, vessels veering round in sight of the Longships Lighthouse, the whole of the Atlantic Ocean in darkness and space between him and America, he seemed a little excited and pleased with himself, watchful, thrilled, veering along in a sense of mastery and of power in conflict. (108)

What is Lawrence doing with 'veering' here? How does this work in the larger context of the story?

Originally the story was entitled 'The Prodigal Husband', but Lawrence later altered it to 'Samson and Delilah'.[35] As Jacques Derrida reminds us, 'a title is always a promise'.[36] As such it is characterized by a certain excess, hanging over the text and our reading, as we wait in some hope and expectancy of discovering why the work has the title it has. The problem with the original titling is that it rather gives the game away. To any reader familiar with the return of the prodigal son (in Luke 15), this title effectively reveals the enigma that propels the narrative. Within a week or so of dispatching the manuscript of 'The Prodigal Husband' to J. B. Pinker (in November 1917), Lawrence has 're-christened it'.[37] But in a sense 'Samson and Delilah', as it is now generally known, remains haunted by the earlier title: Lawrence veers, there is veering in the title.[38] Indeed we might even think of 'Veering' *as* another, albeit imaginary or ghostly title for the story, for this word perhaps more than any other marks or remarks the reflexive nature of Lawrence's writing, the way in which the narrative depends at once on movement and on the withholding of knowledge.

Numerous words recur in the opening four paragraphs of Lawrence's story, including 'darkness', 'twinkled', 'curiosity', 'lights' and 'looking' (or 'looked'), but the repetition of 'veering' has decisive significance. Within the same sentence 'veering' veers from the external to the internal, from the nautical to the psychological. The 'vessels veering round in sight of the Longships Lighthouse' at once prefigure and give way to a more enigmatic veering. Now external now internal, the recurrence of this participle ('veering along in a sense of mastery and of power in conflict') signals the moment at which the narrative most clearly seems to cross over into the mind and body of the as yet unnamed man. Veering is irreducibly double. It crosses and even, we might say, it double-crosses what Roland Barthes calls the hermeneutic code and the proairetic code. Why is this man 'excited', 'watchful', 'thrilled, veering along'? What are we to make of this quietly ecstatic moment?

This singular, singularly double figure, 'veering', at once specifies the real ('the vessels veering round in sight of the Longships Lighthouse') and what is literary, what makes this text a work of narrative fiction. With 'veering' we shift into the mind and body of this character: it marks the irruption of the telepathic, the magical 'thought-adventure' and 'emotion-adventure' of a work of fiction in which the narrator or narrative voice relates a character's thoughts and feelings as if from within.[39] And at the same time *veering* also describes the governing narrative strategy of the text, namely its veering between the perspective of one character (Willie, or 'Samson') and another (Alice, or 'Delilah') while resisting or avoiding until very close to the end of the story the disclosure of their relation to one another.[40] 'Veering' figures as a sort of cryptic beacon of avoidance. It comports secrecy and absence or avoidance of relation, and in this way it signals, in turn, the literary. Without this strangely duplicitous veering there would be no story.

*

Perhaps more than any other writer we have discussed in this book, Lawrence is interested in veering as a strategy of *avoiding*. You veer in order to avoid obstacles. It is not the only reason for veering, of course, and indeed *reason* may not even be in operation. But veering can be, crucially, a way of getting round and away from things. *Aaron's Rod* (1922) provides compelling material in this context.[41] The opening two chapters ('The Blue Ball' and 'Royal Oak') culminate in a remarkable cluster of veerings, a proliferation that makes this verb ('to veer', 'veered') a curious kind of violence. It is a sort of flailing flourish or paraph, a nodal word in which the energies of Lawrence's writing up to this moment at once converge and diverge.

Aaron Sisson is a Miners' Union secretary, a troubled man unable to adjust to home life after the war, manifestly alienated from his wife and young daughters. It is Christmas Eve: 'this was home, this was Christmas: the unspeakably familiar. The war over, nothing was changed. Yet everything changed' (11). He has difficulty interacting with those about him: he eats the dinner his wife has made for him, plays his piccolo flute (the 'rod' of the novel's title), then goes off alone to the pub, the Royal Oak, where he engages in some heated discussion about 'the common good', money, education, British colonial rule in India, and other topics. The atmosphere is sexually heated too: there has evidently been something going on between himself and the landlady. Heated but also icy cold. For this evening 'his innermost heart was hard and cold as ice . . . [H]e disliked his whole circumstances. A cold, diabolical consciousness detached itself from his state of semi-intoxication' (23).

The narrative does not allow us to attribute the sense of trouble to any single cause, any more than it rests within any single perspective. It veers between, within and away, avoiding any clear or explicit revelation of what is driving the protagonist or where the narrative is going. It is closing time and (leaving the landlady yellow-faced with 'passion and rage') Aaron Sisson departs. The chapter concludes with these three short paragraphs:

> Outside it was dark and frosty. A gang of men lingered in the road near the closed door. Aaron found himself among them, his heart bitterer than steel.
> The men were dispersing. He should take the road home. But the devil was in it, if he could take a stride in the homeward direction. There seemed a wall in front of him. He veered. But neither could he take a stride in the opposite

direction. So he was destined to veer round, like some sort of weather-cock, there in the middle of the dark road outside the 'Royal Oak'.

But as he turned, he caught sight of a third exit. Almost opposite was the mouth of Shottle Lane, which led off under trees, at right angles to the high-road, up to New Brunswick Colliery. He veered towards the off-chance of this opening, in a delirium of icy fury, and plunged away into the dark lane, walking slowly, on firm legs. (25)

The repetition of *veer* here ('he veered', 'to veer', 'he veered') partakes of the delirium and fury described. The peculiar, as if stabbing insistence of this verb indeed seems to encapsulate the nature of Lawrence's novel up to this point. Of this verbal knot or nodal point let us note, first of all, that *veering is not one*. There are three veerings, and veerings in three directions. We could provisionally designate these as: (1) external veering (the way the world is described, Aaron's veerings viewed from the outside); (2) internal veering (the character's interior thoughts and feelings, veerings within); and (3) narrative veering or narrativeering (storytelling as veering, avoiding revelation, specificity or explicitness).

The force of Lawrence's writing devolves from this veering multiplic-ity. Moreover the multiplicity cannot, in fact, be simply divided up in this pseudo-trinitarian manner: the pleasure of reading Lawrence has to do with the ways in which the very specification and differentiation between these categories is *avoided*. The external veers into the internal, and/or *vice versa*. It is the pleasure of a text that avoids telling you where the external (the voice of the narrator, veering about in the outside world) passes over into the internal (the feelings, thoughts or inner dis-course of a character), as well as where any of this is leading (or who, in fact, knows): the proairetic and hermeneutic codes are crossed by another force. Where is Aaron or, indeed, the narrative going? Where or perhaps, more veeringly, *wheer*?[42] And wheer does the narrator's voice end or Aaron's begin?

'So he was destined to veer round, like some sort of weather-cock, there in the middle of the dark road outside the "Royal Oak".' This is a bizarre sentence. Especially given its position at the end of the paragraph, it evokes something vertiginous and mad, final but unend-ing. And at the same time we cannot tell whether this destiny is being ascribed to Aaron by the narrator, or if it is what Aaron himself thinks and feels. Narrative voice: veering in the dark.

Even the internal (the space of magical thinking, the structure of telepathic narration that enables the reader to learn what a character is thinking or feeling) is at odds with itself, at odds, that is to say, with any model of characterization based on reason, identity and the primacy of consciousness. As the final paragraphs of 'Royal Oak' make clear,

Aaron Sisson is a veering character. This 'veer[ing] round like some sort of weather-cock' recalls the evocation of him some ten or so pages earlier: 'He never went with the stream, but made a side current of his own' (14).[43] The veering is not only physical and literal (the man in the road veering about) or emotional and erotic (the man unwilling or unable to return to his wife, *or* to turn to the woman in the pub). There is also something demonic about it: the sense that 'the devil was in it', the feeling of being 'destined to veer round' as if endlessly, mad as a weather-cock, diabolically.

It is difficult not to suppose there is something faintly Oedipal about the road junction in Lawrence's text. Like the Sophoclean crossroads in *Oedipus Rex*, the divergent routes presenting themselves are suggestive of free will, a matter of choice, but also of chance: 'But as he turned, he caught sight of a third exit . . . He veered towards the off-chance of this opening . . .'. There is an air of hallucination or fairy tale in this third exit, as well as apparent randomness in 'the off-chance' it embodies. And as a sort of *détournement* of this Oedipal scene, veering is foregrounded as a delirious 'plung[ing] away' *in* the moment, *of* the moment.

In an essay entitled 'Looking at Obstacles' Adam Phillips argues that, from the perspective of Freudian psychoanalysis, the unconscious is 'a place without obstacles'.[44] Thus, he argues, jokes are important to Freud because they are 'the most ingeniously efficient way of rescuing our pleasure from the obstacles' (90). Correspondingly, Phillips suggests, literature – and *Oedipus* in particular – teaches us that we can 'never know whether obstacles create desire, or desire creates obstacles' (87). This gets us close, I think, to a sense of what makes veering pivotal for thinking about literature and about its relation to psychoanalysis. From the perspective of what I have been calling the literary turn, the unconscious is perhaps not so much 'a place without obstacles', in Phillips's phrase, as a veering *of* place, a tilting, swerving, spinning, whirling that literature gives us, on the off-chance, a sense of vertigo, *jouissance*, queerness and telepathy that cannot be corralled within a where or who, within the terms or terminology of the consciousness or the unconscious of *someone*.

'He veered towards the off-chance of this opening . . .': we cannot tell to whom this 'off-chance' is being ascribed, whether it is to be read, in effect, as Aaron Sisson's word or as the narrator's. In the unfolding of the novel we do not know what kind of off-chance this is, where it will lead, or indeed whether it is as much an off-chance in the moment of writing as in the moment of reading, an off-chance phrase as unexpected and enigmatic to the author as to the reader. An off-chance is 'A remote chance, a possibility; a contingency out of the probable course' (*OED*,

'off-chance', n.). There is an oddity about this compound ('off-chance')
similar to that of the 'outside chance': it is a chance or possibility that is
at the very edge of chance, off or outside it, no longer merely or simply
chance. The *OED*'s 'out of the probable course' helps sharpen a sense
of the *off-chance* as, itself, a sort of veerer. It catches up the 'delirium'
ahead, veering back towards the verb and making it newly duplicitous
and strange: is this veering external or internal, actual or psychological,
real or fictive? What does it mean, 'in a delirium', to veer towards an
off-chance?

*

If veering entails 'a sense of mastery and of power in conflict' (to recall
Lawrence's words in 'Samson and Delilah'), there is also something of
the devil in it, a sense of being possessed, delirious, at a loss. It figures
in turn what we might call a deconstructive force of literature in the
moment of letting go, letting words and feelings veer and swarm, pleasure in a sense of secrecy or the unknown that does not belong or return
to anyone (author, narrator, character, reader). 'Veering' thus becomes
a sort of by-word for the cryptaesthetic character of the literary work,
as the reader is embroiled in the chiasmatic strangeness of whether
(in Adam Phillips's phrase) 'obstacles create desire, or desire creates
obstacles'. In short (though Phillips, I suspect, would not put it in this
way), *veering* engages us in an experience of the undecidable.[45] And in
the ghostly quick of this veering it is no longer a question of any nar-
ratological fantasy of omniscience, any single point of view, any 'stable
character of [an] ego' or, indeed, any fixed *place* that could be called 'the
unconscious'. There is a kind of magic: we are both inside and outside
Aaron Sisson's thoughts and feelings, and such narrative telepathy or
magical thinking is the very oxygen of the novel. At the same time, in
declaring that, prior to leaving the pub, Aaron himself 'was in a state
of semi-intoxicated anger and clairvoyance' (24), the text installs a sort
of internal mirror for magical thinking. Clairvoyance is a wavering and
uncertain element internally as well as externally.

But such magic can never be simply a cause for wonder. As Lawrence
remarks elsewhere, 'Nothing is wonderful unless it is dangerous.'[46] And
the wonder and danger of veering are never a matter of literature or 'the
novel' as a closed space, separated off from the real. On the contrary, it
is the very trembling or tremulation of life. As he says in 'Why the Novel
Matters', novels are strange 'tremulations on the ether': 'the novel as a
tremulation can make the whole man [or woman] alive tremble'.[47] It is a
question of 'trembling with a new access of life' – not going 'in any one
direction' but being 'startle[d] . . . into change'.[48] You have to veer and

keep on veering. And if the novel or 'bright book of life' (in Lawrence's famous phrase) is a veerer, this has to do with a sense of what is dangerous, with off-chance and uncanny surprise.[49] The novel would be a veerer, then, (1) on account of its flickering, fleeting affirmations of promise and potential (what might be called, after Hélène Cixous, literature's weird '*might*'[50]); (2) in its explorations of the literary itself as a space of magical thinking and feeling, the devilish and clairvoyant, strange shiftings between 'desire' and 'obstacle'; and (3) in its dynamic but uncertain, uncanny commingling of the magical with the real.

The novel has to do with the time out of joint *right now* – provoking transformations in the very moment of reading. The sort of mad veering at the end of chapter 2 of *Aaron's Rod* is intimately bound up with the real – with an abhorrence of war, in particular, and of the strangulating power of money. It is an eerily posthumous novel in that sense – a ghost work about capitalism over our dead bodies. As Aaron puts it: 'It's money we live for, and money is what our lives is worth – nothing else. Money we live for, and money we are when we're dead: that or nothing' (21). And at the same time, in the same breath, *Aaron's Rod* seeks to affirm the singular and anomalous, the sheer oddness and freakishness of people, especially English people. Chapter 2 concludes in Aaron's veering towards the off-chance of an opening; chapter 3 gives another opening, veering off in a new and quite different tone: 'It is remarkable how odd or extraordinary people are in England. We hear continual complaints of the stodgy dullness of the English. It would be quite as just to complain of their freakish, unusual characters . . .' (26).

*

Receiving a photograph of Mark Gertler's painting *Merry-Go-Round*, Lawrence writes to him from Cornwall, on 9 October 1916: 'Your terrible and dreadful picture has just come. This is the first picture you have ever painted: it is the best *modern* picture I have seen: I think it is great, and true. But it is horrible and terrifying.'[51] As 'a man of words and ideas', Lawrence can hardly say what he 'read[s] in the picture' (660). Gertler's painting depicts a lurid blue, fiery orange, red and yellow whirling array of men and women with frozen gaping-mouthed expressions, endlessly circulating on model horses. It is a sort of pictorial apocalypse, 'a real and ultimate revelation', declares Lawrence, a 'combination of blaze, and violent mechanical rotation and complex involution, and ghastly, utterly mindless human intensity of sensational extremity' (660). Gertler's painting demonstrates for Lawrence 'the great articulate extremity of art' (661): it is the pictorial equivalent of war poetry, we might say, and it is *veering*.[52]

Lawrence does not use the word in his letter of October 1916, but it shows up a year or two later, in the strange and violent story, 'Tickets Please' (1918). Gertler's painting seems to haunt this wild wartime piece, with its coldly erotic fairground scene, lit up on 'a drizzling ugly night':

> The roundabouts were veering round and grinding out their music, the side-shows were making as much commotion as possible. In the cocoa-nut shies there were no cocoa-nuts, but artificial war-time substitutes, which the lads declared were fastened into the irons. There was a sad decline in brilliance and luxury. None the less, the ground was as muddy as ever, there was the same crush, the press of faces lighted up by the flares and the electric lights, the same smell of naphtha and [of new-] fried potatoes, and of electricity.[53]

Veering: a sort of password, in short, for what we might consider all the love letters of Lawrence's reality literature, his singularly perverse literary vorticism.

Concerned to evoke 'the most dangerous tram service in England' (35), 'Tickets Please' opens with a remarkable single sentence that, in its 'plunging' and 'tilting' rush, prefigures the veering roundabouts at the fair and thus generates a vortiginous narrative figure weirdly resembling the doubling movements of 'violent mechanical rotation and complex involution' Lawrence attributes to Gertler's great painting:

> There is in the Midlands a single-line tramway system which boldly leaves the county town and plunges off into the black, industrial countryside, up hill and down dale, through the long, ugly villages of workmen's houses, over canals and railways, past churches perched high and nobly over the smoke and shadows, through stark, grimy, cold little market-places, tilting away in a rush past cinemas and shops down to the hollow where the collieries are, then up again, past a little rural church, under the ash trees, on in a rush to the terminus, the last little ugly place of industry, the cold little town that shivers on the edge of the wild, gloomy country beyond. (34)

The very title of this story, 'Tickets Please', is a soliciting: welcome aboard, you're on your way, veering with Lawrence.[54]

*

A merry-go-round or roundabout can veer, like the universe in miniature. So can a laden coffin. Thus, in the painfully abrupt and unnervingly condensed passage at the end of part one of *Sons and Lovers* (1913), we read about the death of Paul Morel's brother, his body being brought into the house by Paul's father and five other men. Twice we are told how 'the great dark weight' of the coffin 'swayed' as its bearers came up the garden and door steps. As the coffin 'rode like sorrow on their living flesh' and 'Paul saw drops of sweat fall from his father's brow', there is the constant foreboding of a ghastly inappropriateness, the coffin falling (open). And then:

> Six men were in the room – six coatless men, with yielding, struggling limbs, filling the room and knocking against the furniture. The coffin veered, and was gently lowered on to the chairs. The sweat fell from Morel's face on its boards.[55]

The eerily active 'veered', suggesting that the coffin has a life of its own, is in uneasy tension with the passive 'was gently lowered'. The ghostly animism of this active verb-form evokes a cryptic, unreadable corpse.[56] Veering with Lawrence, the uncanniness of death would never be far away. Knocking on would: veering between 'wood' and 'would'. As the text goes on: 'The family was alone in the parlour with the great polished box . . . Paul thought it *would* never be got out of the room again. His mother was stroking the polished *wood*'.[57] Returning from the funeral, Mrs Morel is said to be unable, 'after this, to talk and take her old bright interest in life. She remained shut off.' But then a turn of telepathic narration lets us in: 'All the way home in the train she had said to herself: "If only it *would* have been me!"'[58]

*

Veering: it is the very play and force of desire. (And so I veer about, in and out of Lawrence's extraordinary writings, from so-called 'post-war' to 'pre-war' to 'wartime', from later to earlier and sideways and inside out, wanting in doing so also to veer in time, to respond in my own way to his affirmations of veering in time, to his 'pagan' characterization, for example, in *Apocalypse*:

> we have to drop our own manner of on-and-on-and-on, from a start to a finish, and allow the mind to move in cycles, or to flit here and there over a cluster of images. Our idea of time as a continuity in an eternal straight line has crippled our consciousness cruelly. The pagan conception of time . . . allows movement upwards and downwards, and allows for a complete change of the state of mind, at any moment.[59]

Such, I have tried to suggest, is the time of veering.) Lady Chatterley and the gamekeeper have made love for the first time in his hut. She goes back the next day but does not find him. She goes back the day after that and still there seems to be no sign of him.

> Night was drawing near again; she would have to go. He was avoiding her.
> But suddenly he came striding into the clearing, in his black oilskin jacket like a chauffeur, shining with wet. He glanced quickly at the hut, half-saluted,

then veered aside and went on to the coops. There he crouched in silence, looking carefully at everything, then carefully shutting the hens and chicks up safe against the night.

At last he came slowly towards her. She still sat on her stool. He stood before her under the porch.

'You come then,' he said, using the intonation of the dialect.

'Yes,' she said, looking up at him. 'You're late!'

'Ay!' he replied, looking away into the wood.[60]

Evidently he has seen her (having 'glanced quickly at the hut', he 'half-saluted'), but he veers away to attend to the safety of the chickens 'against the night'. 'He veered aside': he wants her, so he avoids her – to want wanting, veering with veering, wanting intensified by avoiding. A few moments later: '"Is it," she stammered, "is it that you don't want me?"'[61] Does the gamekeeper's 'veer[ing] aside' suggest that he does not want her or redouble the sense that he does? His veering aside corresponds to his 'looking away' ('"Ay!" he replied, looking away into the wood'). The literary work keeps secret – averted. It is a matter, as Rei Terada says apropos the figure of 'looking away', of a sense of beauty in what is *singular* and *evanescent*.[62]

*

To desire, to fear, to desire to fear, to fear to desire: veering.

*

'An Island', chapter 11 of *Women in Love* (1921), opens with Ursula chancing upon Birkin by a large deserted pond. He has been mending a punt and he solicits her help in getting it into the water: 'There were two small islands overgrown with bushes and a few trees, towards the middle. Birkin pushed himself off, and veered clumsily in the pond.'[63] You can veer clumsily or you can veer gracefully, but with Lawrence, of course, the distinction between them is not necessarily hard and fast: clumsiness can become a form of grace, just as readily as Ursula's feelings about Birkin are susceptible to shifting and transforming. She is 'rather repulsed' (138) by Birkin at this point, as well as 'troubled and bewildered' (140), but soon enough she is finding what he says 'attractive', indeed *really* desirable' (142). He is talking about love as a word that 'we hate . . . because we have vulgarized it' (145). She is feeling 'a fine hate of him' while also finding him 'utterly desirable': he is 'priggish and detestable' and yet, at the same time, 'so quick and attractive' (144). The clumsy veering of Birkin in the punt at the outset gives way to something quite different:

Again they looked at each other. She suddenly sprang up, turned her back to him, and walked away. He too rose slowly and went to the water's edge, where, crouching, he began to amuse himself unconsciously. Picking a daisy he dropped it on the pond, so that the stem was a keel, the flower floated like a little water-lily, staring with its open face up to the sky. It turned slowly round, in a slow, slow Dervish dance, as it veered away.

He watched it, then dropped another daisy into the water, and after that another, and sat watching them with bright, absolved eyes, crouching near on the bank. Ursula turned to look. A strange feeling possessed her, as if something were taking place. But it was all intangible. And some sort of control was being put on her. She could not know. She could only watch the brilliant little discs of the daisies veering slowly in travel on the dark, lustrous water. The little flotilla was drifting into the light, a company of white specks in the distance. (145)

It is like 'The Ancient Mariner' in reverse, as what is perceived as boat- or ship-like (a 'flotilla') recedes into 'specks'.[64] Veering in love: *Women in Love* turns around this figure. When we read about how Birkin 'veered clumsily in the pond' we perhaps do not pause to wonder about so-called point of view or focalization: is it Birkin himself who realizes he is veering clumsily, or is it Ursula's perception, or is it the perspective of what used to be called an 'omniscient narrator' but is rather the telepathic animal-machine, the magical thinking in multiple voices of narrative fiction?

Veering is the word. It comes back in this passage about the daisies as they veer in an almost hypnotically beautiful way and thus seem to supplement, displace or substitute for the earlier clumsiness. It is the dancing drifting pivot: the word 'veer' ('veered', 'veering') is the erotic crossover, the figure or movement in which the man and woman are drawn into one another. Drawing in, drawing on a language of what is unconscious or unknown ('he began to amuse himself unconsciously', 'it was all intangible . . . She could not know'), the passage entwines the perspectives of Birkin and Ursula in a telepathic turn that belongs or comes back to no one. The only 'open face' is of the veering daisy, 'staring . . . up to the sky'. The man and woman can 'only watch'. The whirling Dervish dance, with its connotations of trance, drifts into the 'strange feeling' that 'possessed' Ursula. 'A strange feeling possessed her, as if something were taking place.'[65] And the ghostliness, the haunting or entrancing strangeness of this 'taking place' is in the 'veering': 'She could not know. She could only watch the brilliant little discs of the daisies veering slowly in travel on the dark, lustrous water.' No one says anything. It is writing, a magical thinking in multiple voices, a veering subvocal oddity. In this silent telepathic citation of the daisy that slowly 'veered away' from Birkin, Ursula watches the daisies 'veering slowly' away.

*

Veering with Lawrence has to do with machines and stars, beasts and flowers, as much as humans. And it has to do with writing itself – in other words, with death and a kind of magic. What I have called his perverse and singular literary vorticism is about the queer turns of reading. The literary work is open but cryptic, like a daisy. 'Lawrence's literary vorticism' is not a modest recataloguing suggestion for filing away in the dusty annals of modernism. It is about the chancy and strange dangers of reading, about new and undiscovered whirls of thinking and feeling. Lawrence's queer vorticism is quite different from what he refers to as the *'mere noises'* of Italian futurist poetry or 'mere jags and zig-zags' of 'futuristic paintings', in which art becomes 'pure accident, mindless'.[66] He writes this in a letter to the American poet Amy Lowell in November 1916. Of course 'veering' can always seem empty, mindless. As tactfully as he can (in a letter that begins by thanking her for the precious donation of a cheque for £60), he intimates that that is just what Lowell comes close to in her poem 'An Aquarium', which he quotes:

> Streaks of green and yellow iridescence
> Silver shiftings
> Rings veering out of rings
> Silver – gold –
> Grey-green opaqueness sliding down[67]

Vortiginous Lawrence: neither mindless nor merely artful.

In a remarkably consistent manner, across novels and stories, poems and essays, Lawrence's work compels us to read and imagine a veering – figures and effects of veering – not confined to the human. If there is something beautiful (or clumsy) about veering, this involves a sense of aesthetics of motion that is not only or perhaps not at all human. We might here recall Gerald Doherty's cautionary suggestion that 'the aesthetic is the realm that most effectively "erects a barrier between species"'.[68] The force and value of veering as I have sought to explore it in this book entails the constant questioning, dismantling or avoidance of such a barrier. Animals, non-human creatures can veer, as we have seen in numerous contexts in the preceding pages. Birds, reptiles, insects, mammals, aquatic creatures: all veer.

The greatness of Lawrence's writing has to do with its realizations of a veering universe and veering life. Figured as turning away or turning to avoid, veering is what living creatures do. As he remarks in *Studies in Classic American Literature*:

> The difference between life and matter is that life, living things, living creatures, have the instinct of turning right away from *some* matter, and of

blissfully ignoring the bulk of most matter, and of turning towards only some certain bits of specially selected matter.[69]

Veering with Lawrence, as I have called it, entails a newly critical sensitivity to anthropocentrism, and a heightened apprehension of the sorts of responsibility to otherness that 'human veering' peculiarly entails. Veering is about desire and fear, the idiom and singularity: everyone veers in their own way. If Lawrence gives us something new, this has to do with the experience and event of veering as a thinking and becoming beyond self or ego. As Deleuze summarizes: 'Stop thinking of yourself as an ego in order to live as a flow, a set of flows in relation with other flows, outside of oneself and within oneself.'[70] Veering *with* Lawrence, however, also means going beyond him or (perhaps) behind his back, doing new things with his words. It means engaging with what I have tried to sketch out in this book as a kind of ethics of veering, and elaborating questions of responsibility regarding the singularity and absolute otherness of, for example, a Galapagos green turtle.

Veering is what language does, with us and without us. Words veer in sense, in the twists and turns of their own strange materiality. Syntax veers. We are all a-veer in the Lucretian dance of atoms, subjects of – but also to – the downpour of words and signs. Adventuring in English, it is about what happens to our language as we read or write. Hélène Cixous describes this strangely erotic and affirmative encounter with the book (a novel or poem or, perhaps, an essay) that is writing you:

> It makes a fool of me while creating itself. This too is its secret: the proof of creation is laughter. It is a marvel to feel the innumerable vibrations of the soul make themselves, collect themselves, crystallize themselves into words, to witness the rain of atoms Lucretius made us dream of. Millions of signs rain down and in their flood they stick to one another, they kiss.[71]

Veering is not only in the words but, even more perhaps, in the spaces and spacing, in the silences. Veering in Lawrence's work is about all the velocities and shifts, alterations and gaps, switches and doublings in narrative flux.[72] It is also about the more specifically poetic veerings I have attempted to note elsewhere in this book: the turning of a line or sentence, the turning of a word within itself and between its various appearances ('relativity', for example, or 'veering' itself). But veering in Lawrence is never simply a linguistic or literary thing: it is insistently about life, desire and danger, dying and death, the world and others, the future. To veer with Lawrence is to acknowledge and reflect on what makes the distinction between the real and the fictional tremble: veering also just *is* that tremulation or trembling. Which is also to say that it cannot be stilled or fixed into a time or place or identity: it is ghostly, veering in itself, out of itself.

It corresponds with the figure evoked in Lawrence's poem 'St Matthew' (1923), a creature at once human and non-human, amoebic and protean, a messianic veerer,

> Face downwards
> Veering slowly
> Down between the steep slopes of darkness, fucus-dark,
>   seaweed-fringed valleys of the waters under the sea,
> Over the edge of the soundless cataract . . . (*CP*: 321–2)

Soundless, verging on darkness, it is conjured as human, even a saint, a Jesusoid fish, a bat, an uncanny heart with wings, a ghostly ray.[73]

*

I conclude with another poem, 'Tortoise Family Connections' (*CP*: 356–8), written in Italy in 1920. This extraordinary little text begins (or 'goes on') as follows:

> On he goes, the little one,
> Bud of the universe,
> Pediment of life.
>
> Setting off somewhere, apparently.
> Whither away, brisk egg?
>
> His mother deposited him on the soil as if he were no more than droppings,
> And now he scuffles tinily past her as if she were an old rusty tin.
>
> A mere obstacle,
> He veers round the slow great mound of her—
> Tortoises always foresee obstacles.
>
> It is no use my saying to him in an emotional voice:
> 'This is your Mother, she laid you when you were an egg.'
>
> He does not even trouble to answer: 'Woman, what have I to do with thee?'
> He wearily looks the other way,
> And she even more wearily looks another way still,
> Each with the utmost apathy,
> Incognisant,
> Unaware,
> Nothing. (*CP*: 356–7)

This poem is, as Lawrence himself nicely observed, 'so queer'.[74] As always with his so-called 'animal poems' we are caught up, challenged and haunted by the experience of a question perhaps most neatly encapsulated by Timothy Clark: 'What is the "literal" language for describing the behaviour of an animal?'[75] For all the 'emotional' projections of 'voice', *it is no use*: this 'brisk egg' does not speak. It veers in silence.

Perhaps the funniest and most illuminating account of 'Tortoise Family Connections' is in Deleuze and Guattari's *A Thousand Plateaus*. It is a question of what they call 'becoming-tortoise' and the 'anomalous':

> Lawrence's becoming-tortoise has nothing to do with a sentimental or domestic relation. Lawrence is another of the writers [like Melville] who leave us troubled and filled with admiration because they are able to tie their writing to real and unheard-of becomings. But the objection is raised against Lawrence: 'Your tortoises aren't real!' And he answers: Possibly, but my becoming is, my becoming is real, even and especially if you have no way of judging it, because you're just little house dogs . . . The anomalous is neither an individual nor a species; it has only affects, it has neither familiar or unsubjectified feelings, nor specific or significant characteristics. Human tenderness is as foreign to it as human classifications.[76]

The anomalous is the singular and singularly odd. 'A mere obstacle, / He veers round the slow great mound of her— / Tortoises always foresee obstacles.' In this lovely off-chance of off-rhyme (*mere, veers*), the tortoise veers round and away from the mother (and father), veering off from every known or specifiable relation. 'On he goes', this 'bud of the universe', 'this atom' in 'the dark-creation morning' (*CP*: 357–8), a veering in verse, a poetic creature veering past us, without a word, veering in the direction of new and unheard-of relations and relativities. Lawrence's queer baby tortoise recalls – but also perhaps projects a new angle on – what the Mock Turtle says in *Alice's Adventures in Wonderland*: 'We called him Tortoise because he taught us.'[77] In its deliberations on the etymology of 'tortoise', the *OED* suggests a derivation from the Latin *tortus*, meaning 'twisted'.

Notes

1. Henry Thoreau, *Walden*, in *Walden and Resistance to Civil Government*, 2nd edn, ed. William Rossi (New York: Norton, 1992), p. 158.
2. Maurice Blanchot, 'The Great Reducers', in *Friendship*, trans. Elizabeth Rottenberg (Stanford: Stanford University Press, 1997), p. 67.
3. Introduction to *The Cambridge Companion to D. H. Lawrence*, ed. Anne Fernihough (Cambridge: Cambridge University Press, 2001), p. 6.
4. This is the phrase that appears on the CUP website, applying to many of the thirty-eight titles listed under 'The Cambridge Edition of the Works of D. H. Lawrence'. Lawrence's playful phrase 'bookfarming' comes to mind: see his *Studies in Classic American Literature* (New York: Viking Press, 1971), p. 105.

5. Harold Bloom, *The Western Canon: The Books and School of the Ages* (1994; London: Macmillan, 1995), pp. 3 and 458. Further page references are given parenthetically in the main body of the text.

6. Lawrence, *Studies in Classic American Literature*, pp. 137–8.

7. See *The Complete Poems of D. H. Lawrence*, ed. Vivian de Sola Pinto and F. Warren Roberts (New York: Viking Press, 1975), p. 148. Further page references to poems by Lawrence are to this edition and appear parenthetically in the main body of the text, abbreviated 'CP'.

8. Letter to Carlo Linati, 22 January 1925, in *The Letters of D. H. Lawrence, Volume 5, March 1924–March 1927*, ed. James T. Boulton and Lyndeth Vasey (Cambridge: Cambridge University Press, 1989), p. 201.

9. Gilles Deleuze and Félix Guattari, *Anti-Oedipus: Capitalism and Schizophrenia*, trans. Robert Hurley, Mark Seem and Helen R. Lane (London: Athlone Press, 1984), and *A Thousand Plateaus: Capitalism and Schizophrenia*, trans. Brian Massumi (Minneapolis: University of Minnesota Press, 1987); Gilles Deleuze, 'On the Superiority of Anglo-American Literature', in Gilles Deleuze and Claire Parnet, *Dialogues II*, trans. Hugh Tomlinson and Barbara Habberjam (London: Continuum, 2006), pp. 27–56, and 'Nietzsche and Saint Paul, Lawrence and John of Patmos', in *Essays Critical and Clinical*, trans. Daniel W. Smith and Michael A. Greco (London: Verso, 1998), pp. 36–52.

10. See Deleuze, 'Dead Psychoanalysis: Analyse', in *Dialogues II*, p. 99.

11. For the Freudian formulation, see Sigmund Freud, 'Beyond the Pleasure Principle', in *SE* 18: 39.

12. On twiddle-twaddle, see Lawrence's 'John Galsworthy', in *Phoenix: The Posthumous Papers of D. H. Lawrence, 1936*, ed. Edward D. McDonald (New York: Viking, 1972): 'All the critical twiddle-twaddle about style and form, all this pseudo-scientific classifying and analysing of books in an imitation-botanical fashion, is mere impertinence and mostly dull jargon' (539).

13. See Deleuze, 'On the Superiority of Anglo-American Literature', p. 41. Further page references to this essay are given parenthetically in the main body of the text.

14. See Deleuze and Guattari, *Anti-Oedipus*, p. 49.

15. See Deleuze, 'Preface to the English Language Edition', in *Dialogues II*, p. vii.

16. I borrow the term 'self-shattering' from Leo Bersani, in particular *A Future for Astyanax: Character and Desire in Literature* (Boston: Little, Brown and Company, 1976) and *The Freudian Body: Psychoanalysis and Art* (New York: Columbia University Press, 1986).

17. See in particular Gerald Doherty's two excellent studies, *Theorizing Lawrence: Nine Meditations on Tropological Themes* (New York: Peter Lang, 1999), and *Oriental Lawrence: The Quest for the Secrets of Sex* (New York: Peter Lang, 2001), as well as his essay, '*Women in Love*: Sacrifice, Sadism and the Discourse of Species', in Earl Ingersoll and Virginia Hyde (eds), *Windows to the Sun: D. H. Lawrence's 'Thought-Adventures'* (Madison: Fairleigh Dickinson University Press, 2009), pp. 69–98.

18. Doherty, *Oriental Lawrence*, p. 7.

19. See Jacques Lacan, 'A Love Letter', in *Feminine Sexuality: Jacques Lacan*

and the école freudienne, ed. Juliet Mitchell and Jacqueline Rose, trans. Jacqueline Rose (London: Macmillan, 1982), p. 154.

20. Doherty, *Oriental Lawrence*, p. 11.

21. Letter to Edward Garnett, 5 June 1914, in *The Letters of D. H. Lawrence, Volume 2, June 1913–October 1916*, ed. George J. Zytaruk and James T. Boulton (Cambridge: Cambridge University Press, 1981), pp. 182–4: here, p. 183. Further page references appear parenthetically in the main body of the text.

22. See C. P. Ravilious, 'Chladni Figures', *Notes and Queries*, 20 (1973): 331–2. Ravilious describes how E. F. F. Chladni (1756–1827) was concerned with investigating vibration in sonorous bodies and, in experimenting with horizontal plates of sand and a violin-bow, came to witness what (in Chladni's words) 'no mortal had previously seen', the sand suddenly shifting into 'a star with ten or twelve rays' (332). Ravilious concludes: 'The Chladni Figures are therefore in some sort "lines unknown", outside the control of the experimenter, just as the novelist's creations resist his conscious will' (332). He then cites Lawrence's veering and demonic poem, 'Song of a Man Who Has Come Through': 'Not I, not I, but the wind that blows through me!' (*CP*: 250).

23. For another reading of the 'allotropic' in Lawrence, see Garrett Stewart, 'Lawrence, "Being", and the Allotropic Style', *Novel*, 9: 3 (1976), 217–42. In ways that correspond closely to what I have been calling the art of veering, Stewart finds in Lawrence's work 'a vocabulary and grammar' that are 'self-generating' and emphasizes what he calls 'a keeping underway – and under self-investigation – of diction, syntax, and imagery whose separate momentums reinforce and impel each other' (221).

24. D. H. Lawrence, *Fantasia of the Unconscious* and *Psychoanalysis and the Unconscious* (Harmondsworth: Penguin, 1971), p. 25. Further page references appear parenthetically in the main body of the text.

25. See in particular, Doherty, 'Lawrence and Jacques Derrida: A Dialog Across the Abyss', in *Theorizing Lawrence*, pp. 145–61. Doherty contends that, in contradistinction to Derrida, Lawrence 'accepts as unproblematic the transactions between signifier and signified, consciousness and speech, selfhood and utterance: he takes for granted the role of language, as a transparent mediating agent, though he sometimes recognizes its function as one code among others' (147).

26. See Lawrence, 'Art and Morality', in *Phoenix*, p. 525.

27. See Lawrence, 'The American Edition of *New Poems*, by D. H. Lawrence' in *Phoenix*, pp. 218–22.

28. The word 'banditry', we may recall, comes from the Latin verb 'to proclaim, to proscribe'. The *OED* gives the following etymology: 'Italian *bandito* "proclaimed, proscribed," in plural *banditi* n. "outlaws," past participle of *bandire* = medieval Latin *bannīre* to proclaim, proscribe' (see *OED*, 'bandit', n.).

29. See Deleuze, 'On the Superiority of Anglo-American Literature', p. 52.

30. See Lawrence, 'Sinners', in *CP*: 223–4.

31. Quoted in Alicia Arinas, 'Episodic or what Lacan's teachings are not', *Psychoanalytical Notebooks 8* (2002), 51–6: here, 54. My thanks to Lauren Lumby for this reference.

32. D. H. Lawrence, 'Samson and Delilah', in *England, My England and Other Stories*, ed. Bruce Steele (Cambridge: Cambridge University Press, 1990), pp. 108–22. Further page references to this story will be given parenthetically in the main body of the text.

33. See letter to Ernest Collings, 3 March 1917, in *The Letters of D. H. Lawrence, Volume 3, October 1916–June 1921*, ed. James T. Boulton and Andrew Robertson (Cambridge: Cambridge University Press, 1984), p. 100.

34. I am thinking of the deployment of the word 'sexier' and the playful parenthesis that follows it when Doherty talks, at the beginning of *Oriental Lawrence*, about Lawrence's rejection as early as 1908 of 'his Christian affiliation (Congregationalism) as too repressive, too dogmatic and rational, too bound to social conformity, and too life-denying and negative in its sexual attitudes'. Doherty then adds: 'Already he was in quest of something sexier (how he would have loathed that word!), something richer and more impulsive, more compulsive and exotic than (what he saw as) Christianity's parched and pedestrian doctrines' (3).

35. See letter to J. B. Pinker, 17 November 1916, in *Letters* 3: 34.

36. See, for example, Jacques Derrida, *Mémoires: for Paul de Man*, trans. Cecile Lindsay, Jonathan Culler and Eduardo Cadava (New York: Columbia University Press, 1986), p. 115.

37. See Bruce Steele's Introduction to *England, My England*, p. xlii.

38. Indeed, having told Pinker that he has 'rechristened it', Lawrence immediately adds: 'If you like the old title better, take it back.' See *Letters* 3: 34.

39. For the characterization of 'a novel' as not only a 'record of emotion-adventures [but] also a thought-adventure', see D. H. Lawrence, *Kangaroo*, ed. Bruce Steele (Cambridge: Cambridge University Press, 1994), p. 279. These phrases arise in a curious passage about non-human telepathy ('There can't be much telepathy about bullocks . . . Telepathy! Think of the marvellous vivid communication of the huge sperm whales' (278–9)), which practises telepathic narration ('. . . thought Richard . . . said Richard to himself . . .' (279)) without, however, making any explicit connection between these telepathies or forms of 'thought-adventure'.

40. And even this 'end' and 'disclosure of relation', of course, is elliptical, as I have tried to suggest: a pausing of aposiopesis and *jouissance, jouissance* in aposiopesis, aposiopesis of *jouissance*.

41. D. H. Lawrence, *Aaron's Rod*, ed. Mara Kalnins (Cambridge: Cambridge University Press, 1988). Further page references appear parenthetically in the main body of the text.

42. On the opening page of the novel, when Aaron Sisson's daughters ask him to set up the Christmas tree, he asks: 'Wheer is it?' (5). It is as if the text is already hinting at a 'veer' in 'wheer', a where that veers. Lawrence gives this dialectal version 'wheer' elsewhere: see, for example, 'Odour of Chrysanthemums' and 'Wintry Peacock', in *The Collected Stories of D. H. Lawrence* (London: Heinemann, 1974), pp. 276, 281, 363 and 364.

43. The associations of veering and weather cocks are well established. Under the heading for 'weather-cock' as 'changeable, inconstant' (sense 3a), for example, the *OED* cites a novel from 1801, entitled *Marvellous Love-Story*: 'Miss Harrison was one of those every-day sort of weather-cock

characters who veer about with every varying gust of prejudice, folly, or envy.' But cf. also the much earlier image of the veering 'Weather-cock of government' in John Dryden (discussed earlier in this book). In a more contemporary vein (if you will pardon my homophone), veering is evoked in Stephen King's '1922' when the narrator remarks that 'the years between childhood and adulthood are gusty years, and those living through them spin like the weathercocks some farmers in the Midwest used to put atop their grain silos': see Stephen King, '1922', in *Full Dark, No Stars* (London: Hodder and Stoughton, 2010), p. 8.

44. Adam Phillips, 'Looking at Obstacles', in *On Kissing, Tickling and Being Bored* (London: Faber and Faber, 1993), pp. 83–98: here, p. 97. Further page references are included parenthetically in the main body of the text.

45. I mean this in the sense that 'the undecidable' is a phrase or concept generally associated with deconstruction and the name of Jacques Derrida; and reference to the writings of Derrida constitutes an intriguing absence in Phillips's work. Extensive reflection might be given to the question of what sort of 'obstacles' Derrida's work presents to him.

46. See Lawrence's review of *A Second Contemporary Verse Anthology*, in *Phoenix*, p. 324.

47. See Lawrence, 'Why the Novel Matters', in *Phoenix*, pp. 533–8: here, p. 535.

48. See Lawrence, 'Why the Novel Matters', p. 536. It is perhaps worth noting here that Lawrence's use of the term 'novel' is hardly conventional: the 'supreme novels' (536), for him, include the Bible, Homer and Shakespeare.

49. See Lawrence, 'Why the Novel Matters', p. 535.

50. For a rich and detailed reading of Cixous's work from this perspective, see Jacques Derrida, *H. C. for Life, That is to Say . . .*, trans. Laurent Milesi and Stefan Herbrechter (Stanford: Stanford University Press, 2006).

51. See letter to Mark Gertler, 9 October 1916, in *Letters* 2: 660–1: here, 660. Further page references appear parenthetically in the main body of the text. Gertler's *Merry-Go-Round* (1916) is currently on display at Tate Britain, in London. The Tate website notes: 'This work was painted at the height of the First World War, which seems to be its subject. Men and women in rigid poses, their mouths crying in silent unison, seem trapped on a carousel that revolves endlessly. Gertler was a conscientious objector. He lived near London's Hampstead Heath, and may have been inspired by an annual fair held there for wounded soldiers. The fairground ride, traditionally associated with pleasure and entertainment, is horrifically transformed into a metaphor for the relentless military machine. He explained, "Lately the whole horror of war has come freshly upon me."' See http://www.tate.org. uk/servlet/ViewWork?workid=5130&tabview=work.

52. Going to see Gertler's painting, in February 2011, I was overwhelmed, first of all, by the sheer scale of the painting (189.2 x 142.2 cm). I was struck, too, by the fact that the title has no definite article (contrary to its occasional designation elsewhere). It is simply *Merry-Go-Round*. I subsequently jotted down the following, in no particular order: 'The red-uniformed young man (bell-boy?) in the centre foreground has a faintly expectant expression, otherwise the faces all open-mouthed, showing their (bad) teeth, their expressions more obviously of terror, horror, perception

aghast. The solitude of the sailor, the only one (on the left) with his back to us; his buttocks, however, rhyming with those of the horse – the most erotically explicit aspect of anatomical presentation. The bell-boys' slant-edly odd caps (like face-on breasts, or medical instruments). The cut-off, as if lobotomized backs of the figures. The strange flaming cones emerging from the heads of two of the figures in the centre foreground. The devilish expression on the face of the horse just right of centre foreground. The dis-turbing, weapon-like transversal metal tubes (?) in the centre to upper-left of the merry-go-round. The eyes of the horses in the background (upper left and upper centre) looking backwards like something out of Fuseli. The monstrously non-representational or anti-representational vortex of the horses within the seemingly fixed frame provided by the almost semi-circular golden-red transversal strip at the bottom of the painting. The huge silver veering slugs, metal tubes, floodlighting or mushroom tops occupying the uppermost fifth of the canvas. There are no feet in the painting – neither for the horses nor for their riders.'

53. See Lawrence, 'Tickets Please', in *England, My England and Other Stories*, pp. 34–45: here, p. 37. Further page references appear parenthetically in the main body of the text.

54. The sexually charged nature of the story – a satirical if also disturb-ing account of phallic power – is explicitly marked in the punning of Lawrence's initial title, 'John Thomas': this name refers to the principal male character, John Thomas Raynor, but is also (as in *Lady Chatterley's Lover*) a colloquialism for 'penis'. (On the variation in titling, see Bruce Steele's Introduction to *England, My England*, pp. xxxiv–xxxv.)

55. D. H. Lawrence, *Sons and Lovers* (Harmondsworth: Penguin, 1984), p. 173.

56. On the enigmas and resistances of the 'readable corpse' in Lawrence, see Garrett Stewart's admirable *Death Sentences: Styles of Dying in British Fiction* (London: Harvard University Press, 1984), p. 251 and *passim*. Stewart is marvellously alert, among other things, to 'the paradoxically fluid friction of Lawrence's prose' and to the ways in which Lawrence is 'quick to implant an ambiguity of diction in his flexible death sentences' (219).

57. Lawrence, *Sons and Lovers*, p. 173, emphases added.

58. Lawrence, *Sons and Lovers*, p. 174, emphasis added. As I have sought to make clear elsewhere in this study, it is not primarily a matter of whether such a homophone ('would'/'wood') is intended or not. It is rather a ques-tion of the veering effects of language, especially as these can be tracked and analysed in that obscure obstacle of desire, the novel or other literary work. In addition to this, we could suggest that Mrs Morel's 'would' ('If only it would have been me!') corresponds with Shakespeare's 'woo't', in *Hamlet* and *Antony and Cleopatra*, and Hélène Cixous's 'might'. For more on this, permit me to refer to Nicholas Royle, 'Woo't', in *In Memory of Jacques Derrida* (Edinburgh: Edinburgh University Press, 2009), pp. 68–88.

59. D. H. Lawrence, *Apocalypse* (Harmondsworth: Penguin, 1976), p. 54.

60. D. H. Lawrence, *Lady Chatterley's Lover* (Harmondsworth: Penguin, 1961), p. 128.

61. Lawrence, *Lady Chatterley's Lover*, p. 128.

62. See Rei Terada, *Looking Away: Phenomenality and Dissatisfaction, Kant to Adorno* (London: Harvard University Press, 2009), p. 68, n.36. Terada is talking here about the 'reverie' of 'the phenomenophile', but her remarks are intriguingly apt also as a characterization of the experience of reading – of veering about with Lawrence. While it might appear hyperbolical to suggest that Lawrence's gamekeeper is a phenomenophile, this passage from *Lady Chatterley's Lover* does seem, in its singular and erotically charged fashion, to bear out the force of Terada's proposition that looking away can be not only 'respectable' but '*its very desire to withdraw from what it perceives is worthy of respect*' (29).

63. D. H. Lawrence, *Women in Love* (Harmondsworth: Penguin, 1960), p. 138. Further page references are given parenthetically in the main body of the text.

64. See Chapter 6 'On Critical and Creative Writing', above.

65. This is a weirdly Beckettian moment, calling to mind that exchange in *Endgame* when Hamm, '*anguished*' (as the stage direction has it), asks 'What's happening, what's happening?' and Clov replies: 'Something is taking its course'. See Samuel Beckett, *Endgame*, in *The Complete Dramatic Works* (London: Faber and Faber, 1986), p. 98.

66. See letter to Amy Lowell, 14 November 1916, in *Letters* 3: 31.

67. Amy Lowell, 'An Aquarium', quoted in *Letters* 3: 31. The 'veering' in 'An Aquarium' is perhaps echoed in Lawrence's poem 'Street Lamps' (*CP*: 253–4), first published in early 1917 (see *Letters* 3: 29n.), in which the transition from sunset to the lighting up of 'gold' and 'silver' street lamps is evoked: 'The globe of the day, over-ripe, / Is shattered at last beneath the stripe / Of the wind, and its oneness veers / Out myriad-wise.'

68. See Doherty, '*Women in Love*: Sacrifice, Sadism and the Discourse of Species', p. 90. The figure of 'erect[ing] a barrier between species' is drawn from Olivier Richon's 'The Hunt', *Public*, 6 (1992), 89, and Cary Wolfe's *Animal Rites: American Culture, the Discourse of Species, and Posthumanist Theory* (Chicago: Chicago University Press, 2003), p. 176.

69. Lawrence, *Studies in Classic American Literature*, p. 164. This remark comes in a funny if slightly 'ghoulish' passage near the end of the book, in which Lawrence is reprimanding the ghost of Walt Whitman. In particular he is questioning and pulling apart Whitman's three-line poem: 'I am he that aches with amorous love: / Does the earth gravitate, does not all matter, aching, attract all matter? / So the body of me to all I meet or know.' (See 'I Am He that Aches with Love', in *Walt Whitman: Complete Poetry and Selected Prose and Letters*, ed. Emory Holloway (1860; London: Nonesuch Press, 1971), p. 103.)

70. Deleuze, 'Nietzsche and Saint Paul, Lawrence and John of Patmos', p. 51.

71. Hélène Cixous, 'Writing Blind: Conversation with the Donkey', trans. Eric Prenowitz, in *Stigmata: Escaping Texts* (London: Routledge, 1998), p. 141.

72. Deleuze offers a succinct formulation of the Lawrentian flux in this context: 'a flux is something intensive, instantaneous and mutant – between a creation and a destruction' (Deleuze, 'On the Superiority of Anglo-American Literature', p. 37).

73. Another book might be written on the subject of veering and marine life.

Suffice here simply to add to the examples from Amy Lowell and Lawrence one other recent literary instance. In Philip Roth's *Nemesis* a man called Bucky Cantor sees a large glass aquarium: 'A neon light shone down on the tank, and inside he could see the population of tiny, many-hued fish, more than a dozen of them, either vanishing into a miniature grotto, green with miniature shrubbery, or sweeping the sandy bottom for food, or veering upward to suck at the surface, or just suspended stock-still near a silver cylinder bubbling air in the corner of the tank.' Mr Cantor, we are inclined to suppose, is looking at a multivarious image of his life. See Philip Roth, *Nemesis* (London: Jonathan Cape, 2010), pp. 45–6.

74. See letter to Amy Lowell, 3 October 1920, in *Letters* 3: 607. 'Tortoise Family Connections' is one of the so-called *vers libre* poems later published as *Tortoises* (in December 1921): see *Letters* 3: 605, n.2.

75. See Timothy Clark, *The Cambridge Introduction to Literature and the Environment* (Cambridge: Cambridge University Press, 2011), p. 44. It is in this context also that we might note the veering logic of 'fantastic transversality' that Akira Mizuta Lippit describes, apropos the way 'animal metaphor' seems to breathe at the very heart of language: 'One might posit provisionally that the animal functions not only as an exemplary metaphor but, within the scope of rhetorical language, as an originary metaphor. One finds a fantastic transversality at work between the animal and the metaphor—the animal is already a metaphor, the metaphor an animal. Together they transport to language, breathe into language, the vitality of another life, another expression: animal and metaphor, a metaphor made flesh, a living metaphor that is by definition not a metaphor, antimetaphor—"animetaphor".' See Lippit, *Electric Animal: Toward a Rhetoric of Wildlife* (Minneapolis: University of Minnesota Press, 2000), p. 165.

76. Deleuze and Guattari, *A Thousand Plateaus*, pp. 244–5; and cf. pp. 251–2. See, too, Gerald Doherty's '*Women in Love*: Sacrifice, Sadism and the Discourse of Species', which alludes to the poem in the context of 'a Deleuzean "becoming", which, in dissolving nonhuman and human identities, precipitates the free flow of libidinal energies across species bounds' (82). The silhouette of another book lurks here: a reimagining of Darwin and the veering of species.

77. Lewis Carroll, *Alice's Adventures in Wonderland*, in *Alice in Wonderland*, ed. Donald J. Gray, 2nd edn (New York: Norton, 1992), p. 75.

Appendix: A Note on Nodism

Nodism presents an immediate difficulty for the English speaker, who is faced with the tongue-knotting question of whether the first syllable is to be pronounced 'nod' or 'node'. The fact is you can say it either way and not be wrong. This is because nodism is a kind of nudism that bears and bares both nod and node. Perhaps this will sound like mere wordplay, but you would be quite mistaken in thinking so. Nodism is a profoundly serious affair. In a sense everything rests on it. If you are going to use the word, be vigilant. Remember Heidegger's little dictum: 'Every mere *ism* is a misunderstanding and the death of history'.[1] Nodisms (for they are legion) should always be approached with care. The origin of the term is uncertain, but I can here confirm that it occurred to me during dinner on the evening of 12 April 2010, at my favourite Spanish restaurant, Casa don Carlos, in Brighton.

Nodism is a practice of reading that takes its orientation from a single word, phrase or syllable in a work of literature. The word or phrase is not necessarily obvious: often it may seem a small detail, peripheral to the main action. It might occur only once but that 'once' is always complicated. Usually it will turn up elsewhere in the text or in other writings by the same author. This word or phrase, this little clipping then comes to form a pivot for an analysis of the work *in extenso*. If the term 'nodism' itself has an author it would be a multiple collaboration. You would probably have to hand it to Shakespeare, first of all, and then perhaps to Sigmund Freud, William Empson, Raymond Williams, Hélène Cixous and Jacques Derrida. But nodism belongs to nobody. Indeed you could very readily say that the 'nod' is a squashing up of 'nobody'. Never forget Emily Dickinson's nuggety lines: 'I'm Nobody! Who are you? / Are you – Nobody – too?' Nodism is no diss to anyone – but if you want to try to pin it on a single author or proper name, it is no dice. It is a dreamy word, no doubt, and dreams are strangely knotty, as Freud saw.

If you want to explore nodism, then, it helps to have a slightly dreamy disposition, or at least an interest in the oneiric. A bottomless love of the *Oxford English Dictionary* is also a boon. Even the briefest flirtation with 'node' can lead to a love tangle. The *OED* tells us that it comes from the Latin *nodus*, a knot or point of intersection of two or more lines, perhaps from the same Indo-European base as 'net' (to bind or twist together). Here are just four definitions of 'node' that contribute to an understanding of nodism:

> A knot, a knob, a protuberance; a knotty formation. (sense 1)
>
> *fig.* A knot or complication; an entanglement. (*obsolete*, sense 3)
>
> A point of significance; a crux, a critical turning point; a focal point. (sense 8)
>
> [In *Computing* and *Telecommunications*.] A junction in a local area network, a wide area network, or any similar system of components interconnected by telecommunication lines; a device occupying such a position. (sense 9e)

Each of those definitions is a point of convergence and divergence sending you off in different directions. And the same goes for 'nod': it takes you all the way to the East of Eden and round back to the Land of Nod.

The term *nodism*, I was saying, condenses Shakespeare's nod and Freud's nodal point. A dream is, as Freud puts it, 'a factory of thoughts'. In *The Interpretation of Dreams* he talks about 'nodal points' in dreams, where 'a great number of dream-thoughts converge'.[2] He also refers to words themselves as nodal points: 'Words, since they are the nodal points of numerous ideas, may be regarded as predestined to ambiguity.'[3] In my nodding state I realise I am also making a novel reading of Freud's nodal as his navel, because the ambiguity of words for nodism goes beyond straightforward equivocation, double-meaning or polysemia, and thus inevitably connects up with what he elsewhere evokes as the 'navel of dreams', where the dream 'reaches down into the unknown'.[4] Nodism does not ultimately distinguish between the domain of one word and another: as in dreams, so in literature, a word is never only itself, it is constantly veering off into something or somewhere else. And the navel or nodal point might be anywhere. While nodism keeps saying yes (yes to life and to literature), it is also always concerned with what is secret, unknown or, in Freud's phrase (almost as difficult to say as 'nodist'), 'unplumbable'.[5]

You can trace nodism to the ways Shakespeare works with 'nod'. In *Antony and Cleopatra*, for example, Antony, near his end, likens himself to a cloud or vapour in the process of dissolving:

Sometime we see a cloud that's dragonish,
A vapour sometime like a bear or lion,
A towered citadel, a pendent rock,
A forkèd mountain, or blue promontory
With trees upon't that nod unto the world
And mock our eyes with air.[6]

Shakespeare appreciates how plant life nods: in *A Midsummer Night's Dream*, Oberon dreamily observes, 'I know a bank where the wild thyme blows, / Where oxlips and the nodding violet grows . . .'.[7] He also lets trees and flowers speak for people. Antony's trees that 'nod unto the world / And mock our eyes with air' are hallucinatory, perhaps, but they recall other moments in the play where 'nod' occurs: Antony is said to nod towards Cleopatra (after promising her 'All the East', Alexas tells us, 'So he nodded, / And soberly did mount an arm-gaunt steed': I, v, 47–50), and Caesar later disparagingly speaks of how Cleopatra 'Hath nodded [Antony] to her' (III, vi, 68).[8] One nod gives a nod to the other, as if they were so many nodding plumes (to recall a beautiful image from *Coriolanus*).[9] There is a sort of telecommunication between them, an eerie network. Nodism is a practice of reading and writing attentive to the strange and magical knots of life that Shakespeare, Wordsworth, Melville and others pass on to us.

Notes

1. Martin Heidegger, *What Is a Thing?*, trans. W. B. Barton, Jr. and Vera Deutsch (Chicago: Henry Regnery, 1967), pp. 60–1.
2. Sigmund Freud, *SE* 4: 283.
3. Freud, *SE* 5: 340. For an extended exploration of the ineluctable nodalities of Freud and modernist writing in general, see Maud Ellmann's excellent book, *The Nets of Modernism: Henry James, Virginia Woolf, James Joyce, and Sigmund Freud* (Cambridge: Cambridge University Press, 2010).
4. Freud, *SE* 5: 525. We might also recall here Paul de Man's remark on 'the manifest bisexuality' of the navel: it is a 'mark', he suggests, 'which separates as much as it unites, and which escapes the difference between the genders'. See de Man, letter of 23 August 1983, cited in Shoshana Felman, 'Postal Survival, or the Question of the Navel', in *Yale French Studies*, The Lesson of Paul de Man, 69 (1985): 68.
5. See Freud, *SE* 4: 111.
6. William Shakespeare, *Antony and Cleopatra*, ed. David Bevington (Cambridge: Cambridge University Press, 1990), IV, xiv, 3–8. Further references to *Antony and Cleopatra* are to this edition.
7. William Shakespeare, *A Midsummer Night's Dream*, ed. R. A. Foakes, updated edn (Cambridge: Cambridge University Press, 2003), II, i, 249–50.
8. For an extended reading of *Antony and Cleopatra* in this context, see

Nicholas Royle, 'Nod', in *How to Read Shakespeare* (New York: Norton, 2005), pp. 106–20.

9. William Shakespeare, *Coriolanus*, ed. Lee Bliss (Cambridge: Cambridge University Press, 2000), III, iii, 134.

Index